Larry Writer is the author of the Ned K[
Tilly Devine, Kate Leigh and the razor
Australia at the 1936 Nazi Olympics, which was shortlisted for
the William Hill Australian Sports Book of the Year; the Mark and
Evette Moran Nib History prize–winning *Cecil Healy: A Biography*;
Pitched Battle: In the frontline of the 1971 Springbok tour of Aus-
tralia; *Never Before, Never Again: The story of St George's 11*
straight rugby league premierships, 1956–66; *Bumper: The life and*
times of Frank 'Bumper' Farrell; and *The Golden Era: The extra-*
ordinary two decades when Australians ruled the tennis world (with
Rod Laver). Larry has also collaborated with tennis legends Rod
Laver, John Newcombe and Margaret Court, and rock star Chrissy
Amphlett, on their memoirs.

The
SHIPWRECK

The true story of the *Dunbar*, the disaster that broke the
colony's heart and forged a nation's spirit

LARRY WRITER

ALLEN&UNWIN
SYDNEY•MELBOURNE•AUCKLAND•LONDON

Allen & Unwin
83 Alexander Street
Crows Nest NSW 2065
Australia
Phone: (61 2) 8425 0100
Email: info@allenandunwin.com
Web: www.allenandunwin.com

We acknowledge all First Nations lands on which we work.

 A catalogue record for this book is available from the National Library of Australia

ISBN 978 1 76087 910 5

Internal design by Midland Typesetters, Australia
Charts by Mika Tabata
Index by Garry Cousins
Set in 11.5/16 pt Sabon LT by Midland Typesetters, Australia
Printed and bound in Australia by Griffin Press, part of Ovato

10 9 8 7 6 5 4 3 2 1

The paper in this book is FSC® certified. FSC® promotes environmentally responsible, socially beneficial and economically viable management of the world's forests.

For Carol, a sailor,
And to Tom and Casey,
With love

Contents

CONTENTS

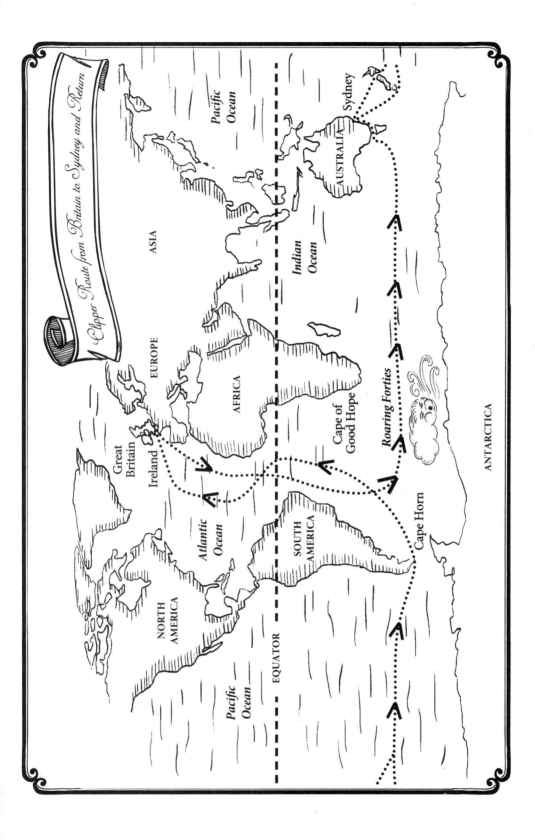

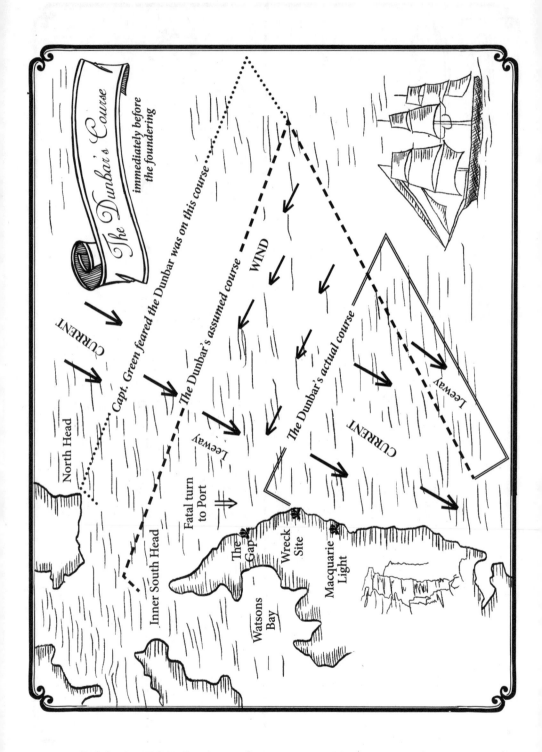

The Dunbar's Course

immediately before the foundering

CURRENT

North Head

Capt. Green feared the Dunbar was on this course

The Dunbar's assumed course

WIND

The Dunbar's actual course

Leeway

Leeway

CURRENT

Inner South Head

Fatal turn to Port

The Gap

Watsons Bay

Wreck Site

Macquarie Light

Prologue

Dawn. Friday, 21 August 1857. The south-easterly gale that had come in the night still blasted Sydney, knocking down trees and causing flooding from the city's west to the Blue Mountains and north to the Hunter Valley. A local man had rugged up against the elements and was walking along the beach below Georges Head, between Middle Head and Bradleys Head in Port Jackson. Fifty metres or so offshore, he saw something he didn't see every day. Amid floating debris and cargo that could only have come from a large ship, the carcass of a red shorthorn cow with white spots floated in the iron-grey chop. Thinking he'd drag the dead beast in to the shore and butcher it, he waded out towards it through the swirling foam. As he drew nearer, he realised that the cow was jerking and twisting and there was blood in the water. He saw the sharks' fins and the snapping jaws tearing chunks from the animal. Leaving the sharks to their feast, the shaken man returned to the headland to raise the alarm.

As the corpses of women, men and children and the carcasses of livestock, wooden spars and beams and cargo bobbed in the harbour and washed up onto the shores, news was spreading through the colony that a large ship had been wrecked and, as Sydneysiders were well aware, four such passenger and cargo vessels were due from Britain, the *Duncan Dunbar*, the *Vocalist*, the *Zemindar* and, the finest and most famous of them all, the *Dunbar*.

1

This hard land

Since near enough to forever, colossal twin sandstone headlands, rearing 60 to 80 metres high like slabs of striated honeycomb, have guarded the entrance to Sydney's Port Jackson. South and North Heads, 1.1 nautical miles (2 kilometres) apart, are Triassic-era bulwarks, protecting the harbour within the Heads from the massive swells that power in from the Tasman Sea and hurl themselves upon the coast.

The craggy towering cliffs of Outer South Head extend 7 kilometres south from its northern tip to Ben Buckler on Bondi's northern headland, and then another 16 kilometres south to La Perouse on the northern edge of Botany Bay. The southern headland was the landmark that voyagers coming from Britain to the colony of New South Wales at the end of the eighteenth century and long into the nineteenth century kept their eyes peeled for. As it materialised, they knew that at last, after many months at sea, they were soon to reach their destination, for worse or better. Now all their ship had to do was round the southern headland and they would be safe inside Port Jackson.

South Head is where, wrote P.R. Stephensen and Brian Kennedy in their *History and Description of Sydney Harbour*, 'the ocean abruptly meets the land, with no shelf of shallows to reduce the impact of the surf. The cliffs are grandly beautiful as sighted from seaward, especially so to the homecoming sailor . . . The South Head peninsula is a massive breakwater in Nature's design of the Port of Sydney. It breaks the force of the ocean's swell, and of easterly gales, to shelter the Main Harbour.'

After the long and perilous voyage from England, after storms, turbulent seas, baking heat and icebergs, the serene waters of Port Jackson were sweet relief. Once safely inside the Heads, the officers and crew, the convicts cast from the British Isles, the free settlers and, in the 1850s, the prospectors who staked all to discover if the streets of Bathurst, Sofala, Hill End and Bungonia really *were* paved with gold, all realised what Indigenous people had known for untold thousands of years: this waterway was a magnificent haven.

Port Jackson, named by Lieutenant (later Captain) James Cook after Sir George Jackson, a Lord Commissioner of the British Admiralty, extends to the west from its single entry point, the fairway between South Head and North Head, and comprises the tidal waters of North Harbour, Middle Harbour and Sydney Harbour, as well as into the Lane Cove River, the Parramatta River and Darling Harbour.

In modern-day terms, what Captain Arthur Phillip of the Royal Navy and his small party of First Fleet officers could see as they ventured through the Heads aboard their pinnaces—small sailing boats with oars—on 22 January 1788, was North Harbour bounded by North Head, Manly Cove and Dobroyd Head; Middle Head and Middle Harbour reaching north-west past Balmoral Beach to Clontarf and The Spit; and, unfolding to the left of Middle Head, Sydney Harbour.

James Cook did not enter the Heads when he sailed up from Botany Bay on the HMS *Endeavour* in 1770, satisfying himself with the view of the harbour from 3 kilometres offshore. But when Captain Phillip arrived in the mysterious southern land eighteen years later with his First Fleet, he immediately saw the potential of

Port Jackson. With Britain's gaols full and North America being no longer an option for a British penal colony after Britain's defeat in America's War of Independence in 1783, Phillip's mission was to investigate locations in the continent then known variously as 'New Holland', 'Terra Australis Incognita' and 'Unknown South Land' for a place to send hardened criminals along with unfortunates whose crime had been to steal food or clothing to stay alive in an age of poverty and hunger. (It was British explorer Matthew Flinders who coined the name 'Australia' on completion of his circumnavigation of the continent in 1804.)

On 22 January, Phillip, Captain John Hunter, navigators James Keltie and David Blackburn, marines commanded by Captain David Collins and a handful of sailors left the fleet behind in Botany Bay (which Phillip, contrary to Cook's and his botanist Sir Joseph Banks' recommendations, had deemed unsuitable for a settlement because it had no secure anchorage, too-sandy soil and no reliable fresh water source) and sailed 11.8 nautical miles (22 kilometres) north in three pinnaces to the entrance to Port Jackson. There they gave a wide berth to the wave-smashed cliffs of Outer South Head and entered the harbour. It was dark when they beached their boats at the western end of the crescent beach at Inner South Head. There they stayed the night, observed intently by the local Aboriginal people, and gave the beach a name, Camp Cove. South Head was where the Birrabirragal clan lived and died, and their rock carvings can be found in the area today. The Birrabirragal called Outer South Head *Tarralbe* and Inner South Head *Burra-wa-ra*.

Next morning at four, Phillip's party ate a quick breakfast, boarded their pinnaces, and rowed further into Port Jackson to explore the shoreline and take depth soundings to locate safe channels for the fleet.

On laying eyes on the placid cobalt blue waters, white sand coves, beaches and bays and deep, sheltered anchorages, Phillip believed that he had discovered 'the finest harbour of the world, in which a thousand sail of the line may ride in the most perfect security'.

He had found his site for a penal settlement, but his words indicated that he also envisioned one day a thriving colony on these shores for free settlers and merchants. Phillip and his party returned to Botany Bay to tell the rest of the First Fleeters the good news.

Four days later, on a rainy, windy and humid 26 January 1788, after a 258-day, around 12,950 nautical mile (23,983 kilometre) voyage from Portsmouth, the First Fleet anchored in the small bay which would become Sydney Cove (which Phillip named for his mentor, Thomas Townshend, First Viscount Sydney) and Circular Quay. The First Fleet comprised eleven ferry-sized sailing vessels— the 35.5 metre, 549 tonne, twenty-gun flagship HMS *Sirius*, the naval escort *Supply* (to which Phillip transferred from *Sirius* on departing the Cape of Good Hope), the storeships *Fishburn*, *Golden Grove* and *Borrowdale* and the convict transports *Scarborough*, *Prince of Wales*, *Alexander*, *Charlotte*, *Lady Penrhyn* and *Friendship*. Crammed on board were, according to records, 568 male and 191 female convicts (mostly British but also African, French, Indian, North American, West Indian and Chinese), 206 marines, 210 navy seamen, 233 merchant seamen, 27 wives and 19 children. Some 47 convicts died en route, including one who was washed overboard. Those convicts who survived suffered terribly on the nine-month voyage, chained together in foetid holds, fed food that the ships' pigs and goats may have shied from, and routinely assaulted by guards. Their shipmates were 32 pigs, 4 goats, 7 cows, 2 bulls, 44 sheep, 7 horses including a stallion, and live poultry purchased at ports along the way.

There was enough equipment and stores, Captain Phillip prayed, to last until the arrival of the Second Fleet—a six-ship convoy bringing more supplies, convicts and officials; or until his settlement became self-sufficient.

The *Supply* anchored in Sydney Cove in water 10 metres deep, and Phillip was rowed ashore on the western side of the bay. He would have inhaled the pungent eucalyptus fragrance of the bush wafting from the banks, tasted the bracing fresh water of what would be known as the Tank Stream that flowed down through a forest to the muddy beach. Around 7 p.m., flanked by his officers, Phillip raised St George's flag with its red cross on a white background, claimed the land for King George III, and toasted the health of the king and the success of the new settlement. Phillip would explain why he chose Sydney Cove. 'The different coves of the harbour were examined with all possible expedition, and the preference [to site the colony] was given to one which had the finest spring of [fresh] water, and in which ships can anchor so close to the shore that at very small expense quays may be constructed where the largest vessels may unload.'

The disembarkation and unloading of the ships at Sydney Cove was watched with both trepidation and amusement by scattered groups of the Gadigal clan of the Eora nation. They knew the cove as Warane. Each confronted by exotic strangers, it's arguable whether the interlopers or the inhabitants were most disconcerted. The stiff-backed officers in their tricorne hats or high-plumed black helmets, red tunics, white breeches and knee-high boots, musket- and sword-wielding marines and the convicts, deathly pale from months locked below decks, emaciated, filthy and querulous. And to the British the Indigenous people were just as alien as Martians. Lieutenant William Bradley recorded his impressions.

> The men we met with here were . . . stout and well-limbed, the women were young in general, shorter than the men, very straight-limbed and well-featured, their voice a pleasing softness, they were all entirely naked . . . The men had their beards long and very bushy . . . some of them had teeth of some animal and pieces of bone stuck in their hair with gum, they were so dirty it was hard to tell the real colour of their hides . . . Most of the men had lost one of their fore teeth and their skins are much scar'd.

On 7 February, at the spot where St George's flag fluttered in the harbour breeze, the king's commission proclaiming the colony of New South Wales and appointing Arthur Phillip governor, empowered to implement British government policy and maintain order in the colony, was read aloud by judicial officer Captain David Collins.

From that moment, Sydney Cove was forever changed. Collins would chronicle the first days of the colony as trees were felled, animals tethered and tents pitched.

> The run of fresh water stole silently along through a very thick wood, the stillness of which had then, for the first time since the creation, been interrupted by the rude sound of the labourer's axe, and the downfall of its ancient inhabitants—a stillness and tranquillity which from that day were to give place to the voice of labour, the confusion of camps and towns, and the busy hum of its new possessors.

As the colonists laboured, the Gadigal, naked bodies painted and carrying spears and boomerangs, did as they had always done. They hunted and gathered, paddled their hollowed-log and bark-and-twine canoes, caught fish and eels and prised oysters off the rocks. They cooked their food on open fires lit by fire sticks, as wispy spirals of pungent wood smoke ascended into the vast skies. They were at home on the sandy beaches, among the jagged sandstone outcrops, spinifex-covered sandhills, marshes and swamps, mud banks, scrubby heath, woodlands of soaring blackbutt, apple gum and red gum trees, banksias, fig trees, acacias, casuarinas, bangalow and cabbage tree palms, ferns, vividly coloured and delicate flowers and shrubs. For the Gadigal people, the fauna—kangaroos, possums, goannas and echidnas, wombats, snakes, whales, tortoises, cackling kookaburras and screeching cockatoos, rainbow-hued lorikeets and parrots— was commonplace. But for the First Fleeters, so much was new and wondrous. Having known only the muted greys and greens, the cuddly, harmless fauna, the low clouds and close horizons of home, they were dazzled. Some of those convicts delivered from the shadow of the gallows and, once the colony was established, free settlers, must have felt they'd been transported to paradise.

Yet for all its natural beauty, the settlement that sprang from sydney Cove would prove to be paradise hard won. In the colony's first decades, many new immigrants and emancipated convicts survived and thrived; for others, every day was a life-or-death struggle. The most optimistic spirit was crushed by the ceaseless back-breaking toil that building Sydney Town demanded, homesickness and isolation, wretched living conditions, disease, and starvation for the soil was not fertile.

These strangers in the strangest of lands got by as best they could. They scrounged food from the stingy earth, and did their best to follow the Gadigal people's lead in hunting kangaroos and other wildlife, and fishing. The *Charlotte*'s captain and First Fleet chronicler Lieutenant General Watkin Tench noted the variety of fish in the harbour, 'everything from a whale to a gudgeon . . . sharks of a monstrous size, skate, rock cod, grey mullet, bream, horse mackarel and innumerable others unknown in Europe'.

The American First Fleeter Jacob Nagle was a member of a fishing party sent to catch fish for Governor Phillip's household.

> Our customary method was to leave Sydney Cove about four o'clock in the afternoon and go down the harbour and fish all night from one cove to another. We would then make a fire on the beach, cook our supper, and take our grog, lay down in the sand before the fire, wet or dry, and go to sleep till morning, though we would be often disturbed by the natives heaving their spears at us at a distance, and being in the night, it would be by random. In the morning we would return, taking the fish to the Governor's house, where they would be shared out, as far as they would go.

Phillip and his colonists, barely surviving on dwindling rations, waited and waited for the ships of the Second Fleet, indeed *any* ship, to bring food, cargo and livestock. To ensure that a vessel carrying precious supplies did not sail right past the Heads, on 20 January 1790, a signal station was established on South Head, high on a cliff-top 1.75 kilometres south of the northern tip. At first, the station was just a few tents scattered around a fig tree, a wooden flagstaff wedged in rocks from which fluttered semaphore flags, and a brick column or obelisk marker. On fine days the flags could be seen with an eye glass or a telescope from Observatory Hill above Sydney Cove, at Ben Buckler headland at the northern end of Bondi bay, and from out to sea. (In January 1791, members of the Birrabirragal clan stole the coloured semaphore flags to decorate their bark canoes.) In years to come, at night, a flashing lantern was used to signal the arrival of ships at the Heads. As well as alerting maritime and immigration officials, the signal station warned vessels that they were nearing the coast. The station was overseen first by Captain John Hunter of the First Fleet flagship *Sirius* and staffed by up to a dozen *Sirius* marines. Among them were Lieutenant William Bradley (after whom Bradleys Head would be named), midshipman Daniel Southwell, and quartermaster and sailmaker Robert Watson, after whom Watsons Bay would be named in 1811.

No more important job did those at the signal station have than to keep watch for the arrival of the Second Fleet. There were fears that the six vessels would put into Botany Bay and find nobody there or sail past the Heads, so the station had to constantly be on the lookout for the fleet. Daniel Southwell recorded how

The purpose for which the Lookout was established was fulfilled on 3 June 1790 with the sighting of *Lady Juliana*, the first vessel of the Second Fleet. The flag was raised and Sydney settlement responded. At length the clouds of misfortune began to separate, and on the evening of the 3rd of June, the joyful cry of 'the flag's up' resounded in every direction. I was sitting in my hut, musing on our fate, when a confused clamour in the street drew my attention. I opened my door, and saw several women with children in their arms running to and fro with distracted looks, congratulating each other, and kissing their infants with the most passionate and extravagant marks of fondness. I needed no more; but instantly started out, and ran to a hill, where, by the assistance of a pocket glass, my hopes were realised. My next-door neighbour, a brother-officer, was with me, but we could not speak. We wrung each other by the hand, with eyes and hearts overflowing.

The Second Fleet was not the godsend that the starving colonists prayed for. The settlers were desperate for the supplies and convict manpower that the fleet would deliver, but the *Guardian*, the main supply ship laden with stores and plants, had struck ice at Table Bay, near Cape Town, was wrecked on the coast and lost much of its cargo. And, of the 928 male and 78 female convicts in the ships, 273, or 26 per cent, died during the voyage. Some 486 arrived too ill to be anything but a burden to the colony. Making matters worse was that other supply ships from India, Indonesia and Africa bringing food and livestock to the colony were wrecked on the way or simply failed to arrive.

On 23 July 1790, the month after what remained of the Second Fleet had shambled into Port Jackson, tragedy struck the signal station. Daniel Southwell and fellow staffer James Bates and two friends, Thomas Harp and John Wilkins, set off in a flat-bottomed rowboat for Sydney Cove to fish and buy provisions for the signallers. Between what is now Nielsen Park and Bradleys Head, the boat was charged and tossed into the air by a whale, maddened from being wounded by harpooners earlier that day. Only Southwell made it to shore.

It was also the responsibility of South Head Signal Station to advise the Marine Pilot Service, which had been established at Camp Cove in 1792, when a ship was preparing to enter the Heads. Once alerted to an approaching vessel by a blue flare from the ship or the raising of a flag at the signal station, the chief pilot and usually a crew of five and a coxswain would row out in their whaling boat and draw alongside the vessel. Back then, pilotage was a haphazardly organised operation with pilots of varying levels of competence and sobriety. Rival pilot crews would race each other to the ship to win the pilotage. The victorious pilot would haggle with the captain over a price and once a deal was struck, he would clamber up a rope ladder onto the deck, and, utilising his knowledge of Port Jackson, guide the vessel home. On a clear day with gentle seas, approaching and rounding South Head and entering Port Jackson from the south (the traditional route of sailing vessels from Britain) presented few problems for the experienced master and his crew with a pilot on board who knew Port Jackson. Pilot boat crews, however, were reluctant to assist incoming vessels when the sea was running heavy, or even at night, fearing that their unstable open-decked whalers would be swamped or capsize. Of course, at these times before any lighthouses, when poor visibility, a miscalculation or unfamiliarity with Port Jackson could see a ship founder on the unlit Outer South Head cliffs or run aground on the unlit North or Middle Head, or Sow and Pigs reef, or Clark, Shark and Pinchgut islands, was when a pilot boat was needed most. Even after 1840 when it was made compulsory to assist ships at night, some pilots refused to do so. In the absence of a pilot, ships' masters were advised to remain outside the Heads until morning or until the weather abated. Another service these cutthroat competitive entrepreneurs vied with each other to provide was taking newspapers from newly arrived ships and passing them, for payment, to a horseman who would rush them to the city.

* * * *

Phillip sited Sydney Town across the two ridges now occupied by The Rocks and Hyde Park, with the colony's vital artery, the freshwater stream, running through the scrub between the ridges into Sydney Cove. Convicts, unless repeat offenders and many were, were not locked up but housed in tents and one-room wooden and reed- and cabbage palm–thatched huts ('wretched hovels' according to officer Watkin Tench), and made to work five days a week from dawn until they collapsed exhausted in the dark of night. Under the stern direction of the governor and his marines—and from 1791 the New South Wales Corps—the convicts in their ill-fitting government-issue cotton 'slops' stamped with arrow shapes or the letters 'PB' for 'Prisoner Barracks', cleared the land, quarried sandstone and made bricks, felled trees, built roads, wharves, bridges and footpaths. They carried the sandstone and bricks and mortar for the public buildings and banks. On Saturdays, convicts considered to be on the way to rehabilitation could be paid for their toil as carpenters, builders, blacksmiths, barbers, tailors, cobblers and servants.

After serving their time, emancipated convicts enjoyed the same rights as free settlers. They were welcomed into the community, no stigma attached, and encouraged to move west of the harbour settlement and take up farming. To help ex-convicts on their way, they were given tools (a hatchet, two hoes, a spade, a shovel, a cross-cut saw), food, a firearm and access to medical care, and up to 12 hectares of arable land (more if they had married) on which to farm wheat, corn and vegetables and raise cattle, and sheep for meat and wool. The wool became the colony's first lucrative export. In years to come, many former convicts would make valuable contributions to the colony. Architect Francis Greenway, a convicted forger, designed and supervised the construction of buildings that remain among Sydney's most impressive more than two centuries later.

Anyone struggling to survive Sydney Town's hard-scrabble fledgling decades could have no inkling of its illustrious future. Home for the majority of emancipated convicts and British settlers and their first-generation Australian children was typically a one-room, earth-floored tumbledown shack with no running water, ill lit by candle or oil lamp. The unilluminated dirt alleys at night harboured thieves and stray dogs and cats. Human waste was buried in a pit or those responsible left it where it lay; rubbish was burned, enshrouding the settlement in thick, choking smoke. Black rats, an unwelcome gift to the colony from the First and Second fleets, skittered through garbage piles, which also attracted squadrons of flies. Bodies were dumped in rough graves on the western shore of Sydney Cove and the carcasses of slaughtered cattle and sheep were slung into Sydney Harbour, to be devoured by sharks or washed up on the shore where they were left until decomposition.

There was drought and blistering summer heat. Torrential storms turned dirt roads into rivers and lightning struck livestock. A plague of caterpillars feasted on crops. Snakes, sharks, jellyfish, spiders, ants and mosquitoes bit and stung, sometimes fatally. Crooked officials and merchants cheated settlers of money they could not afford to lose, and homesickness drove colonists to despair.

The colony was certainly no place for the meek. Despite Phillip's best intentions, the Aboriginal people of Sydney Cove and west to the emerging settlement at Parramatta quickly came to resent the usurpation of their land and food sources, and there were skirmishes with woundings and fatalities on both sides. And the New South Wales Corps and rebellious convicts were endlessly at each other's throats.

The governor worked to create the new colony, despite being surrounded by lazy and malcontent convicts, incompetent and corrupt officers and administrators, and widespread defeatism. He asserted his authority by meting out punishment, corporal and capital.

Despite the threat of the gallows and the cat o' nine tails for perpetrators, theft was rife, as was assault and prostitution and disobedience to superiors. Work shirking was a whipping offence. If repeated, laziness, like killing an Aboriginal or stealing cattle or food, meant the scaffold. Despite such deterrents, lawlessness reigned in Sydney, Other law-breakers left town and took their chances in the bush, becoming bushrangers or simply disappearing forever.

2

A brave new world

In those years between Governor Lachlan Macquarie becoming governor in 1810 and the tragedy of the *Dunbar* in 1857, the society that would feel its loss so keenly was formed. It is worth understanding how that society was shaped.

Despite all the tribulations, like a plant that defies harsh conditions to burst into bloom, Sydney Town began to thrive. In 1800, the colonial population was 3000; in 1820, 12,000; and in 1856, the year before the *Dunbar* calamity, 53,358.

Into the nineteenth century, with the arrival of hard-working free settlers, the colony founded by Governor Arthur Phillip was showing signs of becoming much, much more than a dumping ground for convicts. The governors who succeeded Phillip made varying contributions: Captain John Hunter (1795–1800), Captain Philip Gidley King (1800–1806), and Captain William Bligh of *Bounty* notoriety (1806–1808). Bligh was ousted from office by the New South Wales Corps in the Rum Rebellion of 1808, after the powerful colony paymaster, wool industry pioneer and politician John Macarthur and Major George Johnston of the New South Wales Corps, who could not abide Bligh's decision to ban the use of rum as currency and also possession of stills. But the man who, with his enlightened planning and sturdy oversight, kickstarted New South Wales was the colony's fifth governor, Major-General Lachlan Macquarie, who took office in 1810 after two years of military rule by the Corps' Major Johnston.

Born the son of a carpenter in 1762 on the island of Ulva, Argyllshire, in the Scottish Hebrides, Macquarie became a career officer in the British Army serving in North America, Europe, the West Indies, India and Egypt. His orders from King George III were clear: 'To improve the Morals of the Colonists, to encourage Marriage, to provide for Education, to prohibit the Use of Spirituous Liquors, to increase the Agriculture and Stock, so as to ensure the Certainty of a full supply to the Inhabitants under all Circumstances'.

First, Macquarie and his own regiment faced down John Macarthur and Major George Johnston's New South Wales Corps, and the governor set about transforming parts of the rough-hewn settlement by the harbour into a Georgian-style city. By the time he was succeeded by Major-General Sir Thomas Brisbane in 1821, to Macquarie's credit were 265 mostly convict-built public buildings, Macquarie Light on Outer South Head, cemeteries and such major thoroughfares as Macquarie, George and Pitt streets, a road to Parramatta and one from Sydney over the Blue Mountains, South Head Road from Sydney Town to the escarpment above Watsons Bay, and then a road linking that thoroughfare to the fishing and pilot boat village. Under Macquarie, a metropolis took shape.

* * * *

Since 1790, the collection of sheds and shacks that grew into what we now know as the village of Watsons Bay had been connected to Sydney Cove by an 11 kilometre dirt track with potholes that could snap a horse's leg and a buggy's axle. Bushrangers and runaway convicts lurked in the undergrowth to relieve travellers of their belongings at gunpoint. In 1811, Governor Macquarie ordered to be built a wide, hard road of hand-packed stones from Sydney Town along the route of present-day Old South Head Road to the top of the hill above Watsons Bay to provide a more accessible and safer thoroughfare for the horses, horse-drawn cabs and carriages and bullock drays of those coming from Sydney to meet arriving family and friends, collect mail and newspapers from Britain from the ships, or to picnic at the beach, Camp Cove or along the cliff-tops on weekends. The *Sydney Gazette* editorialised that the new road to South Head 'presents to the inhabitants of the town a beautiful avenue of recreation, either as a pleasure ride or promenade, that attracts the wonder of the meditating passenger'.

Another reason Sydneysiders flocked to Watsons Bay was to visit The Gap, adjacent to the village, the dramatic indentation in the sandstone cliff face some 650 metres from the northern extremity of Outer South Head. To many, it seemed as if a gargantuan sea monster had taken a bite out of the headland. The lookout above The Gap (or Gap Bluff) offered views out to sea, to North Head and Manly and west to Sydney Cove and beyond. Those untroubled by vertigo could edge close to the precipice and peer down onto the table rock below, upon which toppling waves crashed, the impact shooting spray high into the air, before receding in a gurgling white-water backwash.

Joseph Lycett's 1824 painting, *View of the Heads at the Entrance to Port Jackson*, shows the South Head Signal Station and flag-staff on the cliff-top. In the painting, as well as both Heads and calm blue seas, some of the Birrabirragal mob gaze from the high ground down to Watsons Bay's sandy beach. The terrain is scrubby heath, xanthorrhoea grass trees spearing up out of low scrub, rocky outcrops, eucalypts and fig trees—described as 'massive' by First Fleeters when they sailed past—shading the flatlands that edge the harbour waters. Lady Macquarie enjoyed picnicking under the figs by the beach.

For the first 30 years of the colony, there was no lighthouse on South Head. Approaching ships' captains had to take their bearings from, first, a wood fire in a cauldron on the cliff-top, and then, from

1797 when coal was discovered, a coal-fired flame in a tar barrel atop a tripod. In July 1816, Governor Macquarie and engineer Captain Gill laid the foundation stone for a lighthouse. Two years later, there shone at the 82 metre high point of Outer South Head, 2.2 kilometres south of the northern tip of the promontory at South Reef and 490 metres south of the signal station, a 23-metre-tall sandstone lighthouse. So impressed with it was Macquarie that he named it after himself—Macquarie Light, or Macquarie Tower—and partially pardoned its convict architect, Francis Greenway.

Macquarie Light had an interior spiral staircase, balanced by two domed wings at its base containing a guard-house and barracks. Three groups of three revolving whale oil–burning lamps set in parabolic reflectors, all powered by a clockwork mechanism, flashed every 60 seconds. Despite Greenway fretting about the flaky quality of the lighthouse's sandstone, Macquarie touted the new light-house as an 'elegant and strong stone tower'. Elegant, definitely, but Greenway was right. Before long, steel bands had to be added to the light to fortify the crumbling stone.

A local poet celebrated the lighthouse:

Behold, on yonder cliff, a beacon shines
Whose torch-light thus a brilliant blaze displays.
It shines to guide the sea-tossed mariner
Across his trackless, rough and watery ways.

Macquarie Light's beacon, shining from 105 metres above the ocean, could be seen in fine weather by ships up to 35 kilometres away approaching from all directions, and from as far to the west as Parramatta. It was an impressive light, but had a fatal flaw. It identified the cliffs of Outer South Head, but it did not mark South Reef at the entrance to the harbour, 2.2 kilometres to the north. Put simply, Macquarie Light was a guide *to* Port Jackson but not *into* Port Jackson. The flaw did not go unnoticed. Complained Captain J. Lort Stokes in 1838, 'Its site has been admirable chosen for indicating the position of the port from a distance at sea, but it has been placed too far from the entrance to be of much service to vessels when close inshore.' It would dawn on the government, too late, that a second light was needed at the tip of Outer South Head to guide ships safely through the Heads and into Port Jackson.

The first superintendent and keeper of Macquarie Light when it began operating in 1818 was Robert Watson, a First Fleeter. Watson had been quartermaster on Phillip's flagship *Sirius*, worked at the signal station, been a pilot boat captain and—until he was dismissed for drunkenness and stealing canvas—the harbour master. He also sold spirits to supplement his annual wage of £50. This colourful colonist's transgressions proved no impediment to his being granted a stone cottage by Governor Gidley King, or having Watsons Bay named after him.

A more sober and law-abiding pillar of the Watsons Bay community was another Watson: Captain Thomas Watson who, like his namesake, was a harbour pilot and Macquarie Light superintendent. He became keeper of the light in 1822, and was a chief pilot from 1826 to 1837. Watson's subsequent success in commercial shipping and trading bought him a mansion by the beach at Watsons Bay with servants for himself and his wife, Hannah. The Watsons' establishment was one of the first of a number of grand houses that would be built at the onetime fishing and signal outpost.

The signal station's tents were replaced in 1838 by a two-level stone signal house above a cellar, designed by the official colonial architect, Mortimer Lewis. Staff continued to fly semaphore flags by day and signal with a light that shone well enough on a fair night and dimly or not at all in bad weather.

By 1839, a second road to South Head from Rushcutters Bay, just east of Sydney Cove, through Double Bay and Rose Bay and on to Watsons Bay was in use. Old South Head Road and New South Head Road converged near Macquarie Light. From there, a wide track led down to the anchored ships, Watsons Bay beach, The Gap and Camp Cove. In 1854, the Sydney and Melbourne Steam Packet

Company began a twice-daily ferry service from Sydney Cove to Watsons Bay, replacing the erratic service of earlier days. Travel time was around 45 minutes.

For the first couple of decades of the colony, only a few pilots, fishermen, and the staff of the signal station lived in Watsons Bay and neighbouring Vaucluse, but as time went by, the villages' population was swelled by the wealthy occupants of the grand new homes being built and their servants, lighthouse staff, and, living in small whitewashed timber cottages, those who maintained the tall ships, the boat builders, tradesmen, shopkeepers and hoteliers and their families. By the 1850s, around 300 people lived in the community.

Immigrants and emancipated convicts alike were finding that if they were prepared to bend their back and had a little luck, they and their family might prosper and live a better life than the one they'd left. Certainly, the climate was kinder ... most of the time. They wrote home to loved ones in Britain, many of whom followed them out. From the 1820s, the British government subsidised the emigration of workers and their families fleeing famine and poverty wrought by the population explosion in the British Isles and mass unemployment. Emigration to Australia eased overcrowding in Britain while providing much-needed workers in the colony. Assisted emigration schemes were also offered to women to sail to Australia to marry and raise a family or be domestic servants, so correcting the gender imbalance that had existed since the days of the First Fleet. The passenger list of an emigrant vessel that sailed to Sydney in 1820 listed farmers and farmhands, seamstresses, labourers, servants, cabinetmakers, carpenters, gunsmiths, shoemakers, warpers and packers, dressmakers, schoolmasters, policemen, brewers, teachers, confectioners, bakers, butchers, shepherds, gardeners, rope makers and tailors.

Getting around the colony was by boat or on foot, until the horse population increased and riding or being drawn in a buggy or dray by a horse or horses or bullocks became the way to travel. Seven horses had landed with the First Fleet, and historian Robin

Derricourt has noted that horse numbers had multiplied to twenty in July 1794, and to 517 by 1805.

In parts of Sydney, handsome two-, three- and four-storey sandstone and brick buildings were replacing rickety timber and palm leaf–roofed shacks and there were wide straight paved roads where once were dirt tracks. Stately Macquarie Street was laid in 1810 and came to host Sydney Hospital in 1811, Parliament House in 1816 and, in 1824, at the junction of King Street, St James' Church. There was a law court on Macquarie Street and a Classical Greek–styled courthouse at Darlinghurst, where those found guilty were despatched to nearby fortress-like Darlinghurst Gaol.

Hyde Park Barracks was another impressive structure built in Macquarie Street between 1811 and 1819 to hold male convicts caught terrorising Sydney Town after dark. The barracks building, designed by Francis Greenway, would also serve as a mint, a hospital, a law court and an asylum for destitute women. When an infirmary, it was called 'the slaughter house' because of a spate of dysentery deaths there. From 1817, the Bank of New South Wales was a safe repository for Sydneysiders' savings (Macquarie had introduced the colony's own currency in 1813, replacing rum) and, in a growing number of cases, fortunes.

The foundation stone of St Mary's Cathedral was laid in 1821. The Australian Museum showcased 'many rare and curious specimens of natural history', first in the post office in Macquarie Place and then in a noble building at the corner of William and College streets, which, like so many other convict-built buildings and public spaces, exists today as an enduring reminder of the past. In the next couple of decades, cemeteries sprawled in The Rocks, in George Street (where Sydney Town Hall is now), Devonshire Street in Surry Hills and then, in 1848, at O'Connell Town in Newtown, 8 kilometres west of the city. David Jones (established in 1838 'to sell the best and most exclusive goods') and Farmers department stores and other emporiums and specialty shops in Market, Pitt, Hunter and George streets sold products manufactured locally and imported from Britain. George

Street with its teashops and restaurants was where Sydney café society gathered and gossiped. Two-storey Gothic Revival–style Government House, with its castellated towers, was built from 1836 to 1845 in the lush open space of the Domain on the eastern side of Farm Cove. The University of Sydney was founded in 1850. Remarkably, despite the high number of illiterate colonists, the colony boasted many newspapers—the *Sydney Herald*, which became the *Sydney Morning Herald*, the *Sydney Gazette* and the *New South Wales Advertiser* (described by critics as 'moral to the point of priggishness'), *The Monitor*, the *Weekly Register*, *The Atlas*, *The Australian*, *Freeman's Journal* and *The Empire*—to keep the community informed about local news and what was happening in Britain and the rest of the world.

During these decades, the settlement radiated from Sydney Cove west along Parramatta Road, which was laid in 1811. The Rose Hill Packet steam ferry chugged passengers to the fertile pastures of Rose Hill, which grew into Parramatta. Settlements were established at Windsor and Richmond, Liverpool and Campbelltown and west of the Blue Mountains after they were traversed by the expedition of Gregory Blaxland, William Charles Wentworth and William Lawson in 1813. Ferries linked the south and north shores of Port Jackson, connecting Sydney Town with the villages that dotted the foreshores.

Sydney grew into a cluster of communities, and where people made their homes sprang shops and factories, foundries and mills, wharves, wool stores and warehouses, pubs, brothels and sporting venues to cater to their needs and peccadilloes. In 1858, William Stanley Jevons, an economist and logician employed at Sydney Mint, published his *Remarks upon the Social Map of Sydney*. Jevons reported that prosperous merchants, shopkeepers and professional men lived in mansions or villas, usually on elevated land just outside Sydney Cove, such as in Macquarie Street and Lower Fort Street, in Paddington's Glenmore Road, Darlinghurst, Elizabeth Bay and Glebe. The middle classes, by which Jevons meant skilled workers,

lived in four- to five-roomed cottages clustered in Surry Hills, Straw-
berry Hills, Redfern, Glebe, Pyrmont, Balmain and Millers Point.
The worst housing, generally for unskilled workers and current and
ex-convicts, festered at The Rocks, the lower end of Sussex Street
and around Druitt and Goulburn streets, where the labyrinthine dirt
alleys and lanes were perpetually strewn with garbage. Jevons was
affronted by conditions there:

> I am acquainted with most of the notorious parts of London ...
> but in none of these places, perhaps, would lower forms of vice and
> misery be seen than Sydney can produce. Nowhere too is there a
> more complete abandonment of all the requirements of health and
> decency than in a few parts of Sydney.

Then, as now, Sydney was a city of startling contrasts, of rich and
poor, poverty and opulence, industry and indolence.

French explorer, artist and writer Jacques Arago experienced the
best and worst of the settlement when the ship on which he was sailing
the world, the *Freycinet*, anchored in Sydney in 1819. Arago's valu-
ables were stolen by light-fingered locals on his first day, but he was
still able to be 'enchanted' by the town's 'magnificent hotels, majestic
mansions, houses of extraordinary taste and elegance ... Fountains
ornamented with sculptures worthy of the chisel of our best artists,
spacious and airy apartments, rich furniture, horses, carriages, and
one-horse chaises of the greatest elegance, immense storehouses'.

The mansions of Macquarie Street were modelled on the
imposing yet graceful Georgian town houses of London's Belgravia
and Mayfair. Traveller John Askew described the scene lyrically in
his 1857 memoir *A Voyage to Australia and New Zealand*:

> The best time to see this neighbourhood in all its glory is on a summer's
> evening, about an hour after sunset, when the drawing rooms are
> in a blaze of light. Then the rich tones of the piano or some other
> musical instrument are heard gushing forth from the open windows,

accompanied by the sweet melody of female voices . . . Beautiful ladies, dressed in white, may be seen sitting upon the verandas, or lounging on magnificent couches, partially concealed by the folds of rich crimson curtains in drawing rooms which display all the luxurious comforts and magnificence of the East, intermingled with the elegant utilities of the West.

Colonists made the most of what little leisure time they had.

Just like today, public houses were where the people gathered. In 1811, there were more than a hundred ale houses in Sydney, a good number of which were places that upstanding citizens avoided. These were crowded, nasty drinking dens, dirt- or sawdust-floored blood-houses where patrons got drunk and gambled and might reasonably expect to be entertained by a bare-knuckle boxing bout, a cock fight in which the spurred birds made each other's blood flow and feathers fly, a rat pit where wagers were taken on which dog could catch and kill the most rodents, and a drunken brawl (usually over a spilled glass of ale or a slight, real or imagined). Particularly in sailors' pubs, drinks were spiked and groggy boozers mugged when they staggered outside. Occasionally someone was murdered. It was said of lawless Sydney that while God might have created the harbour, Sydney was the work of Satan.

But increasingly in the first half of the century there were, as well, respectable establishments where well-behaved drinkers sipped fine imported wines and spirits, and debated politics and sport without drawing a gun or knife, played cards and dice, and sang songs. Sentimental Irish, English, Welsh and Scottish ballads, such as 'Auld Lang Syne', 'Barbara Allen' and 'Home Sweet Home', accompanied by accordion and violin reduced the homesick to tears. New lyrics, reflecting life in the colony, were added to traditional compositions, and original Australian songs, such as 'Currency Lasses' and 'I Think of Thee', were sung.

On summer evenings and weekends, citizens donned their finery and promenaded along grand Macquarie Street. They patronised the theatre and opera and dined in restaurants on Anglo, French and Indian fare. Dunsdon's, an upscale eatery in King Street East, distributed a poem purportedly written by a satiated diner who wrote of the restaurant's 'soups, hashes, curries, ragouts, puddings, pies/ Geese, fowls, turkeys, ducks, beef, pork, mutton veal/ Salmon, whiting, stew'd oysters, bream, collar'd eel . . .'.

Sydneysiders of every style and strata visited Hyde Park, at the southern end of Macquarie Street, which took shape between 1810 and 1827. It was the settlement's recreation area, named after London's Hyde Park and dedicated by Governor Macquarie 'to the recreation and amusement of the inhabitants of the town'. The vast park was used for fairs and picnics, and, Sydney then as now being a sporting town, cricket, running and jumping, boxing and wrestling matches (until the inebriated antics of spectators and disappointed bettors saw bouts in the park relocated), quoits, football and the racing of imported Arabic and thoroughbred horses (again, until the inebriated antics of spectators and disappointed bettors saw racing relocated). Conmen would batten onto sporting events like fleas on a rat, setting up pea-and-thimble and card-sharp booths to relieve punters of any funds they'd not lost on the horses or pugilists. To ensure the comfort and safety of park-goers, carts and buggies, cattle, goats, pigs and sheep were banned. Red-jacketed, high-hatted soldiers of the New South Wales Corps paraded in the park in the shadows of marble statues, fountains and monuments. There was political spruiking under the fig trees, and frequent brawls between the spruiker and those who disagreed with them. Colonists, soldiers and Aboriginal people alternatively got along and waged pitched battles under the palm trees. More serious arguments were resolved in Hyde Park, with duelling pistols.

Parramatta Road was another playground for colonists. Horse-races, running and piggyback races, rock-rolling contests and, in a grotesque emulation of fox hunts in England and Ireland—mounted hunters pursuing wild native dogs—drew crowds there. Royal Botanic Gardens at Farm Cove was established in 1816 and the adjoining Domain, once the governor's farm, became a public park and cricket ground in 1810. Cricket, and other sports, were played on the sandy wasteland that would soon become the Sydney Cricket Ground.

A famous cricket match took place in Hyde Park in March 1830 between a team of soldiers and one comprised of sporty settlers and emancipated convicts. A reporter from the *Gazette* was there: '[The settlers] took the field bareheaded, with a handkerchief tied around their heads, or with the popular cabbage tree hat encircled with its broad blue ribbon, and with long streamers floating behind, and in most cases played either barefooted or in their stocking feet.' A healthy crowd wagered 'money, pigs [presumably admitted for the match], sawn timber, boots, dripstone, maize, snakeskins, shoes, fish and butter'. The settlers amassed 170 runs to the soldiers' 134, and afterwards all gathered to celebrate at Toby Green's pub in Pitt Street. The *Sydney Herald*'s resident poet eulogised 'noble and scientific' cricket: 'Since cricket is a manly game/ And Britons' recreation/ By cricket we will raise our fame/ 'bove every other nation'.

Especially coveted were invitations to a musical soiree at a prominent colonist's home, where Mozart, Bach or Beethoven may be performed on harpsichord or piano, and violin. Government House hosted balls and feasts, and officers, gentlemen and their ladies glided and dipped to the latest minuet or exerted more energy reeling to 'The Dashing White Sergeant'.

'The colony was not the cultural wasteland often portrayed. Yes, there was violence and deprivation, but many people, free settlers and emancipated convicts alike, enjoyed a variety of cultural pursuits,' says historian and genealogist Annette Lemercier, a fifth-generation descendant of James Cheers, brother of Marian Egan who would book passage for herself and her children on a magnificent clipper named the *Dunbar* in 1857. Lemercier's portrait of Marian Egan for the *Dictionary of Sydney* proves her point. Like many of her fellow colonists, Marian endured tragedy and hardship yet displayed resilience to reach a prominent position in society and enjoyed the finer aspects of colonial life.

Marian Egan was born Marian Cheers in Sydney in 1818, the daughter of Jane and Richard Cheers, Jane having been transported to Sydney for theft in 1814. Richard was one of twenty convicts who helped sail the Second Fleet provision ship *Guardian* to port after it hit ice off Cape Town in 1789. Cheers was pardoned, and given land grants in Sydney on which he set up a butchery, the Black Bull Inn and farms. Marian, a dark-haired beauty, married Henry Cahuac on 29 July 1834. They had two children, Henry, born in 1837, and Gertrude, in 1839. Cahuac managed farms in the Kempsey region 430 kilometres north of Sydney. Their property, Euroka, was described by the Commissioner of Lands as comprising 'a good slab house, huts, well-fenced paddocks, a piggery and a stock yard with 30 acres [12 hectares] of maize under cultivation and watered by the McLeay River and creeks'. Marian's farm life ended when her husband was thrown from his horse and killed.

With her children, Marian moved to Sydney where property in Hunter Street had been left to her by her parents. On 17 July 1843, she married Daniel Egan, a wealthy magistrate, merchant ship-owner, businessman and alderman in Sydney Municipal Council. She being Anglican and he Catholic, they had two weddings, at Sydney's finest churches, St James' and St Mary's. Daniel Egan would become mayor of Sydney in 1853. The couple lived an existence that would have been the envy of any wealthy Londoner. Says Annette Lemercier, Marian 'enjoyed a busy social life'. At the Mayoral Ball of 1844, she turned heads with her elaborate fancy dress, and at the same event in 1847, she went as the gypsy Arline, a character in the opera *The Bohemian Girl* that was a smash hit in Sydney at the time. In 1853, to mark Egan's election as mayor, Sydney musician and music vendor Henry Marsh composed 'The Marian Waltzes', in Marian's honour. Writes Annette Lemercier:

Anne Hale Chapman, a relative, recalled 'delightful parties; given at the Egan home in Hunter Street around 1850 where [Marian] met, among others, the widower Governor FitzRoy and his son

George. And: 'Mrs Egan took me to a great Race Ball, given by Mr & Mrs R. Fitzgerald of Windsor. We stayed there a fortnight and went to the races in the open Carriage and cut a great dash. Mrs Fitzgerald, Mrs Egan, Miss Egan [Marian's stepdaughter], Harriet Walsh [Marian's niece] and myself—lots of young Gentlemen came to the Carriage, the Fitzroys, Hassells, Sam Terry, James Martin, Pantons (3). Then the Ball, and Champagne suppers every night for the week; then we returned to Sydney after a 'Pic Nic' down part of the Hawkesbury River. How we did enjoy ourselves!!

Marian Egan could kick up her heels at a party or ball while remaining 'a lady of eminent charity and piety'. She collected donations for the Free Hospital and for a residence for the Sisters of Charity, and helped to establish these institutions. She helped to found the Destitute Children's Society and donated a substantial amount of money to the Children's Asylum at Randwick. She cared for the dying Catholic Bishop of Maitland, Bishop Davis, and supported her son Henry's candidature as a postulant with the Benedictines.

Marian enjoyed the theatre. Plays, classical music and opera had been performed in Sydney Town since Arthur Phillip's day. First in a makeshift playhouse in The Rocks then, from the early nineteenth century on, at the gilded Theatre Royal, the Pitt Street Theatre and the Royal Victoria Theatre, which were modelled on the glittering theatres and concert halls of London's West End, Shakespeare's *Henry IV Part 1*, *Macbeth*, *Hamlet* and *Romeo and Juliet* were performed for an erudite and respectfully silent audience, undoubtedly including the Egans.

Those less culturally inclined could be found at the lowbrow theatres and music halls of the town, where broad comedy, juggling and magic tricks, novelty songs, bawdy pantomime and melodrama were performed. These patrons were somewhat less than reverent. Drunken roughnecks raucously heckled the poor performers, threw vegetables and invaded the stage.

* * * *

Since Arthur Phillip's day, Sydney Harbour had been the beating heart of the colony. Tall ships came and went, depositing convicts and immigrants, food and supplies. And some immigrants, after initial trepidation, learned to sail and row and explore the bays and inlets and the rivers that ran from the heart of the harbour like blue veins. On weekends, the colony's best oarsmen raced their boats the 5.6 nautical miles (10.4 kilometres) from Sydney Cove to Shark Island and back. And on a breezy summer Saturday in 1838, a sailing regatta was held to celebrate the colony's Golden Jubilee. 'The whole stream in front of Fort Macquarie [at the tip of Bennelong Point] and the bay to the eastward was crowded with sailing and rowing boats in constant motion, to and fro, and filled with gay parties of pleasure,' recorded the *Gazette*. Possibly Marian and Henry Cahuac made the long journey to Sydney to see the celebrations, or, perhaps with a baby and the demands of nineteenth-century farming, maybe not.

There were swimming races for men across Woolloomooloo Bay from the Domain to Garden Island and back from around 1830, but despite swimming being acknowledged as a healthy and refreshing recreation, few colonists indulged. Stripping off or wearing a flesh-exposing swimming costume was deemed obscene by the self-appointed moral guardians of Sydney. And perhaps staying out of the water was just as well because there were enormous sharks in the harbour, attracted not only by the plentiful fish but by the dumped cattle and sheep carcasses, garbage and raw sewage. It was not for nothing that the original names of today's Nielsen Park and Bottle and Glass Point were Shark Beach and Shark Point. Shark Island retains its colonial name to this day.

The detritus dumped overboard at Watsons Bay at Inner South Head by arriving ships at anchor awaiting a berth in Sydney Cove attracted sharks in number and there are reports of locals sitting on the harbourside beaches and the rocky foreshores watching the flashing dorsal fins of large sharks as they cruised the waters.

3

Bound for Sydney Cove

Farewell native island, from thee I must sever,
To dwell where no longer thy charms I shall see;
When afar o'er the ocean forget thee I'll never,
Sweet home of my fathers, dear land of the free.

The sails are unfurl'd now, and all is commotion;
The wind's playful whistle, the sea-birds' shrill cry;
The song rolls afar from the sons of the ocean,
Bringing tears fondly streaming from many an eye.

The anchor is weighed, and the tide is swift-flowing,
Farewell native island! Dear England, adieu!
Deep is my heart's anguish, as from thee I'm going,
I weep as thy green hills dissolve from my view.

'The Emigrant's Farewell', Traditional

The sailing route from the old world to the new for convict and emigrant vessels to Sydney in the 1830s and '40s had not changed since Arthur Phillip's day. Some 11,950 nautical miles (22,130 kilometres) from Britain southwards through the North and South

Atlantic, around the Cape of Good Hope at the southern extremity of South Africa, then east across the Indian Ocean in the 30–40-degree south latitudes, along the southern coast of Australia, then northwards along the east coast to Sydney Town. A voyage could take as long as ten months. The roughly 15,000 nautical mile (27,780 kilometre) return route was north-east from Sydney across the Pacific, around hazardous Cape Horn on Hornos Island in Southern Chile's Tierra del Fuego archipelago, then back north through the South and North Atlantic to Britain.

Because on such a lengthy voyage a ship would need to replenish stocks of food and livestock and undergo maintenance, ships put in at ports, many of them with inhabitants and customs, that, going by voyagers' journals and diaries, left indelible impressions. Las Palmas and Tenerife in Spain's Canary Islands, whose soaring volcanic peaks reared from a deep ocean floor; São Miguel, an Azorean island with tea plantations, blue hydrangea groves and volcanic lakes; the rugged Portuguese island of Madeira with its clamorous harbour and insistent locals who, for a few coins or an item of clothing, thrust upon visitors coconuts, pineapples and oranges, sheep, cows, ducks and chickens and bottles of the fortified wine that takes its name from the island; the volcanic archipelago of Cape Verde in the middle of the Atlantic; South Africa's Cape Town—described by one sailor as 'a welcome island of European culture on the edge of a dark and forbidding continent'—with its landmark Table Mountain and white cloud brooding atop it. James Bell, a 21-year-old who sailed to Australia on the *Planter* in 1838, was entranced by Rio de Janeiro in the shadow of Sugarloaf Mountain. He wrote in his diary: 'We are near the coast of Brazil still, which is lovely beyond description—at every mile a beautiful peak rises in almost a perfect cone, and that again overtopped by another beyond on whose lofty summit rest eternal mists. I would never tire of looking at such a scene, and I could almost wish to climb every mountain and cast anchor in every bay.' On departure, Bell rhapsodised, 'So farewell to this land of slavery and despotism which defile as interesting a country as ever lay to the sun. Farewell

31

to her dark-eyed beauties whose mild features delight the fancy and lead captive the heart. If ever I return to England again it shall be my endeavour to spend a month at Rio de Janeiro.' A number of Bell's fellow passengers enjoyed Rio for more prosaic reasons. The young man was dismayed by their drunkenness as they staggered back on board, and took secret pleasure in their hangovers.

Yet, notwithstanding the wondrous experiences it offered, sailing to Australia in a wooden ship over many months was inherently dangerous and often unpleasant, especially for convicts shackled together below the waterline, enduring squalor and brutality from officers and guards, and those travellers in low-cost or government-assisted steerage class. But no landlubber, even those in first class, escaped being terrified by storms and pounding waves that made the vessel pitch and plunge, and even moved atheists to pray for land. To be endured, too, were seasickness, disease and homesickness, foul food and water, fierce heat and bitter cold. Passengers and crew falling overboard was not uncommon in turbulent seas. Many a voyager desperate to reach their destination spent brain-numbing weeks becalmed on oil-slick smooth seas in the windless doldrums of the Atlantic. And, no matter how hard ships were scrubbed by crew and steerage passengers, they grew dirty as the voyage wore on and filth caked every crack and cranny. Vermin took up residence in food stores and bedding. There was constant noise: chains clanking, waves slapping the hull, sails flapping, officers shouting orders and sailors cursing, timbers groaning, livestock mooing and honking. Pirates were a threat, as were the warships of whatever country was England's enemy at the time. Colliding with an iceberg or a whale, or a fire on board, unless there was another vessel nearby, would be disastrous, as no ship carried sufficient lifeboats for its full complement. No one embarked on a voyage unmindful that ships sailing the same waters, ships just like theirs, such as the *Cataraqui*, *Edward Lombe*, *Waterloo*, *Madagascar* and *Guiding Star* and hundreds more had foundered and sunk with many lives lost.

Second mate Henry Macdonald was one of only three of 429 passengers and crew to survive the sinking of the Duncan Dunbar–owned ship the *Cospatrick*, which caught fire and sank south of the Cape of Good Hope on its way to Auckland. Macdonald, who was on a lifeboat, told the Inquiry into the disaster a harrowing tale.

Thirst began to tell severely on all of us. A man named Bentley fell overboard while steering the boat and was drowned. Three men became mad that day and died. We threw the bodies overboard. On the 23rd, the wind was blowing hard and a high sea running. We were continually bailing the water out . . . Four men died, and we were so hungry and thirsty that we drank the blood and ate the livers of two of them. We lost our only oar then. On the 24th, there was a strong gale . . . There were six more deaths that day. She shipped water till she was nearly full. On the 25th there was a light breeze and it was awful hot. We were reduced that day to eight, and three of them out of their minds. We all felt very bad that day. Early on the morning of the 26th, not being daylight, a boat passed close to us running. We hailed but got no answer. She was not more than 50 yards off. She was a foreigner. I think she must have heard us. One more died that day. We kept on sucking the blood of those who died. The 27th was squally all round, but we never caught a drop of water, although we tried to do it. Two more died that day. We threw one overboard, but were too weak to lift the other. There were then five left—two able seamen, one ordinary, myself and one passenger. The passenger was out of his mind. All had drunk sea water. We were all dozing, when the madman bit my foot, and I woke up. We then saw a ship bearing down upon us. She proved to be the *British Sceptre*, from Calcutta to Dundee. We were taken on board and treated very kindly. I got very bad on board of her. I was very nigh at death's door. We were not recovered when we got to St Helena.

The passenger and an ordinary seaman both died soon after the rescue. Only Henry and two able seamen survived.

* * * *

Before boarding their vessel, emigrants signed a Contract to Sail, agreeing to abide by the rules and regulations of the voyage, indemnifying the ship-owner against injury or death, and instructing them to bring on board their own soap, knife, fork and spoon, crockery, cotton and needles, cards, books and writing materials. Women needed six blouses and as many pairs of stockings, two thick flannel and two light cotton petticoats, two pairs of shoes or boots, a cloak with a hood, a hat and a light bonnet. For men: six shirts, a pair of stout shoes and boots, a light jacket and a heavy coat.

A ship became a village on the waves, with the same class divisions that existed within communities on land. Observed *Planter* passenger James Bell, 'There exist the same grades—the same heart-burning after distinction, the same oppression of the poor and hatred of the rich, the same jealousy of the aristocrats among themselves. And nowhere are all these more apparent or the cause of more annoyance than during a sea voyage of considerable length. Everything is exacerbated . . .' In *The Voyage Out: 100 Years of Sea Travel to Australia*, a compendium of entries from voyagers' diaries, Anne Gratton on the *Conway* in 1858 found herself 'in a dead calm sea . . . Not a single wave or the least breeze and our ship standing quite still. It is also intensely hot and it is with great difficulty we can keep ourselves clean as there are some filthy people on board and I am sorry the unwelcome travellers have found their way to our part of the ship. The scenes at bedtime are far beyond description.'

* * * *

Voyagers from Britain to Australia, depending on their budget, could travel first or cabin class, second or intermediate class, or—the cheapest fare—steerage. Fares varied depending on the ship, but in the 1830s and '40s it might have cost from £40 to £70 to travel first (or cabin) class, £20–30 for an intermediate passage, and £7 for a steerage ticket. (To put these prices in perspective, at the time a labourer might earn £27 for a year, while his wife and children added £13 to the family's income.)

Those who could afford only steerage, the claustrophobic compartment below the waterline, were sardined into a dark and dirty verminous cramped space of single-tiered, straw-filled coffin-like cots. One cabin class passenger of the early 1840s, Albert Fell, slummed it for a short time in the steerage compartment of his vessel and took pity on those who would be stuck there for the entire voyage. 'Poor creatures, it is a horrible place . . . so many people in so small a space, I wonder how they live.' Down the centre of the steerage compartment ran a common table where passengers squabbled over meagre portions of low-grade, adulterated meat and bread and drank water from algae-caked barrels fouled by vermin that had crawled in and drowned. In bad weather, steerage passengers could find themselves confined to their quarters for weeks on end. Bathing facilities were restricted or non-existent, so those inclined to cleanliness had to make do with a quick scrub with a damp cloth, often under the bed covers for privacy. Consequently, typhoid, cholera, tuberculosis, scarlet fever, dysentery, scurvy, measles, smallpox and pneumonia were commonplace. Seasickness was not fatal, although sufferers were heard to moan that death would be preferable. Candles and oil lamps were banned because they could set aflame tarred timber planking and straw bedding, so in the evening there was no light by which to read or play cards or board games.

Steerage passengers relieved themselves in pots and buckets by their cot, over the side of the ship, or on the tiny section of the deck, far from intermediate- and cabin-class passengers, that was available to them. Those who chose the latter option swept their excrement overboard or into the bilge with a bucket of salt water and vinegar or chloride of lime.

Steerage was divided into three sections. For their own safety, single women, sometimes watched over by a matron, were confined to the area towards the stern. Married couples and their children were in the middle compartment, and single men were housed in the forward area, as far as possible from the single women. Usually, the segregation was maintained. Occasionally it was not. In his book,

The Blackwall Frigates, maritime historian Basil Lubbock told of a near-mutiny on another Duncan Dunbar line vessel, the *Dunbar Castle*, a sister ship of the *Dunbar*.

> She was taking emigrants to Sydney, 10 married couples and 90 single girls. One evening . . . a terrible hullabaloo broke out below, and the girls' matron came chasing up on deck in a state of panic. She was followed a few minutes later by the ship's medico, a nervous little man who narrowly escaped having all his clothes torn off. Captain Carvosso was then compelled to take a hand. At the foot of the hatchway, he was met by a strapping north country girl who, stripped to the waist and with fists clenched, stood like a boxer ready for battle. But the little captain had an impressive personality, and, with his reef topsail voice, soon succeeded in silencing the furious mob of women. 'What the devil next!' he roared . . . he threatened to turn the hose on the girls unless they went to their bunks at once and knowing only too well that he would be as good as his word they quieted down and the mutiny was quelled.

Intermediate class, usually in the middle deck between steerage and cabin class, was superior to steerage, but not by much. Its occupants had compact compartments with small, basic bunks from which they could reach up and touch the ceiling. Latrines and bathing facilities were rudimentary and malodorous. An intermediate-class emigrant, according to one 1840s ship's manifest, would receive strictly rationed quantities of meat, vegetables and bread. Lemons, limes and oranges were available as it was believed that citrus fruit prevented scurvy.

Full-fare-paying cabin-class passengers had their own cabin on the deck with a comfortable bed, a basin in which to wash and enough space to relax in private. The ship's cooks prepared and served them generous portions of hearty food—lambs and sheep and cows loaded in England or purchased at ports of call were slaughtered on board and vegetables were as fresh as they could be in those pre–cold storage days—accompanied by tea, coffee and alcohol. Meals could be served in their cabin or they could dine with the captain and officers. They were encouraged to socialise with each other on the poop deck (the elevated deck at the stern).

The British government's emigration commissioners issued to shipping companies a list of shipboard regulations 'with the view of promoting order and health onboard passenger ships to the colonies'. Captains adhered to the rules to a greater or lesser degree, depending on circumstances and their ability—or inclination—to enforce them. Broadly, passengers rose at 7 a.m., unless they had a medical reason to remain in their bunk, and breakfasted at 8 a.m. Lunch was at 1 p.m. and dinner at 6 p.m. Passengers were expected to be in bed, lights off, by 10 p.m. No naked flame was allowed 'at any time or on any account'.

Steerage and intermediate passengers were responsible for keeping their quarters as clean as possible and aired their own bedding twice a week. Males fourteen years and older were assigned cleaning and basic maintenance duties.

Passengers' firearms, gunpowder, swords 'or other offensive weapons' would be confiscated. There was no smoking allowed between decks, and 'gambling, fighting, riotous and quarrelsome behaviour' would not be tolerated.

While steerage passengers were expected to entertain themselves, efforts were made to make cabin- and intermediate-class voyagers' passage enjoyable. There might be school lessons for children and lectures for adults on religion, geography, nature, history and the benefits of temperance. There might be a grievance meeting where shipboard gripes were aired and mediated by an officer. Steerage people sorted out their own issues.

There was free time in the afternoon and early evening to read the Bible, the works of Shakespeare, novels by Charles Dickens and books about Australia and what emigrants could expect when they arrived there. As the voyage progressed, the latter were passed around and much discussed.

An emigrant named Arthur Wilcox Manning, sailing from England on *Earl Grey* in 1839–1840, wrote in his journal, now in the archives of the State Library of New South Wales, of a typical evening.

> After dinner all the ladies were on the poop, and Payne and myself sang several songs to them. In the evening dear Fanny wrote to her Mother, and I played two games of chess, losing both. It was the first time I had played since my illness, and I soon found that my head had not yet recovered the shock. It is painful to me to keep up my attention for any length of time. Before going to bed we read as usual from the Old and New Testaments.

Passengers wrote to those they may never see again (their letters were thrown in a bag onto the deck of a passing Britain-bound ship or left in a port for collection and delivery) and painted or drew scenes from the voyage or remembered people and places from home. They passed the time with whist and bagatelle, chess and draughts, sewing and smoking, while children played hide-and-seek, tag, ball games, skipping and quoits. All on board rushed on deck to admire a glorious sunset, an island looming on the horizon or a whale breaching nearby. Literate passengers were encouraged to write for the ship's newspaper. One such publication was *The Cockroach,* in honour of the pests that far outnumbered passengers and crew. In the early evening, officers briefed those who were interested in the day's progress.

Going to bed on time and actually sleeping were two different matters. Tropical heat and the noise of the ship—and, in steerage, the reek of close-packed bodies and the bilge sloshing underfoot—could make sleep elusive. So many people jammed together with no privacy led to resentments that could degenerate into verbal and physical conflict.

'On Sunday,' read the emigration commissioners' rules, 'the passengers are to be mustered at 10am when they will be expected to appear in clean and decent apparel. The day to be observed as religiously as circumstances permit.' Passengers and crew gathered on deck to hear Bible readings from the captain and, if there was one, the ship's chaplain. Hymns would be sung as the service wound down:

There's a land that is fairer than day,
And by faith we can see it afar.
For the Father waits over the way
To prepare us a dwelling place there.
In the sweet bye-and-bye,
We shall meet on that beautiful shore;
In the sweet bye-and-bye,
We shall meet on that beautiful shore.

4

For posterity

To mark all they had seen and done, many emigrants to the colonies of Australia kept a journal or diary to record the pleasures and travails of their trip. As well as creating a keepsake to last a lifetime, jotting regular entries gave structure to each day and helped occupy tedious hours.

If passengers on the *Dunbar*'s ill-fated voyage to Sydney Town in 1857 kept diaries, and surely many did, the entries, like those who penned them, are lost. From what we do know, the *Dunbar*'s was a speedy, 'prosperous' and 'uneventful' journey, but those on board, as with all who sailed from Britain to Australia, would have experienced and seen remarkable things. So, although we cannot know precisely what transpired between when the grand clipper set sail from Plymouth on 31 May 1857 until the night 81 days later when it foundered on Outer South Head, the writings of others, who did arrive safely on other sailing ships in the first six decades of the nineteenth century, leave us a valid idea of what life on the *Dunbar* was like for those 121 souls whose memories and dreams died with them in the stormy seas off Port Jackson.

Some diarists tell vividly of storms and onboard mishaps and tragedies, others make lyrical and deeply reflective entries. A selection of
seafarers' journal and diary entries follows and it is valid to imagine
Dunbar voyagers experiencing similar emotions and insights.

James Bell, who had so enjoyed Rio de Janeiro, was a highly literate
and devout 21-year-old adventurer who sailed to Australia on the
emigrant ship the *Planter* in 1838, leaving his family and loved ones
in England for what he hoped would be a bright future in Australia.
Sadly, this was not to be. Bell died just two years after his arrival,
which makes his words all the more poignant. Bell's journal was
found in a country bookshop in England a century and a half after
it was written, and bought at auction by the State Library of South
Australia. The entries were edited by Sydney publisher Richard Walsh
and published in 2011 as *Private Journal of a Voyage to Australia*.
Bell was moved to flights of eloquence by the sea and the heavens.

> The sky is most beautiful by day and quite delightful at night. The
> moon shines with extreme lustre in the north, the planets much
> larger in appearance than I have been accustomed to see them, while
> the whole are reflected from the sea, presenting to the eye a picture
> on which it loves to repose with rapture . . . and leads the mind to
> contemplation while it sets all the passions at rest and spreads a
> feeling of pleasure and happiness over the whole soul.

Arthur Wilcox Manning, son of John Edye Manning, registrar of
the Supreme Court in Sydney, sailed cabin class with his new wife.
He would become a government official in Sydney and Brisbane.
Manning was mesmerised by the night sky on his voyage from
Plymouth to Sydney on the *Earl Grey* in 1839–1840:

> We are now making south latitude fast. Several nights ago, we lost
> sight of the 'North-Star' which is only visible to a certain degree of
> northern latitude; and now we may shortly expect to get the first sight
> of the 'Southern Cross', which is considered by far the most brilliant

and beautiful constellation in the Heavens. It is mainly composed of four large stars in the shape of a cross—hence the term 'Crux Australis'. So long as the 'Great Bear' was visible to our sight at the same time that our dear friends in England could see it, we seemed to have still one link connecting us with the land we had left behind us; and it was a pleasing fancy to think that a dear friend in England might be gazing at the same object as ourselves and at the very same moment, our eyes meeting as it were at the apex of the angle. But now this gratifying fancy is done away with, and the last links are broken. We are in different hemispheres, and gaze on different Heavens at night. There is certainly something melancholy in the idea, although I am going to my home, where I know I shall be happy. I know not how it is, but I feel that I have no business to be where I am, and a small, still voice tells me that I ought to be in England.

Being at sea intensified feelings of sadness and regret. While many were glad to be leaving Britain, others, like Manning, spent melancholy moments gazing at the horizon and contemplating the life and loves left behind. Excitement about what lay in store as they made a new life in a far-flung and mysterious land was tempered by fears that moving to Australia might prove to be a terrible mistake. James Bell wrote in his diary:

I found myself shedding a flood of tears. With all my fortitude I could not restrain them, and again and again would the memory of some one of my relations or friends separated from me, perhaps for ever, force upon me and cause my tears to flow afresh, until I had recourse to the source of all consolation and poured out my heart in prayer to God for a blessing upon them all.

Sinclair Thomas Duncan on the *Sussex* was stunned by the grandeur of a tropical sunset and remarked that sunsets at home paled in comparison. His diary, published as *Journal of a Voyage to Australia*, contains the following entry:

As [the sun] began to touch the western horizon, the sky around him got into a fiery-like illuminating blaze; and as he began to vanish from our view, his rays sprang up in a golden-like beauty, far surpassing any sunset I had seen in other latitudes. Then, as there is little or no twilight in the tropics, he no sooner disappeared below the waters, which at times lay peaceful and smooth, than, as if to make up for the light we had lost, the vault of heaven bespangled with millions of stars suddenly presented a spectacle grand and glorious to look upon. And to add to the beauty of the scene, at times the moon hung out suspended between the clear sky and the globe on which we live with a brightness and a beauty such as she has never seen in the northern hemisphere. Being glad of the cool refreshing breeze of the evening, I often sat for hours at a time admiring the heavenly bodies as they shone out in their splendid array; and when the moon was full, it was delightful to see how she illuminated the waters with her silvery-like beams which appeared to dance on the broad and ever-changing ocean around us. At times like these I often wished that some of my own relatives and old acquaintances had been near me, with whom I could have conversed, and who would have enjoyed the grand scene along with me. Knowing well, however, that I was deprived of that pleasure, I endeavoured the thought from my mind by thinking of the strange sights that would likely come under my notice in the far distant land to which we were bound.

Britain's gentle grey weather did not prepare voyagers for the dramatic vibrancy of the tropics. Spectacular lightning displays on the horizon awed James Bell.

Thunder rolled in the distance and the constant flashes of the electric fluid amidst the darkness which, from the absence of the moon, was very dense, was awfully grand and majestic. It lighted up the quarter of the heavens from whence it proceeded and, as it merged in the ocean like a solid body of flame, left the beholder lost in amazement, and told of the power of Him in whose hands is the bolt of heaven.

Nature sometimes came too close for comfort. Just as a magnificent sunset or lightning dancing in the distance could elicit tears of joy, it was a rite of every passage to encounter ferocious storms with monster swells, close-by lightning strikes and ear-splitting thunder, and hailstones that peppered the ship like buckshot, breaking timbers and shredding sails. William Millman's recollections of a gale that struck the *Melbourne* were published in *The Voyage Out*.

> The sea had got up to a terrible pitch, it was thumping and banging against the ship's side something fearful . . . a sea came on us with such fearful force that it really seemed enough to smash the ship to pieces . . . the sea was running very high and there were three sails hanging in strips and tatters, there were five sails lost during the night and the sailors say we nearly lost one of the boats. . . The second mate nearly got washed overboard . . . in fact his legs and most part of his body was overboard but he managed to catch hold of the main royal backstay and saved himself.

Seemingly endless languorous days when a ship in steady conditions might progress on the same tack for weeks were broken by bursts of furious activity. Sinclair Thomas Duncan in his *Journal of a Voyage to Australia* chronicled the chaos that ensued when the wind changed direction and caused the *Sussex* to suddenly change tack.

> When the loud ringing sound of the officer's voice was heard giving the order 'about ship', every man ran to his station in double-quick time; all the sheets were made loose, a man stood at each with a turn of the rope around a cleat, and when all was ready and the ship put to the wind there was a minute or two of suspense. The officer in charge standing on the poop glancing at every sail, low and aloft, with an eagle eye, and just as the ship veered in the right direction, away came the order, 'Let go!', when every man at the same moment slipped his rope, and the ship went round with such a sudden lurch as to put all in uproar. Nothing could be heard from between decks

but the screams of children mingled with the noise of pots, pans, knives, forks, plates, spoons, boxes, and a variety of other articles I shall not name, having taken a race to the other side of the ship. The children were crying for their mothers, who had been abruptly separated from them by sliding and tumbling to the opposite side of the vessel, becoming unexpected guests of their fellow passengers, who now knew what it was to have their cabins on the lee side instead of the other.

George French Angas, a world voyager renowned for his drawings and watercolours of the places he visited in the mid-1800s, could not resist leaving his quarters to clamber onto the deck in the middle of a gale to join the crewmen who were lashed to the wheel and stanchions to keep from being swept overboard. Angas survived to write: 'The extreme fury of the wind beat down the sea, which appeared as one mass of boiling surge, the spray drifting along like smoke, whilst all beyond the abyss we were descending, and the side of the next sweeping mountain that seemed as if it would bury us in foam at its approach, was obscured by an impenetrable mist.' In August 1857, Angas was commissioned to illustrate the bestselling booklet, *A Narrative of the Melancholy Wreck of the* Dunbar, and his graphic line drawings may have been informed by his own near-death experiences at sea.

James Bell was snapped from his usual reveries when *Planter* was battered by huge seas.

The gale came with such fury that it burst the main tack in one instant, and away went the sail to pieces with the wind. The mate, who had been so stupid as not to perceive its coming on, called all hands to secure the flapping sail. But while they were attempting this, away went the foreyard in two halves and left all the canvas to chafe about the mast. The jib was reduced to rags, and all that was left was the double reefed main topsail . . . The masts, after the sails had all been rent, quivered and shook in the wind. The sea came on in billows almost as high as our masts and we were at times suspended on the summit of a huge wave, as another plunged down headlong into the gulph [sic] between and, as we had no sails to keep her steady, she was at times almost lying on her side, and the water on both sides spouting over her decks. The captain's cow was thrown over the long boat upon the deck, and is in a deplorable state, as are all the horses and livestock . . . We are in a very disabled state.

John Fitch Clark, whose words were published in *The Voyage Out*, was sure his life had reached its end when the *Nepaul* was battered by a typhoon en route to Australia.

The heaviest lurch . . . happened about 6 o'clock . . . people at one end of the cabin were hurled, if standing, to the other end, and if the door is open right out to the tables . . . and back again with like celerity—boxes, pots, pans, victuals of all kinds, and bits of dirt, following your own course with extraordinary affection. Outside you have displayed in graceful negligence, the plates, mugs, cups and saucers, galley pots, water kegs holding three gallons of water, stone jars of like dimensions, tubs, slop-pails, etc etc . . . This day and night was perhaps the worst we have yet had. We only had three sails out, two reefed as much as possible . . . The bulwarks were stove in on the starboard side, half the length of the main deck washing away, and we were expecting the mainmast to come out for some hours.

Passengers were confined to their quarters during bad weather, but, like George French Angas, Sinclair Thomas Duncan sneaked up onto the *Sussex*'s forecastle during a storm:

to get a full view of the wild and troubled waters. It was terrible, the sea breaking over us . . . pouring columns of water on the main deck with a noise like thunder, while in the midst of all I noticed that the captain was on the poop, two men were at the wheel and others were ready for any emergency; but oh! The large ship was shaking like a leaf as she bounded ahead, throwing and twisting like some living monster in great distress. The truth is, that in taking a look around the horizon, I could compare the sea to nothing else than as it were thousands of hills and mountains covered with snow all running delirious, and now and again falling into caverns, and appearing as if they were drunk. Between the noise of the wind and the sea we could scarcely hear each other speak, and sometimes the heavy seas, breaking and tumbling in over the quarter, came with such force as to send terror to the heart . . . Our gallant ship was so steady and ran through the dreadful seas so well, that I felt little or no fear, but I could not say that of others. It was amusing to hear the sailors speaking to the ship, as she staggered when a sea struck her, and she running before the wind. They never exhibited any symptoms of fear; but I observed a few of them together and after she had recovered from a sea breaking over her, they would say with looks of earnestness, 'Well done, good old ship, keep up your stern, and there is no fear.' The seas we shipped were generally in over the quarter, so that the main hatch had to be battened down; a thing which had a great tendency to frighten the passengers in the second cabin. The greatest danger connected with any vessel when she is running before a heavy rolling sea is just at the time it is breaking over her, and when she is prevented from going ahead, because she is then apt to go down by the stern, as many a good ship has done.

Such hair-raising occurrences, thankfully, alternated with times when the sea was calm and progress was slow and boredom set in. The inevitable tedium of a long sea voyage must have dampened the excitement felt by emigrants at embarkation and brought on home-sickness. At one point of his voyage on the *Planter*, James Bell found himself wondering if it was all worth it. 'There is enough of dullness and monotony; indeed, we are quite the reverse of happy and cannot tell the reason why we are unhappy. The same unvarying round of unemployment occupies them every day . . . nothing to relieve the mind or excite the fancy by its novelty.' While Bell allowed that the sea was 'pleasant', for those longing for land, such as himself:

it seems very tedious to be so idle . . . [That] I have visited several quarters of the globe seems to be but a poor compensation for the loss of a single day of the happiness I have enjoyed at home. We are now fast approaching the country of our adoption—whether for better or worse remains to be determined. I trust for better to some of us, but it has every chance to be worse to many of us. This day commences my 23rd year.

'On reflecting on the past period of my life, I feel many affecting sensations: on looking forward,' pondered Bell, who would not survive two years in the colony, 'the future seems dark and obscure, but is perhaps wisely hid from my sight.'

Ennui's henchmen on a slackly run ship were drunkenness and bad behaviour. James Bell spent one morning on the *Planter* with a headache after being woken at 3 a.m. by a noisy row among cabin-class passengers 'They were all tipsy and quarrelling, singing, dancing, making love, all at once. And the captain worst. I admire innocent and rational amusement as much as any person. But I never saw people indulge in every criminal pleasure and sinful crime so unblushingly as the passengers on board this vessel.'

John Fitch Clark told how a *Nepaul* passenger who was caught stealing a pie was bound hand and foot and 'amidst the jeers and taunts of those on board they carried him to the poop [where he] had his face tarred and was lashed to the mast for an hour and a half, the warning that the next thief would have a rope tied around him and thrown overboard'. Clark also left us a graphic account of a fight between two fellows preparing dinner.

More excitement—pugilism this time. One man washing pork, another wanting to wash his hands. First one would not move, second one endeavoured to pull him away by the hair of his head [and] did succeed in clawing a handful of his hair out by the roots. Therefore the pork washer used his fists upon the other's nose and eyes. Second one retires; brings his son and both set upon the first one till parted.

Committee and captain meet—investigate the case—decided both were in the wrong—cautioned—shake hands very sorry—dismissed.

The combatants were spared the usual punishment for unruly behaviour of being placed in irons without food and water or made to walk the deck for hours.

Shooting birds and fish for sport and food was a popular diversion. Porpoises and dolphins, sharks, cape pigeons, stormy petrels and flying fish that crash-landed on the deck were all fair game. Despite general acknowledgement that killing an albatross brought bad luck, some on board could not resist taking pot shots at the birds, some of which measured 3.5 metres from wingtip to wingtip. James Bell dared to sample cooked dolphin 'but I found it extremely disagreeable to my palate. It had a strong, rancid taste, and smelled something like fish saturated in train oil.'

Seafarers were mesmerised by the lazy undulations of Portuguese man-of-war jellyfish off the bow. 'We were rather sceptical about their alleged stinging properties,' reported the *Henry* emigrant John Wollaston, 'but poor Teddy, having touched one brought up by the ropes, applied his hand to his face and was feelingly convinced for some hours of the truth of the statement.'

Sharks trailed the ships hoping for offal thrown overboard. Sinclair Thomas Duncan wrote of a shark caught on a hook baited with pork and hauled onto the deck. After crew used hatchets and clubs to stop its thrashing, the shark was cut up and eaten. Like James Bell after sampling dolphin, Duncan could not envisage shark becoming a regular part of his diet. 'The flesh of sharks is in general hard, coriaceous and ill-tasted.' Still, the predators had his deepest respect.

They are the most formidable and voracious of all fishes, pursue all other marine animals and seem to care little whether their prey be living or dead. Man often becomes a victim to their rapacity. The sailors hate the shark as their common enemy, and while the one we captured was being cut up, I could easily see that the crew were filled with revenge, and the occurrence led to many a strange and thrilling story being told by parties on board of men having been exposed to attack, and in some cases eaten by the monsters.

Vermin were a bugbear. Fanny Shorter shuddered that her vessel, the *Duke of Buccleuch*:

[had] lots of rats on board. The sub-matron killed one Tuesday. Yesterday she had one on her head; she very pluckily knocked it down and put her foot on it. One of the girls had one scratching her ear in bed. She felt its little cold nose smelling about her face. One feels so very helpless on the sea. There seems to be nothing but a little water between us and God.

Arthur Wilcox Manning seemed in good humour as he told his diary of his pre-bedtime hunting excursions on the *Earl Grey*.

Hardly a night elapses without any killing, plenty of game—It is not hare, nor fox, or stag! It is neither bird, beast or fowl! And yet it is a living creature! . . . What can it be? nothing, more or less, than a—cockroach!! . . . I have plenty of these in my domain, small as it is. Every ship that has ever been laden with sugar will always be overrun with such vermin. The *Earl Grey* brought home sugar and rice from the East Indies last voyage and it is now swarming with cockroaches, which get into the boxes, boots, shoes or any hollow article they can find. Last night I killed 24 in my cabin, much to my wife's amusement—for she sits up in her bed and laughs heartily at the eagerness with which I pursue the blackguards: and the wry faces and chatterings I make whenever I have succeeded in bringing down a monster with my slipper . . . They frequently come right over our heads at night, and fall plump on our noses while we are sleeping.

Mice scampered over John Wollaston in his cot. He grasped what he thought was a piece of string but was instead 'the tail of a mouse which struggled and got away from me'. Yet he preferred mice to 'bugs—some of which I frequently have to hunt at night and keep a candle and match ready for the purpose'.

Rodents chittered and scuttled freely through provisions, maggots, cockroaches and weevils ruined provisions, and lice and fleas multiplied in clothing and bedding. Disease was inevitable. 'Fever,' wrote Arthur Wilcox Manning,

has broken out amongst the Emigrants! Yes, here we are alone, on the wide ocean, far from friends and assistance, and unable to escape, and surrounded by that most direful of all scourges 'Typhus Fever'! I shudder at the thought; for if it once takes firm hold of the ship, God only knows how many now on board will live to arrive in Sydney . . . One man was buried yesterday, and two women are now in the hospital, dangerously ill of the fever. It now appears that our poor steward, who died a few days ago, was a victim of this terrible fever; but the matter was hushed up from fear of alarming the people—I am not at all surprised that we are at last visited by this sickness on board the ship, as she is so very much crowded, and the arrangements so badly managed from the beginning to end. Mr Lunn, who has the management of these emigrants, as surgeon, is no more fit for his station than I am. The heat of these latitudes is very much against us, and by making the 'Tween-decks' close and sultry, fever is more likely to arise, and contagion to spread.

Accidents happened. Passengers and crew alike could be washed overboard and work mishaps on a rocking, pitching and overcrowded vessel were everyday events. James Wilcox Manning:

Today, while the ship was tacking, one of the emigrants was badly hurt by a rope, which swung with great violence against his face. The poor man's lips and face were very much lacerated, and three or four of his teeth were actually knocked out! Mr Lunn was obliged to sew up his lip. He seemed in great pain, and is very much disfigured . . . The poor fellow will not be able to do his work for some length of time.

Admiral Duncan Dunbar-Nasmith, a descendant of Duncan Dunbar II who owned the *Dunbar* and a fleet of other British clippers, examined the logbooks of Dunbar's ships and in a 2005 speech regaled his audience with a litany of recorded mishaps, including, 'John James, ordinary seaman furling the main royal (the highest sail) fell off the yard; overboard, striking the main yard in his descent, and was drowned. It would have been madness to lower a boat.' And he told of the sailmaker's finger that was severed in a pump. Painful, surely, but the logbook noted a happy ending. 'Finger well. Sailmaker resumed duty.' Continued Dunbar-Nasmith, 'There were many cases of stealing, drunkenness and disobedience and the officers had to be tough and handy with their fists to maintain control. Mutiny is recorded and the whole crew walking ashore to put their case to the local magistrate. There were instances of rows with the Pilot and collisions; shortages of food and water and the calculations for reduced rations.'

The tension of existing in a confined space surrounded by seemingly endless sea could take a toll on vulnerable passengers. Sinclair Thomas Duncan witnessed a young man who was returning to Australia with his family after visiting relatives in England jump overboard.

It was very dark, the ship running before the wind at a tremendous rate, and the sea was rolling in huge waves, so that there was no use in making any effort to save him . . . I learned that he had been showing symptoms of insanity while on the voyage and, having had some altercation with his mother, he rushed up the stair leading from the cabin to the poop and jumped over the stern, with nothing on but his nightgown. This alarming affair produced a fearful gloom over us all, especially in regard to his own relatives who, I was told, would not be consoled, their heart-rending screams being heard all over the ship.

Rare was the ship's chaplain who did not have to conduct burials at sea. Whether due to disease, malnutrition, accident or foul play, old age or infant mortality, six or seven deaths per trip was not considered unusual. The gung-ho *Marco Polo* master James Nicol 'Bully' Forbes prayed over 53 coffins on one horrific voyage.

Sinclair Thomas Duncan wrote movingly of a sea burial.

> The little girl in the sick-list died about 4 o'clock in the morning; the funeral took place at 4 in the evening . . . the corpse was sewed up in a piece of thick canvas, some weighty substance [probably lead or iron] being enclosed at the feet; it was then laid on a plank, the one end of which rested on an erection in one of the ports in the bulwark and the other held up by two sailors, one on each side, in silent solemnity. The mother stood at the head as the chief mourner, the captain close by her, reading the burial service according to the rules of the Episcopalian Church; and when he came to a certain part of the ceremony he gave the two sailors a sign, who immediately lifted up their end of the board, the corpse then being instantaneously consigned to the deep, all the spectators withdrawing from the place, except the mother, who stood mourning the loss of her dear little girl, while onlookers were more or less affected, the ship at the same time bounding on in her course at the rate of 10 miles [16 kilometres] an hour.

Earl Grey passenger Arthur Wilcox Manning recoiled with the rest of his shipmates when a burial at sea did not go exactly to plan.

> When the coffin was launched overboard it did not sink, as it was expected to do, but floated on the water, quite upright! This was owing to not putting sufficient weight inside the coffin before nailing it down. Had not the carpenter purposely made several holes in the wood it would have taken days in sinking . . . in a few minutes the coffin disappeared, having filled with water.

When a passenger died, his or her belongings were auctioned. Arthur Wilcox Manning got in on the act:

I bought some *eau de cologne*, a belt and a journal book ... A public auction was held on board this morning, consisting of the property of our poor steward and the emigrant Mahi who died two or three days ago. It is an old and established custom at sea that when anybody died on board or deserts his ship, all the property of which he may have been possessed is sold by auction to the highest bidder. A sale under such circumstances is known by the name of 'Deadman's Sale' ... Passengers subscribed to buy the steward's violin and music, intending to give them to one of the emigrants at the end of the voyage on the condition that he is to play for us when we may choose to call him. Poor Hart, the steward, was a first-rate musician and I heard him playing on the violin most exquisitely only one or two nights before his death.

After months at sea, as the ships neared their Australian destination, excitement was rekindled. A bottle of wine was presented to the first passenger to sight the shore and cry, 'Land ho!' Finally, at last, the voyage ended. Emigrant James Bell, despite his earlier qualms about leaving England, struggled to describe:

the sensations of myself and all on board seeing land. All my past fears and trouble seemed to vanish in an instant. Joy sprang up afresh in my bosom and I hailed the happy prospect of finishing my voyage in safety. I need not say that we have most delightful anticipations of at last ending a long and tedious voyage, which has been anything but agreeable ... As pleasure is sweet after pain, so the pleasure of having gone through so much will be pleasant in the reflection.

While James Bell's hopes and feelings would have been shared by those on board the *Dunbar* as it neared its destination, any pleasant reflection at journey's end would be denied them.

5

A city comes of age

In his introduction to the 1853 *Emigrant's Guide to Australia*, author John Capper assured those emigrants who may be having second thoughts as departure day neared that any fears they had were groundless. Australia, true, had once been 'a place of crime, of chains and stripes, a vast jail in the wilderness, a criminal lazar house, a voyage to which was as much dreaded as a trip to Siberia or Russian Tartary' that attracted 'none but the most wretched to visit its shores'. But that was in the past. Now, in the 1840s and '50s, the Great South Land was:

a land flowing with something better than milk and honey, a region rich beyond exaggeration in gold, copper, timber—prolific to pro- fusion in its yield of corn, wool, wine and oil—teeming with safe and commodious harbours for shipping—with the richest grass land and fertile grain soil—with vast forests of valuable woods sufficient to supply all the world with shipping for the next dozen centuries— and, above all this, blessed with a climate so admirably adapted to the human frame that in most parts of the country the profession of a medical man is a poor and unneeded one. The marvellous tales of boundless wealth, of unceasing prosperity, of unexampled progress, read almost like some story of enchantment from *The Arabian Nights*.

Capper was wearing his rose-coloured spectacles, but there was some truth to his advice. Sydney's days as a benighted outpost where convicts and their keepers scrabbled to survive in shacks and tents on the muddy harbour shore were largely in the past. By the 1850s, the colony was a place where free women and men could lead a civilised life, eat what they grew and raised, and profit from their labour.

When Sydney Town was incorporated as a city in 1842, it occupied 11.65 square kilometres, bounded by Woolloomooloo, Surry Hills, Pyrmont and Chippendale. In 1855, with Sir William Thomas Denison in the governor's mansion, New South Wales attained self-governance. By then, convict transportation from Britain had ceased, bore water provided an adequate water supply and a coal-powered gas works at Darling Harbour had seen gas light replacing oil lamps in homes and on the streets. The now-41-years-dead Governor Arthur Phillip's dream of a self-sufficient colony had come true. Premium-quality New South Wales wool brought high prices in Great Britain and Europe, as did coal, wine, whale and vegetable oil and tallow. The fertile fields west of Sydney were ideal for grazing sheep and cattle and growing vegetables and fruit. Colonists were rolling up their sleeves and constructing roads and buildings, manufacturing ships and trains and laying the tracks they ran on—from 1855, a locomotive sped passengers and goods through tunnels and over bridges built by 650 engineers and labourers brought from England, between what is today Central Station and Parramatta. The colonists felled and milled timber, made garments and footwear, textiles, home furnishings, bricks and tiles; whalers produced the oil for engines, candles and soap. They were creating a foundation for the Sydney of today.

Anyone strolling down Macquarie or George or Pitt streets in the 1850s would see wealthy women in bonnets and long crinoline dresses (with a corset beneath) adorned with buttons and beads. Well-to-do men sported a wide-brimmed straw or felt hat or topper, high-collared shirt, frock-coat over a waistcoat with watch chain, and leather boots. Clenched between most men's teeth was a pipe, cigar or cheroot.

After gold was discovered in California in January 1848, large numbers of Sydneysiders sailed away to the American goldfields. The resultant manpower shortage, coupled with severe drought and a slump in wool, wheat and livestock prices, resulted in an economic depression in the colony in the late 1840s. Yet the downturn did not last. Though James McBrien and others probably beat him to it, on 12 February 1851, Englishman Edward Hargraves found flecks of gold in a billabong at Ophir, Bathurst, and claimed to have made Australia's first 'official' gold strike. Almost simultaneously the precious metal was found elsewhere in New South Wales and Victoria, sparking a prospecting frenzy. The colonists hurried home with their picks and pans from California. With their return, the arrival of big-spending gold-seekers from all over the world who'd been lured by the promise of untold riches, and a surge in immigration, the colony's economy recovered, then boomed.

Those prospectors, whether with pockets full or empty, whether returning to their home country or having remained in Sydney, helped create an international city. At the onset of the gold rush, in 1851, the population of Sydney was 42,700, with another 10,000 or so in outer areas. A decade later those numbers had doubled.

Many who succeeded as merchants, or in manufacturing or farming or who struck it rich in the goldfields bought land and built substantial homes on the shores of Port Jackson. Steam paddleboats ferried the harbourside dwellers to and from Sydney Cove and out to Parramatta. Fears of foreign invaders, notably Russia, at war with Britain and France in the Crimea from 1853, or pirates bent on plundering the city's riches, led to heavy guns being installed at strategic harbour locations. Fort Denison—with its small, round fortress, armoury and barracks—was constructed on the rocky harbour island known as Pinchgut, where troublesome convicts had been sent for execution or solitary confinement.

Parts of Sydney had 'an elegant and uniform appearance that could scarcely be excelled by that of any English town of similar size', wrote John Capper. 'The thickly studded waters swarming with sailing craft and steam vessels, rushing crowds on shore, all tend to impress the stranger most favourably with the beauty and importance of this Australian capital.'

Visiting British novelist Anthony Trollope would concur with Capper. 'I despair of being able to convey to any reader my own idea of the beauty of Sydney Harbour . . . [it] is so inexpressively lovely that it makes a man ask himself whether it would not be worth his while to move his household goods to the eastern coast of Australia.' As would Mark Twain who, in *Following the Equator*, described the harbour as 'a wonder of the world . . . shaped somewhat like an oak-leaf—a roomy sheet of lovely blue water, with narrow off-shoots of water running up into the country on both sides between long fingers of land, high wooden ridges with sides sloped like graves'.

By the early 1850s, Sydney's heart, the harbour, was beating loud and strong. It was a busy waterway crisscrossed by working boats, steam ferries, pleasure boats packed with picnickers, longboats, skiffs, tenders, pilot boats, whaling and sealing boats, Indigenous canoes and small sailing craft. American and British warships visited and the crews they disgorged made the waterfront bars livelier than ever.

Vying for anchorage with the local working and pleasure craft were the sailing ships on the England–Australia–England route. In 1831, some 155 convict and immigrant ships from Britain and other countries entered Sydney Harbour; 30 years later the number was 1327. Sydney Cove bristled with the masts of ships that had delivered emigrants from England, Ireland, Scotland, Wales, Germany, South Africa, China and France, gold-seekers, political, military and naval personnel, livestock, mail and newspapers (albeit months after they were penned, printed or published). Unloaded and transported to stores and colonists' homes were civilising luxuries such as fine furniture, wine, tobacco, books, dining ware, art, jewellery and musical instruments. The merchant ships returned to the northern hemisphere laden with local wool, wheat, textiles and other manu-factured goods.

There were fewer now of the vessels that were throwbacks to the bad old days, ill-maintained, leaky, creaking floating dungeons captained and navigated by, as maritime historian Basil Lubbock put it, 'rum-soaked, bearlike, illiterate officers . . . who trusted to dead reckoning or a blackboard held up by a passing ship for their longi-tude'. These hell ships, if they completed the voyage at all, could be at sea for ten or more unbearable months. But their days were numbered. Now, more and more, there were handsome clippers, brigs, cutters, barquentines, schooners and frigates commanded and crewed by skilled mariners. Another dream of Arthur Phillip, that of 'a thousand sail of the line' riding in Sydney Harbour 'in the most perfect security', had been realised.

Britons were routinely sailing to Sydney to visit loved ones who had emigrated, and colonists who could afford it, like Marian Egan and her children Gertrude and Henry Cahuac, could cure any lingering homesickness or a desire to experience European culture and scenery by sailing back to the northern hemisphere for family reunions and holidays in Britain and on the Continent.

Almost a hundred years before passenger planes and 70 years before telephones—170 years before Skype and Zoom—the great sea voyage was the colony's umbilical cord to the Motherland. The tall ships carrying people, mail and cargo regularly plying from Britain to Sydney and back again—billowing sails harnessing the elements, instilled in the colonists confidence that theirs need not be, after all, lives of isolation at the edge of the globe—reminded them that they still belonged to the world at large.

Marian Egan had turned her fortunes around after the death of her husband, Henry Cahuac. Now, as the wife of Daniel Egan, life was good for her in Sydney. In 1855, Marian booked passage to England for herself, Gertrude and Henry. She was keen, as historian Annette Lemercier says, to 'afford her children an opportunity to see society in its more settled and ancient forms' during an extended stay in Great Britain and the Continent. So, on Christmas Eve, the three sailed from Sydney on the Duncan Dunbar line clipper *Vimeira*, under the steady command of the experienced Captain James Green. Marian's husband, Daniel, remained in Sydney to take care of business and politics.

Considering the many ships on the England–Australia route as the colony found its stride, there were relatively few maritime disasters. For all the long voyage's dangers and discomforts, passengers and merchants were happy to put their trust in a good ship with a good master, and considered the epic journey a risk worth taking.

Of course, ships were sometimes lost. Just kilometres from Sydney Cove, the *Edward Lombe* in August 1834 smashed into Port Jackson's Middle Head at night in foul weather. The human toll was 189 when, in 1842, the Tasmania-bound convict ship *Waterloo* dropped anchor off the Cape of Good Hope to take on fresh food and water and was sunk by a storm. Four hundred passengers and crew perished when *Cataraqui* broke in two on hitting a reef 100 metres off the south-west coast of Bass Strait's King Island in 1845. The Blackwall frigate clipper *Madagascar*, with around 160 passengers and crew and two tonnes of gold on board, vanished in 1853 returning to London from Melbourne. The *Guiding Star* with 543 emigrants and crew disappeared in the Southern Ocean in 1855, most likely after striking an iceberg.

The *Edward Lombe* was a three-masted timber barque of 352 tonnes. It had completed the England–Sydney route in 1830 and 1833. On its third journey to Sydney, in 1834, its master was Captain Stuart Stroyan. On board were 71 crew, emigrants and convicts. In the *Edward Lombe*'s hold were spirits, salt and other goods for the colony. Approaching Port Jackson from due east, its foretop mast staysail and back-stay were smashed by a south-easterly gale and she listed at the mercy of enormous swells, thwarting Stroyan's plan to weather the storm outside Sydney Heads until next day. So, there being no pilot boats willing or able to assist because it was night and the conditions were dangerous, Captain Stroyan ran for Sydney

Cove. The *Edward Lombe* entered the Heads at 9.30 p.m., only to be swept stern first onto Middle Head. Stroyan and eleven others died. The survivors clambered from the foundering ship to the shore and were rescued the following morning. The bloated corpses of the recovered victims were too swollen to fit in small coffin shells. They were piled into an open cart and conveyed through the streets of Sydney Town to Devonshire Street Cemetery.

The *Edward Lombe* was the first large sailing vessel to go down with loss of life in Port Jackson.

A correspondent to the *Sydney Times* blamed:

a want of sharpness both in the shipping regulations, choice of captain and an entire negligence in the Harbour of the Colony. When *Edward Lombe* entered the Heads in such boisterous weather as it was on Monday evening, night signals ought to have immediately been made to the harbourmaster, or a man on horseback despatched *en galloppe* from South Head by land. The revenue cutter or any other boat or boats . . . ought to have been sent away immediately, and so the lives of 12 of our brethren might have been preserved as well as the mail, on the safe delivery of which the more or less happiness of more than a hundred individuals may depend. But the enactment of such regulations requires men of experience, talent and devotion to the public welfare. Poor, neglected, lingering Australia! Whilst ships and men's lives are lost in this way, the officers concerned may be perhaps at their farms, 150 miles [240 kilometres] distance, giving directions how to make some more money, besides a large salary that they get from the public. After the first consternation about *Edward Lombe* will be over, we shall fall again into our usual apathy, until after a shorter or longer time another case of the same nature will occur, burning, as it were, the bowels of every man of feeling.

Prophetic words . . . that came tragically true on another wild August night 23 years later.

6

Greyhounds of the sea

Clippers—long, slim ships with streamlined hulls and gracefully curved bows, built of hardwood with jute or canvas sails billowing from three backward-raked teak masts—were the pinnacle of nineteenth-century sailing-ship design and manufacture. They revolutionised the voyage from Britain to Australia. The first clipper to sail from England to Sydney was the *Phoenician*, which dropped anchor in Sydney Cove on 21 July 1848. Four years later, at the height of the gold rush, it was the first ship to carry colonial gold back to England.

With the *Phoenician*, everything changed. From 1848 till the 1860s when fully steam-powered vessels made of iron superseded sail for long voyages, clippers delivered, to many thousands of emigrants, merchants and gold-hunters, a faster, more comfortable and relatively safer journey to Australia than ever before. In fair winds, a 'greyhound of the sea', as they were known, could average 16–18 knots and at its speediest make 350 nautical miles (648 kilometres) a day; if the weather continued to be kind and there were no mishaps, they slashed the England–Sydney run to a little under three months.

'Clipper' derives from the verb 'clip', to move quickly; and the ships' very names evoke speed, adventure and romance: *Lightning*, *Flying Spur*, *Marco Polo*, *Champion of the Seas*, *True Briton*, *Rainbow*, *Phoenician* . . . In his 1858 publication for White Star Line travellers, *Practical Hints to Intending Emigrants to Our Australian Colonies*, author John Willox touted the line's clippers:

These magnificent clippers, so long employed in conveyance of Her Majesty's mails between Liverpool and Australia, are among the finest, largest and fastest afloat, and have made some of the most extraordinary passages on record. Commanded by men of experience who have been uniformly successful in their respective ships, they offer extraordinary advantages to passengers and shippers of goods who may rely upon them sailing punctually at noon on the advertised dates.

The British version of the softwood American—or Yankee—clippers, which had sailed international trade routes since the early 1840s, were designed to speed low-volume, high-profit cargo, such as Chinese tea, perishable grain, wool and precious metals, such as gold, and passengers. Some of the best British clippers were designed and constructed in London, Sunderland, Plymouth and Liverpool shipyards by Sir James Laing & Sons Ltd. The company built the vessels of the Black Ball clipper fleet and the White Star Line. The *Dunbar*, a classic example of a clipper in the golden age of sail, was built in 1852–53 in Sunderland, north-east England, by James Laing & Sons for the shipping magnate Duncan Dunbar II.

The Australian mariner Alan Villiers, who had sailed on traditionally rigged vessels since age fifteen, was chairman and president of the Society for Nautical Research and governor of Britain's *Cutty Sark* Preservation Society. Villiers authored 44 books, many on the clippers. He wrote that while a clipper could be a schooner, a brig or a barquentine, to him, indeed to all experienced sailors, to truly be categorised as a clipper a vessel had to be built for speed. It had to be 'tall-sparred and carry the utmost spread of canvas'. And it must *use* that sail, day and night, fair weather and foul. 'Optimised for speed, clippers were too fine-lined to carry much cargo.' They did, however, carry extra sails, including 'high-flying skysails and moon-rakers at the top of the mast and studding sails on booms extending out from the hull or yards'. Clippers revelled in high winds that would find other ships shortening their sails. They, wrote Villiers, 'drove on, heeling so much that their lee rails were in the water'.

Unlike the slower ships of earlier eras, clippers on the Australia route usually did not have to make time-wasting landfall for maintenance or to acquire fresh provisions. But, if the master felt there was a need for repairs or decided to replenish water, food and liquor supplies and livestock, or despatch mail and progress reports back home, he might put in at any of the usual ports: Madeira, Cape Verde, Cape Town or Rio de Janeiro.

Cabin- or first-class passengers paid as much as £100 (half of the annual salary of the lowest ranks of commissioned army officers) for a berth on a superior clipper and experienced luxury that cabin classers in previous decades had never known. Their upper-deck cabins had large and comfortable beds, cabinets, dining tables, and bathing and toilet facilities with running water. Weather permitting, cabin-class voyagers promenaded and socialised on the elevated poop deck at the stern, which was as spacious as the ship's narrow dimensions allowed and off-limits to those in intermediate and steerage classes. Cabin-class meals were London-restaurant standard and served in the travellers' quarters or, by appointment, in the captain's or officers' dining area. First-class passengers played deck games, danced to an orchestra and attended classical musical soirees.

Cabin-class and intermediate passengers with theatrical aspirations vied to be cast in shipboard productions of *Macbeth*, *A Midsummer Night's Dream* and *The Merchant of Venice* as well as music hall comedy performances. Singalongs ('The Irish Emigrant', 'The Last Rose of Summer', 'Soldiers Evermore', 'Tell Me Mary', 'Beautiful Erin', 'Far Away O'er Foam' and 'Bob Ridley' and raucous sea shanties such as 'Haul Away Joe' and 'Drunken Sailor') were accompanied by lively fiddle, fife and accordion.

Intermediate and steerage quarters on clipper ships were markedly more comfortable and cleaner than had been the case for lower-paying passengers on vessels in years gone by.

Clippers, being so speedy and well built, could sail the faster, more profitable, but perilous Great Circle Route, or Brouwer Route (named after its seventeenth-century Dutch explorer discoverer Hendrik Brouwer), to the colonies. The Great Circle Route was favoured by traders for whom time was money, by passengers anxious to reach their destination without delay and by prospectors champing to reach the goldfields before the glittering seams expired.

The ships would proceed from England, as usual, south through the eastern North Atlantic Ocean, with Spain and northern Africa on port bow, to the equator. This sector of the voyage typically took around three weeks, although the windless doldrums, where north-east and south-east trade winds converged, could delay the equator crossing by weeks, occasionally months. At the equator, passengers endured the obligatory King Neptune celebrations and tortures. Next, their ship would trace the south Atlantic currents and trade winds to the island of green turtles, Trindade off Brazil, south-east across the South Atlantic, passing the island of Tristan da Cunha, towards South Africa. But then, instead of rounding the Cape of Good Hope at 34–35 degrees south on South Africa's southern tip and sailing due east across the Indian Ocean to Australia on gentle 30–40 degree latitude winds, the Great Circle Route clippers would venture down into the Southern Ocean north of Antarctica with its freezing temperatures, icebergs, gales and blood-curdling 20 metre black-grey swells. There, between latitudes 40 and 50 degrees south, the clippers, with every sail set, hitched a wild ride on the Roaring Forties, strong prevailing westerly winds averaging between 15 and 35 knots and generating 5–10 metre roiling white-capped waves. The winds and swells would propel the vessels east for around 3560 nautical miles (6600 kilometres):

far south of Western Australia's Cape Leeuwin, passing eastwards below the South Australian coast, before arcing up towards Port Phillip in Victoria. Then through Bass Strait (called 'threading the needle'), 430 nautical miles (800 kilometres) north along Australia's east coast, around South Head and finally into Port Jackson. An excellent time for the voyage was 80–90 days. A daring, or foolhardy, master could improve on that time by plunging his vessel past the 40s, down to the shorter-distance 50 and 60 degree south latitudes where the winds were known, with good reason, as the Furious Fifties and the Shrieking Sixties.

In 1850, the clipper *Constance*, commanded by G.B. Godfrey, completed the Great Circle Route voyage from Plymouth to Port Adelaide in an unprecedented 78 days. That record stood until mid-1852, when the black-hulled emigrant clipper *Marco Polo*, captained by James Nicol 'Bully' Forbes, a daredevil martinet to whom speed and profits were more important than the safety and sanity of his terror-stricken passengers and crew, virtually hurtled from Liverpool to Port Phillip in 68 days.

Once in Sydney, marking time while the ship underwent maintenance, a clipper's crew could take their pick of pubs and music halls at The Rocks. Meanwhile, England-bound passengers would embark and the vessel would be loaded with produce, gold and mail, and set sail due east across the Pacific to complete the Great Circle Route. South of the South Island of New Zealand, then around Cape Horn, the southernmost point of Chile, with its Andean gales, freak currents and submerged reefs. When, or if, the Horn was rounded, it was north again, with South America to port, on through the Atlantic to England. The 15,000 nautical mile (27,780 kilometre) return voyage, Sydney–Plymouth, if all went to plan, would take around 100 days.

Thanks to the clipper ships, by the 1850s, passenger and merchant shipping had never been so speedy and risk-free for passengers, or lucrative for owners, agents and traders. Typical of merchants who prospered and attained a quality of life they may never have been able to enjoy in Britain were the enterprising Waller brothers—Kilner Waller in Launceston and John Gough Waller in Sydney—who imported quality liquor, household goods and delicacies for the pantries of the well heeled.

In December 1853, Kilner and his wife, Maria, and their five children could afford to sail to England on the *Great Britain*, an auxiliary steamer, that is, a steamship with sails, for an extended visit. On their agenda was exploring new business opportunities, church work, social reform, family reunions and travel. Mid-1857, after three-and-a-half years away, Kilner and Maria decided it was time for them all to return home. The Wallers decided that they would travel in style, and Kilner booked first-class berths on a ship about which they had heard only good things: the *Dunbar*.

7

'A splendid vessel'

The *Dunbar* was a thing of beauty, in its short life one of the finest British clippers at the zenith of the age of sail. A sleek and majestic Blackwall frigate-built clipper, it was commissioned by shipping magnate Duncan Dunbar II to dash travellers, emigrants, gold-seekers and cargo, provisions and mail to and from Sydney, taking the heavy seas of the Roaring Forties in its stride. The glorious *Dunbar* was the envy of its owner's fierce competitors.

To a din of sawing, hammering, hissing steam, metal striking metal and the shouts and grunts of workers, the *Dunbar* was built at a cost of £30,000 over seventeen months in 1852 and '53 at the James Laing & Sons shipyard on a bend of the River Wear at Sunderland in north-east England, where ships had been built since 1346. It was launched on 30 November 1853.

At 1066 tonnes unladen, the *Dunbar* was the largest [by 272 tonnes] vessel yet constructed in Sunderland, and, according to Duncan Dunbar, even carrying its maximum load of 729 tonnes, it was the fastest of all British ships. It was 61.49 metres long, its beam just 10.66 metres and its depth of hold 6.88 metres. Its hull and internal frames were of sturdy English oak and its deck planking of

East Indian teak. Its three backward-raked Indian teak masts were strong and durable, the 45 metre mainmast weighing 8.1 tonnes, the foremast 7.2 tonnes and the mizzenmast 5 tonnes. At sea, in full flight, the masts carried more than 1579 square metres of white jute and canvas sails: moving aft from the bow, flying jib, outer jib, inner jib, foretop staysail, courses, spanker, staysails, topsails, topgallants, royals, skysails and moonrakers. The height between decks was 2.2 metres. Its hull was fortified with 45-plus tonnes of iron knees, and 16.3 tonnes of protective copper fastening and sheathing, which repelled the timber-devouring clam-like teredo shipworm, the 'termite of the sea'. The *Dunbar* had diagonal trusses and enormously strong breast hooks. Extra reinforcement was provided by six iron orlop beams in the lower hold and 28 iron riders, 5.48 metres long, 12.7 centimetres wide and 7.62 centimetres thick.

The cabin-class (or first-class) compartments below the 25 metre long, 2 metre high raised poop deck at the stern were luxuriously appointed, with splendidly crafted and expensively upholstered chairs, dining tables, desks and commodious beds. The brasswork gleamed.

Steerage- and intermediate-class passengers, used to cramped and miserable quarters on other ships, might have thought they'd wandered into cabin class by mistake. The *Dunbar* offered single and communal baths and ventilating tubes to circulate fresh air. Every bunk was individually lit and the large and airy area between decks was likened to 'a public hall'. The food was an improvement on typical steerage and intermediate fare with, presumably, fewer rats, fleas, weevils and roaches nesting in the bedding and storage barrels.

The captain had his own cabin, as sumptuous as that of the highest paying passenger, and his senior officers enjoyed intermediate-grade accommodation. The crew, as crews always had, roughed it on dormitory cots. Because the ship sailed day and night, as a sailor went on watch, his still-warm bunk was commandeered by a shipmate whose shift was done.

The Dunbar company flag was a red 'Scottish Lion Rampant' in a shield on a blue background with the words *sub spe*, Latin for 'under hope', and this rampant lion, fashioned into a figurehead by the ornamental woodcarver James Brooker, painted scarlet and set in a wooden gilt scroll, reared from the *Dunbar*'s bow. The *Dunbar*'s gunports were painted black and white to imitate the Royal Navy colours, to scare away pirates.

The *Dunbar* underwent three annual surveys on the James Laing dry dock at Sunderland, the last in April 1857, six weeks before its final departure for Sydney. The inspector rated as 'good' its decks, waterways, upper- and lower-deck beams and fittings, its timbers, keel, clamps and shafts, its windlass and capstan and pumps, its lifeboats, masts, yards and sails, its standing and running rigging, its anchors and cables, hawsers and warps. The clipper received the highest possible rating from Lloyd's Register of Shipping: 13 A1. It was said at the time that such was Duncan Dunbar's confidence in the *Dunbar* that he deemed it unsinkable and so did not insure it or its cargo. In fact, it was Dunbar's policy not to insure any of his vessels because the premiums he would need to pay would cost more than any loss of cargo or ship.

To the *Illustrated London News*, the *Dunbar* epitomised:

the mastery which science, capital and perseverance have obtained over natural obstacles in these go-ahead days of free trade and stimu-lating competition . . . She is built for strength, stowage and durability, yet withal is a graceful model . . . The poop [offers a place] for cabin class passengers to socialise and gaze out to sea . . . It is tastefully panelled in front and ornamented with a row of pillars of polished teak . . . Great attention has been paid to ventilation in all parts of the vessel . . . *Dunbar* has been carefully inspected by many of the first shipping authorities, who have unanimously declared her to be the finest merchant ship afloat.

Workers and wellwishers gathered at the dock at Sunderland on 30 November 1854 to see Duncan Dunbar and James Laing launch the *Dunbar*. Perhaps only the superstitious sensed sinister omens when it slid into the water, somewhat unusually for those days, stern-on, rather than bow-first; and when, sailing from the James Laing & Sons shipyard to London to begin its career, the *Dunbar* collided with the barque *Twenty-ninth of May*, and its starboard cathead (a large wooden beam on the bow) and protective bulwarks were damaged.

When the London beer, spirits and wine merchant Duncan Dunbar died in 1825, he left a substantial portion of his £42,000 fortune (valued at around A$2.8 million today) and his business on Dunbar Wharf at Limehouse on the River Thames to his 22-year-old first-born son, on whom he had bestowed his own given name. Dunbar senior was confident that his legacy would be in good hands, for Dunbar junior was a child prodigy who had left school at twelve and distinguished himself at Aberdeen University at just thirteen. Two years after receiving his inheritance, young Duncan, unchallenged by the wine and spirits business, turned his attention to ships and soon owned the largest fleet of three-masted sailing clippers in the world. At his death in 1862, Dunbar was worth £1.5 million.

All told, Duncan Dunbar's ships made between 40 and 50 voyages to Australia, many serving as convict transports, as well as assisted and unassisted emigrant and merchant vessels. While most of Dunbar's ships, like the *Dunbar*, were built by James Laing & Sons at Sunderland, he operated his own shipbuilding yard in Burma (today Myanmar) at the port of Moulmein, 317 kilometres by road south-east of Rangoon (nowadays Yangon), at the mouth of the Salween River. The top-grade teak that gave strength and beauty to his clippers was hewn from the forests on the Salween.

In a 2005 speech, Dunbar's descendant, Rear-Admiral Duncan Dunbar-Nasmith, recalled:

By 1st January 1842, Dunbar's fleet mustered 11 ships with a total tonnage of 5000 tons [4536 tonnes]. From 1842 onwards he proceeded to build at least one new ship a year, often two or three

71

and in 1850 four. In the next 20 years he ordered 42 new ships, three of which were still being built when he died . . . To think up suitable names for all these was a little problem on its own. He named seven after family or Dunbar connections, six were after place names in his family's home county of Morayshire and 27 were named after battles or naval and military commanders.

The Dunbar clan was clearly proud of the name. As well as the *Dunbar*, there was the *Duncan Dunbar*, the *Phoebe Dunbar* (named after Duncan's mother) and the *Dunbar Castle*. According to Dunbar-Nasmith, 'when the younger Duncan Dunbar's sister, Phoebe, married a man also named Dunbar, Captain Edward Dunbar, she said no way was she going to lose *her* "Dunbar" and insisted on being known as "Mrs Dunbar Dunbar"'.

Some of Duncan Dunbar's ships had remarkable longevity. The *Marion* and the *Lady MacDonald* lasted 40 and 50 years. Yet, despite the quality of his vessels and crews, fourteen of his clipper ships were destroyed by storms, cliffs, icebergs, fires, hidden reefs or the inexactitudes of navigation. These included the *Phoebe*, which was wrecked off Madras; the *Randolph*, which went down off Mauritius; and the *Phoebe Dunbar*, which ran aground off Moreton Bay, Queensland. The *Cospatrick* caught fire and sank south of the Cape of Good Hope on its way to Auckland in 1874 after Dunbar had sold it to the Shaw Saville line.

The biggest ship that Duncan Dunbar ever owned, the 1351 tonne clipper, *Duncan Dunbar*, hit a reef off the coast of Brazil on 7 October 1865, on its way from Plymouth to Sydney; all on board survived after the captain sailed 2000 kilometres in an open boat to seek help and left the marooned passengers in the care of former Sydney mayor, politician, businessman and yachtsman George Thornton, about whom more later. Another Dunbar line disaster was when the *Hydrabad* was transporting 118 horses and 250 tonnes of Newcastle coal to Calcutta (today Kolkata) when, said Dunbar-Nasmith:

She struck a shoal in the difficult waters of the Torres Strait, just north of Australia, then slipped off and sank in 15 fathoms. The horses were drowned, but all the passengers and crew were saved. They had to make a five-day passage in the boats, because the captain wouldn't let them land on a nearby island, as he had heard that a ship's crew had been killed there, some time ago, by cannibals, and probably eaten.

As well as overseeing his clipper fleet, Dunbar founded the London Chartered Bank of Australia in 1852 and was chairman until his death. He also chaired the General Shipowner's Society and the Local Marine Board for the Port of London, was deputy chairman and a director of Lloyd's Registry, deputy chairman of the East and West India Dock Company, and a patron of the arts with his own art gallery and publishing imprint. Everyone understood when Dunbar said he was too busy to accept the offer of a Conservative seat in parliament.

After the 58-year-old corpulent bachelor pitched forward in his dressing-room and died in 1862, his obituary read:

Sudden death—an attack of apoplexy—has struck down, in the vigour of life, the eminent London shipowner, Mr Duncan Dunbar, a man whose commercial schemes and transactions literally extended to every quarter of the globe. Though not strictly the architect of his own fortune, for his father, some 30 years since, left him a flourishing business and capital then computed at 30,000 pounds [sic], the deceased so multiplied and enlarged his speculations, and conducted them with such sagacity, spirit and perseverance that he amassed property that cannot be calculated at less than a million sterling, and is even set down (somewhat loosely) at two millions. He had, we believe, about 70 ships, many of them the largest in our mercantile marine, and he was also connected with various banking, dock and insurance undertakings. At the same time, Mr Dunbar lived in a style of liberal hospitality befitting one of the merchant princes.

* * * *

The Crimean War was fought mainly on the Crimean Peninsula by the British empire, the French empire, the Kingdom of Sardinia and the Ottoman empire against the Russian empire from October 1853 to February 1856. At issue were Russia's designs on the Ottoman empire, even though by then the empire was on its last legs. At the outset of the conflict, the Royal Navy offered generous compensation to British ship-owners to requisition their vessels as troop ships, transporting officers, infantry and cavalry, artillery and ammunition, weapons, horses and stores to the Crimea in the Black Sea and to the Baltic Sea. Never averse to profiting from his patriotism, Duncan Dunbar postponed the *Dunbar*'s maiden voyage to Sydney in 1854 and instead deployed it—and fifteen other of his ships—to the Crimea. Dunbar was paid 25 shillings per ton of cargo, reduced to 19 shillings as the war dragged on.

The Crimean War is perhaps best remembered for Florence Nightingale's nursing of wounded British soldiers and the bloody debacle of the Charge of the Light Brigade on 25 October 1854, on the heights above the port of Balaclava. British commander General Lord Raglan's vaguely worded order to attack to his cavalry commander Lord Lucan saw Lucan's 670-strong Light Brigade sent on a suicidal charge through the 'valley of death' into the teeth of the heavily armed Russian forces. Some 110 men of the Light Brigade were killed and 160 wounded.

After becoming a Royal Navy vessel on 8 March 1854, the *Dunbar*, now officially known as *No. 23 Transport*, was placed in the command of Captain Charles Scott. It sailed from Cork, Ireland, on 4 April with fourteen officers and 402 men of the Duke of Cambridge's Own 17th cavalry regiment on board, bound for Scutari (today Uskudar) on the Bosporus Sea in Turkey. Then, on 29 August, the *Dunbar* shipped the regiment to Kalamita Bay, on the Crimean Peninsula, 45 kilometres north of the Russian naval base at Sevastopol. The objective: join the Allied forces in laying siege to, and occupying, Sevastopol. The *Dunbar* took its place in the bay among scores of other transport ships. It looked like a swan among ducks.

The mistakes made during the landing and unloading of the *Dunbar* and some of the other transport vessels at Kalamita Bay were portents of Allied blunders to come. The sea was calm and the wind gentle when the ships dropped anchor, but instead of taking advantage of the kind conditions to disembark the cavalry and their horses, those in charge decided that the infantry should leave the ship first. Of course, when the time finally came for the cavalrymen to lead their mounts off the ship and onto the beach, a rising wind had whipped up the surf and a frantic and time-consuming effort had to be made to save the terrified horses from drowning. It took five days for the British ships to complete the disembarkation and join the French for the march on Sevastopol.

Before Sevastopol, the 17th Regiment would take its place in the first line of the left rank of the Light Brigade in its ill-fated charge at the Battle of Balaclava. Seven officers of the regiment and 63 men were slain.

The *Dunbar* also carried the 79th Cameron Highlanders, under Lieutenant-Colonel Douglas, to the Bulgarian port of Varna and then to Kalamita Bay. The Highlanders fought with the First Division at the Battle of the Alma on 20 September 1854, alongside the 17th Regiment at Balaclava on 25 October, and played their part in the siege of Sevastopol, a brutal campaign that lasted a year. The British and French capture of Sevastopol on 9 September 1855, heralded the defeat of Russia in the Crimea.

Around 900,000 of the 1.6 million soldiers and sailors from all sides, as well as civilians, were killed in the Crimean War or died of typhoid, typhus, cholera or dysentery, starvation or the bitter cold. British historian Orlando Figes called the conflict 'the first "total war", a 19th-century version of the wars of our own age. It was also the first truly modern war—fought with new industrial technologies; novel forms of logistics and communications; important innovations in military medicine; and reporters and photographers directly on the scene. Yet at the same time it was the last war to be conducted by the old codes of chivalry.'

Chivalry notwithstanding, the human toll of the war was heavy and horrific, and the *Dunbar* was involved in one of the most desperate mercy missions of the conflict after the Battle of the Alma. William Russell, *The Times* of London's celebrated war correspondent, reported:

> The number of men sent down from the Crimea was beyond the expectations of anyone ... Nearly 1,500 sick and invalids were placed on board the [transport ship *Kangaroo*] in Kalamita Bay. The captain made signals of distress and remained at anchor from sheer inability to go to sea with his decks encumbered with dying and dead. The vessel was crowded to suffocation. [Soldiers] in all stages of suffering ... The scene is described as appalling—in fact, too frightful for the details to be dwelt upon. At last the *Dunbar* [in his articles, Russell referred to the *Dunbar* rather than *No. 23 Transport*] was sent to his assistance and took off nearly half of what was left of his miserable freight. They arrived [at the Barrack Hospital, Scutari, in Constantinople] on the morning of [25 September], the *Kangaroo* towing the sailing vessel. The *Kangaroo* brought 452, the *Dunbar* 357 sick, who were at once placed in the hospital ... Many deaths occurred on board—many miserable scenes took place, but there is, alas! no use in describing them.

The *Dunbar* had creditably undertaken expeditions through 1854 and early 1855, shuttling troops and artillery from Great Britain and between Kalamita Bay and Eupatoria (today Yevpatoria) on the battle-torn Crimean Peninsula, Varna and Balchik in Bulgaria, Gibraltar, Constantinople (today Istanbul) and Scutari in Turkey. After offloading 450 wounded on the Greek Ionian Sea island of Corfu for treatment, it took on board 148 invalided troops, 151 women and 266 children and sailed to England on 15 February 1855. Three deceased adults and twelve children were taken from the *Dunbar* when she docked at Spithead, near Portsmouth, on 11 April.

One month later, on 9 May, Captain Scott transported on the *Dunbar* a detachment of Polish troops to the Black Sea as a peace-keeping force and to protect Allied interests in the Crimea after the war. Still in service in December 1855, the clipper was despatched to carry powder, shot and shell from Malta to Gibraltar. That completed, the Royal Navy released it back to its owner who must have heaved a sigh of relief knowing that his flagship was finally out of harm's way. Duncan Dunbar saw to it that the *Dunbar*, having done its duty for Queen and country, was cosseted at the Laing shipyard in Sunderland, undergoing repairs and cleaning. It was transformed from a utilitarian troop ship into a luxury clipper again, ready to take on the role it was built for, speeding passengers and cargo to and from Australia. The *Dunbar* was due to sail on its maiden voyage to Sydney in mid-1856. It would be, thought its proud owner, the first of many such voyages.

* * * *

The masters of the England–Australia route sailing ships in the first six decades of the nineteenth century ranged from Basil Lubbock's afore-mentioned 'rum-soaked, bearlike, illiterate officers' whose ships were a floating purgatory, to diligent master mariners, a master mariner being the highest level of qualification for commanding a ship.

Duncan Dunbar would have nothing to do with the former type, and he cherished the latter. When weighing up whether to employ a master, Dunbar examined his experience, character and references. A Dunbar line captain had to be a skilled and experienced sailor, self-confident in his knowledge of the sea and ships and enjoying crew members' and passengers' respect. He had to know every centi-metre of his ship and be able to decisively and calmly deal with the most daunting situations that ocean and weather could throw at him. He needed excellent managerial and communication skills to resolve the inevitable human conflicts that flared in a cramped space over months at sea. A Dunbar line skipper had a hand in selecting the best available officers, mates, seamen, apprentices, riggers and sailmakers. He was familiar with myriad weather patterns, from ferocious storms, infernal heat and cold to the challenges of the Southern Ocean. Should he drop anchor at a port for provisions or repairs, it was essential he understood its politics and customs. He needed to be proficient with a sextant and chronometer, and quickly and accurately be able to decipher complex navigational charts and celestial tables. And as if all this wasn't enough, he was expected to be a shrewd businessman and secure cargo—wool, grain and gold from Australia, teak, spices, tea, rice, jute and ivory from India and China—to keep the holds full on the return journey.

Duncan Dunbar was a hard-driving autocrat when it came to ships and business, but he treated his employees, from captains to labourers, fairly and paid them well. 'I consider that a [captain] who has 20,000 or 30,000 pounds of property under his charge *should* be well paid.' Dunbar's masters' wages were around £10 a month, with a superior cabin and the best food and drink and uniforms all part of the package. A captain in Dunbar's best graces may be awarded shares in his ships. (The first mate on a Duncan Dunbar vessel received around £6 a month, the carpenter around £5 and 10 shillings, the second mate around £4 and 10 shillings and able seamen were paid in the vicinity of £2 and 5 shillings a month—there were 20 shillings to the pound.)

When asked if he devoted as much attention to delving into the capabilities of his masters and senior crew as he did when employing a personal servant to work in his home, Dunbar replied, 'Yes, much more so; because a servant we have always before our eyes: but we know that with regard to captains and mates very frequently we are putting an immense property under their charge, and without any power of control over them in their absence.'

Dunbar's employees, in turn, were loyal to him and his ships. One of his best captains, Henry Neatby, said on Dunbar's death, 'Many thought him a hard taskmaster. He was a good master to me and always gave what he bargained for, to a farthing . . . [although] I wish he had left £100,000 to build alms houses for old captains and mates.'

Rear-Admiral Duncan Dunbar-Nasmith told how

Nine of Dunbar's captains served him for more than 15 years, 10 for 10-to-15 years, 39 for 5-to-10 years and 57 for one to five years . . . I have traced 136 captains who commanded his ships in his lifetime and nine others who commanded his ships after his death. Many were 2nd and 1st Mates before rising to command. Only three of his captains (whose birth dates are known) were older than him and two of these each commanded six or more of his ships for more than 24 years. They were still in command in their sixties. The youngest was his brother-in-law's son, Marmaduke John Tatham, whose captain died at sea, when he [Marmaduke] was still 19, and Marmaduke brought the ship home from St Helena [a remote island outpost in the South Atlantic] to London.

Among the Dunbar line captains, few were as accomplished as James Green, the *Dunbar*'s master. The captain of a Blackwall frigate clipper, such as the *Dunbar*, was regarded as having reached the peak of his profession. Captain Green, a master mariner of course, was entitled to have 'Esquire' and 'Commander' after his name to reflect his exalted standing.

Green grew up a seafarer. Born on 21 December 1821, he was one of two sons and a daughter of fisherman Malcolm Green and Barbara McBeath. Home was the herring fishing island of South Ronaldsay on the Orkney archipelago in the Northern Isles of Scotland. James' brother, Malcolm, would also command Duncan Dunbar's clippers. From childhood, James loved boats and the sea. At age twelve, he served on the *James Paterson* and then the convict ship *Theresa*. When *Theresa* was wrecked, young James Green stayed on board after all hands had left the ship, and just before it went down he took hold of a piece of broken mizzenmast and floated upon it to shore. In 1851, the Lords of the Committee of Privy Council for Trade granted 29-year-old Green his certificate of competency as a master mariner.

By 1856, Green had sailed to Australia seven times. As a younger man he served as first mate to Captain Henry Neatby on the *Agincourt* and the *Waterloo*, and then himself commanded the *Waterloo* and the *Vimeira*. All passages were completed without incident or criticism from crew or passengers. He was a favourite in colonial society, a dashing young captain who was a welcome dinner guest at the best tables. The *Sydney Morning Herald* referred to Green as 'a most energetic, spirited, and gentlemanly man . . . of great character [who] had acquired a large circle of colonial friends'.

So Duncan Dunbar did not hesitate to choose such a fellow for the plum job of helming the pride of his fleet, the *Dunbar*, to and from England and Port Jackson at a time when the run to New South Wales was the most profitable passenger, emigrant and merchant shipping passage on Earth. Further evidence of Dunbar's high opinion of Green was that he awarded him a one-sixteenth share in the profits of the *Dunbar* and a one-eighth share of those of the *Vimeira*.

The *Dunbar*'s maiden voyage to Sydney began at Plymouth, Devon, on the night of 1 July 1856. The ship carried 55 passengers, 41 crew and cargo. Based on Captain Green's log and interviews with passengers and crew, the *Shipping Gazette* of 29 September briefly chronicled the voyage to Port Jackson.

The *Dunbar*, Captain Green, arrived on Saturday after an excellent passage of 87 days. She left Plymouth on the night of July 1 and crossed the equator on the 27th, but from thence down the coast of South America a series of southerly winds retarded her progress materially, and she was 18 days before getting the south-east trades, when the general time usually does not occupy seven or eight. During this vexatious delay the vessel was compelled to tack 30 times. The Cape [of Good Hope] was rounded on the 57th day, southerly winds prevailing the whole way; the greatest latitude being obtained being 41-deg, and that for only three days; had south-east winds four days on the south coast of Australia, and passed Cape Otway at 9am on the 23rd, and was off the Sydney Heads on the 26th, at 10pm . . .

Dunbar is a splendid vessel, sister ship to *La Hogue* . . . The passengers express themselves in very warm terms of the general comforts of the ship and the kind and gentlemanly conduct of Captain Green and his officers, on a very pleasant voyage just terminated.

As remarked upon in the *Gazette*, the captaincy of Green, who was accompanied by Alice, his 23-year-old wife of thirteen months, was exemplary. After arriving at Sydney Cove on 27 September, a delegation of passengers presented him with a sum of money they had collected and the following testimonial:

SIR—We the undersigned cuddy passengers [cabin-class travellers who gather in the cuddy, or saloon cabin, of a ship] on board the ship *Dunbar*, upon the termination of a voyage presently, under Providence brought to a happy conclusion, feel that we have a pleasing duty to perform towards you, the public, and ourselves. Your character as a seaman and a navigator is far too well known in Australia to require any eulogy at our hands; but we are anxious to express our unqualified approbation at your untiring zeal, your urbanity of manner, and your kind attention to all our wants and wishes during the whole time that we have had the pleasure of being passengers on board your fine ship. As a trifling mark of the respect and esteem in which you are held by us, one and all, we beg your acceptance of the accompanying purse of sovereigns, which you will be pleased to expend in the purchase of some token, as a memento of the many happy days which we have spent together. In bidding you farewell, we express a hope that you may long be spared to make many more prosperous voyages between England and Australia, and with our heartfelt prayers for the health of Mrs Green and yourself, we subscribe ourselves sincerely yours . . .

Green's written response was typically gracious.

Ladies and gentlemen—I beg to return you my sincere and heartfelt thanks for your handsome and flattering testimonial. I cannot but feel that the general harmony which has distinguished this voyage throughout is mainly attributable to yourselves, and can assure you that any little kindness or attention on my part I have always felt to be both a duty and a pleasure. Wishing you every success and happiness. I remain, very truly yours, James Green.

Although there exists a late-in-life photograph of James Green's brother, Malcolm, shown to be a heavily bearded and browed man of strong and stern features, we have no images or physical descriptions of the *Dunbar*'s captain, so we cannot know if he resembled his brother, was dark or fair, tall or short, thin or stout. What can be said with certainty is that James Green, over many years and many successful voyages as first mate and captain, was well mannered and genial, and an exceptional seaman who fulfilled his employer's demanding criteria.

At a sad time in the not-too-distant future, Green's passengers and those who served under him on the *Dunbar*'s maiden voyage to Sydney in 1856, and his friends and peers, were moved to offer their impressions. Sir Daniel Cooper, speaker of the New South Wales Legislative Assembly, prominent Sydney merchant and philanthropist, called Green 'a credit to his profession . . . a cautious and vigilant sailor'. Arthur Hodgson, described by the *Australian Dictionary of Biography* as a 'squatter, politician and squire', who, with his family, was a passenger on the *Dunbar* in '56, said that Green and his wife, Alice, who accompanied him:

did all in their power to relieve the tediousness of the voyage, and make all on board comfortable and happy. Both as a sailor and a gentleman, those who sailed with him could have but one opinion, namely, that he was in all respects fully equal to the command of one of the finest ships which had ever entered this port . . . [My] feelings with regard to Captain Green were more those of a brother than of a friend.

Mr Justice Therry and his family were other *Dunbar* passengers in 1856. The Therrys had planned to disembark in Melbourne but chose to sail on to Sydney, he said, simply to spend more time with the estimable master of the *Dunbar*. Therry testified to Green's urbanity and kindness and the 'good feeling which existed between Green and the passengers'.

Another voyager, R.T. Hall, was impressed by James Green's compassion when he, Hall, fell ill and was confined to his bunk for seven weeks: 'during that time no day elapsed in which I was not visited by Captain Green and consoled by his conversation'. Yet Green, said Hall, was strong when necessary. He had shown 'remarkable tact and firmness in checking those outbursts of feeling which sometimes threatened to explode among the passengers'.

'In a profession which often calls forth the noblest characteristics . . . he held a foremost rank,' summed up the *Sydney Morning Herald*. 'He had seen much of ocean life; had a reputation as a bold, generous, and successful sailor; had often cast anchor amidst the 'gratulations of his nautical friends and the grateful acknowledgements of his passengers. He was a favourite in this port.'

On its maiden voyage to Sydney, the *Dunbar* remained in port for more than four months while undergoing minor repairs and Captain Green negotiated with local merchants to ship their goods to England. Then, on 27 December 1856, laden with gold hunters both jubilant and despondent, Sydneysiders returning to the northern hemisphere for a family reunion or holiday, and a hold full of prime New South Wales wool and grain, mail and other goods, the *Dunbar* set sail on the voyage back to London via Cape Horn. To farewell the clipper, the *Sydney Morning Herald* echoed the *Shipping Gazette* in pronouncing it 'a splendid vessel', a verdict shared by all who sailed upon her.

William A. Strang was a shipping clerk at the ship chandlery and sailmaking company Captain James Williamson, Messrs Mitchell & Dixon of Lower George Street, Sydney. He helped to equip the *Dunbar* for the long voyage ahead. He told how:

Dunbar lay in the stream of 'Old Pinchgut', now called the Battery, taking in wool . . . I kept a diary, or, as the sailors would call it, a log book, in which I entered notes of some of the things sent to the ships . . . I received orders to send the steam tank to fill up *Dunbar*'s water tanks, and at 2 o'clock she had then got most of her cargo on . . . I got orders to send some sails to *Dunbar*—one flying jib, one foretop mast stay sail, one main topgallant sail, one coil of 18 thread ratline, one hawser, one large warp, one coil of 4½ inch [11 centimetre] manilla [sic] rope. Soon after this *Dunbar* cleared at the Customs House. I got orders for the tug to take her in tow . . . We were then ready. A number of passengers were on board for London, and many friends saying their goodbyes caused a small delay. Captain Green was on the bridge. Our chief engineer was at his post and Captain Bainbridge (master of the steam tug), was on the starboard side. I was standing right astern awaiting orders. As soon as the last boat left the *Dunbar* for shore, Captain Green called out, 'Go ahead.'

8

Most able seamen

After a seamless passage from Sydney, the *Dunbar* docked at Plymouth on 17 March 1857. Captain James Green farewelled his passengers, and paid off and discharged his crew. He supervised the unloading of cargo and completed paperwork with the Duncan Dunbar line's London shipping broker, Devitt & Moore, and officials of the line. Then he and his wife, Alice, went to their cottage in Hackney in London's East End to regroup with friends and family and, in James's case, recuperate from the relentless demands of command. It was a good time for a short time, for James had signed on to skipper the *Dunbar* on her second trip to Sydney, weighing anchor in only a little more than two months. Alice's intention was to join him again, but she fell pregnant and, when both agreed it would be safer and wiser to spend her pregnancy at home rather than at sea or in the colony, she changed her mind.

Devitt & Moore capitalised on the *Dunbar*'s successful maiden voyage by advertising for passengers and merchants to book a berth or space in the hold on her second passage to Sydney:

For Sydney direct, [the *Dunbar*] has just made her passage home in 78 days, and at the request of several of the merchants will be despatched again on May 20, to enable her to return with the wools for the next February sales (embarks her passengers at Plymouth June 1) . . . the splendid new frigate-built ship *Dunbar*, A 1 . . . register 1,321 tons, James Green, Commander: lying in the East India Docks. This fine ship has been built expressly for the Sydney trade; she has a full poop, with first-rate accommodation for cabin passengers; her 'tween decks being lofty and airy she offers also a desirable opportunity for a few intermediate passengers [there were also steerage quarters], and will carry an experienced surgeon. For terms of freight and passage apply to Capt James Green, on board; to Mr E Gellatly, with the owners, Messrs D Dunbar and Sons, Fore-street, Limehouse; or to Devitt & Moore, 9, Billiter-street.

It was a rapid turnaround. On 24 May, the *Dunbar* took on cargo at London's East India Docks and passengers at Gravesend on the south bank of the Thames Estuary, 35 kilometres south of London. Then it was to Plymouth on the south coast, the clipper's last port of call before setting sail for the South Seas, to board more passengers and load final cargo. At Gravesend, Alice Green bade her husband godspeed and a safe journey. They were glad that James would be back in England for the birth of their first child.

Sunday, 31 May, and the *Dunbar* stood proudly at Plymouth Dock, ready to sail. By now, the ship was a second home to Captain Green, and he took comfort that nine of his crew from the *Dunbar*'s previous voyage to Sydney would again be sailing with him. The *Dunbar* veterans were the ship's surgeon Alexander Bayne, cook James Jack, steward James Ward, and midshipmen John Ridley Jerram—who had left his secure life and job as a London tea dealer to seek adventure on the high seas—William Butler Williams, a midshipman with a distinctive mop of blond hair, Allan Heisch, J.B. Piercey, John Allen and James McGuffie.

Various crew lists differ so precise numbers cannot be known, but it is generally thought that the second-timers were joined by another 43 crew members, including a sailmaker, a carpenter, a cook and a butcher and their assistants. Most crewmen were young, strong and fit, capable of the physical demands of the voyage; only three were past 40. First officer James Struthers, though just 27, was a veteran of the Duncan Dunbar line and renowned for his good humour and prodigious feats of strength. Struthers, like Captain Green, grew up on the Scottish Orkney island of South Ronaldsay. The 24-year-old second officer, John Spence, was another Orkneyman. The Cornish third officer (or mate) was John Pascoe, whose capable seamanship belied his eighteen years. Midshipman Tom Kay of Bedhampton, Hampshire, was just fourteen. George au Vernet, a midshipman, and ordinary seaman John Cummings were all sixteen. Nineteen-year-old George Fish was the butcher's mate and the butcher was 34-year-old Londoner James Parks. Sydney-born midshipman Frederick Weiss, youngest of five sons of J.V.M. Weiss, was seventeen. Although unrelated to Duncan Dunbar, the middle name of seventeen-year-old midshipman Allan Heisch was 'Dunbar'. The oldest crewman was able seaman John Colstone, 46. Charles Sappie, a fresh-faced, brown-haired 38-year-old salt and former Sydney water policeman with anchor tattoos on the back of his hands, was the bosun.

Able seaman James Johnson was a powerfully built, heavily whiskered twenty-year-old from Drogheda, an ancient port on the river Boyne in County Louth on the east coast of Ireland that had been a Viking stronghold from the eighth to eleventh centuries. A seaman since age twelve, Johnson had worked on merchant vessels between Ireland and England and sailed to Australia once before, to Melbourne. On the *Dunbar*, his pay was £2 10 shillings a month.

According to some crew lists, there were two able seamen from Sweden: Alexander Manson, 32, and Royal (or John) Woodworth, 28. Able seaman Ion Amar [or Aman], 24, was from Finland, and there were two German able seamen, Antonio Hoyne, 24, and Thomas Bey, 31.

The *Dunbar*'s crew gathered at the dock at Plymouth as the church bells of the old port city pealed. No doubt some crew members were a little hungover, having honoured the seamen's tradition of last drinks: guzzling the ales of Plymouth's waterfront bars. They drank like there was no tomorrow because on a Duncan Dunbar ship, seamen were allowed only a single glass of grog (rum and water) a day on the voyage to Sydney. (Knowing the iron discipline imposed by Captain Green, it's unlikely that any *Dunbar* sailor was in the wretched condition of a crewman named Spreckett who disgraced himself on the eve of an 1840s voyage to the colonies. He and his cronies did not return to their ship, a shipmate wrote, 'until 2 in the morning . . . in a beastly state of intoxication . . . Mr Spreckett was quite mad with drink. He was taken down to his cabin and laid on his bed where he was lashed plunging about and raving in a most frightful manner.')

Apart from the usual sailors' superstitions predicting dire consequences for whistling, bringing bananas on board and killing albatrosses, none of those on the *Dunbar* had cause to doubt that this passage would be as uneventful and lucrative as the clipper's maiden voyage to the Great South Land.

The *Dunbar*'s cargo was valued at £72,600. In its 6.7 metre deep holds were stowed mail, newspapers, crates of food and casks of alcohol, furniture, machinery, dining ware, clothing and boots, haberdashery, perfume, 'fancy goods', paintings, musical instruments including a piano, candles, paint, oil, stationery, tablecloths, iron rods, saddlery and skins, and the components of 40 stoves that would be assembled on arrival in Sydney. One chest contained coloured dyes for the colony's first postage stamps. There was a package addressed to Reverend John Gale of 'Gunning', Yass, which contained eighteen photographic portraits, letters and books filled with religious poems that Gale had written and collected before emigrating to Australia and making his home 286 kilometres southwest of Sydney. The manifest listed ten cases of Holloway's Pills & Ointment, a popular remedy of the nineteenth century whose maker optimistically claimed they cured 'headaches, sore throats, consumption, dropsy, colic, lumbago, piles, glandular swellings, bad legs, bite of mosquito and sand fly, elephantiasis, fistulas and gout'.

There was livestock on board to be killed and consumed, while other animals—cats, dogs, sheep, pigs, rabbits, two dairy cows, four bulls and a horse—were passengers' pets or destined for farms.

A class above any other beast on board was an elegant, silky-coated Russian wolfhound—or borzoi—that had been rescued from the battlefield at Inkerman during the Crimean War and taken to England where the London newspapers made it a celebrity. The dog had been acquired by twenty-year-old Henry Cahuac, a *Dunbar* cabin-class traveller with his sister, Gertrude, and mother, Marian Egan. Now, after a sojourn on the Continent and Britain, soaking up culture, seeing the sights and having their group portrait painted, the Cahuacs and Marian Egan were returning to Sydney and bringing the Russian wolfhound with them.

It is generally accepted that there were 69 passengers on the *Dunbar* (although, once more, the exact number is unknown because passenger lists were unreliable and the names of servants and late-boarding passengers were not always entered). There were at least twenty children. Some 50 of the voyagers had paid more than £100 for the luxury and perquisites of cabin class. Most of these were wealthy Sydneysiders—English- and native-born Australians—coming home after a visit to the Old Country and, for some like Marian Egan and her children, a Grand Tour of Europe. Travelling in intermediate compartments on the *Dunbar* were emigrants paying a lesser but, compared to the cost of voyaging on inferior ships, substantial fare, assisted passage emigrants, and gold prospectors whose budget stretched only to a basic cot on the way to Sydney but who hoped to be able to afford to breathe the rarefied air of cabin class when they sailed back home. Typically, in 1857, five passenger vessels a week would arrive in Sydney.

After the last crate was stowed and Captain Green had checked and double-checked with his officers that all was shipshape, the passengers embarking at Plymouth ascended the gangway to join those who had come on board at Gravesend. Green, standing statue-stiff in his immaculate uniform, would have tried to put aside his own worries about his pregnant wife, Alice, and welcomed and exchanged pleasantries with his guests, for that was what this gracious captain considered them.

As sailing time neared, a bell was rung to alert friends and relatives of passengers that it was time for last goodbyes. After first mate James Struthers had checked off the Plymouth voyagers' names, stewards and crewmen showed them to their berths. Surgeon Alexander Bayne passed through the ship, checking the passengers for contagious diseases and other medical conditions and offering tips to cope with seasickness. The ship's complement was on deck as a tugboat towed the *Dunbar* past the port's landmark 2 kilometre breakwater and out of Plymouth Harbour. The sonorous chimes of the eighth-century Minster Church of St Andrew afforded the ship and its passengers a funereal farewell. Those bound for, as one put it, 'the opposite extreme of Queen Victoria's dominions', were torn by conflicting emotions: regret at leaving behind friends and family whom they might never see again; trepidation at the long, possibly dangerous, voyage ahead; and excited anticipation for what awaited them in Sydney and for the rest of their life. The devout would have prayed for a safe voyage. 'We placed ourselves in the hands of the Lord and his will,' wrote one voyager about to embark on the same journey on a similar ship, 'whether we should live or die.'

9

So much to live for

Among the *Dunbar*'s passengers were folk who had contributed to Australia's prosperity and growing reputation as an egalitarian society where hard work and enterprise and being a good citizen counted for more than bloodline. Their British and European holiday or business visit over, they boarded the clipper looking forward to resuming on arrival back in Australia where they had left off.

A boundless future seemed assured for Kilner Waller and his wife Hannah (known by her middle name, Maria) and their six children: John, the youngest at three years old; Arthur, four; Maria, six; Kate, eight; Edward, nine; and Mary, thirteen. Wealthy, high achieving, God fearing and with a strong social conscience, the Wallers were among Tasmania's, and Australia's, most distinguished families.

Maria and Kilner had married in Launceston's York Street Baptist Chapel in 1842. It had been a grand occasion in the Tasmanian town. Maria, 24 then, was the daughter of Reverend Henry Dowling, pastor of the chapel, and sister of Henry the younger, a newspaperman and temperance advocate who would become mayor of Launceston. The Dowlings had emigrated from England in the early 1830s. Maria received a finished education at Ellenthorpe Hall, one of Tasmania's pre-eminent schools. Kilner was the son of Captain Edward Waller, who fought with Her Majesty's 87th Regiment, Royal Irish Fusiliers, in the Napoleonic Wars and also served in India. Born in Gosport, Hampshire, Kilner emigrated to Launceston in 1840 on the barque *Cecilia* after organising employment as an apprentice merchant with Perkins Bennett & Co., importer of clothing, groceries, glass and china from Britain and East India. The ambitious young man stayed with Perkins Bennett just eighteen months before starting his own import and export company, Waller Bros & Co., in partnership with his equally sagacious Sydney-based brother, John Gough Waller, importing food, clothing, spices, alcohol and handcrafts from England and India. Simultaneously, Kilner ran a warehouse, Waller & Co., at the back of the York Street Baptist Chapel, retailing imported coffee, tea, spices, ales, wines, pickles, preservatives 'and other dainties'. He was an active member of Launceston's Benevolent Society, campaigned for free immigration, an end to convict transportation and the rehabilitation of convicts currently in prison at Port Arthur.

Maria worked tirelessly for her church and, through the 1840s and into the '50s, schooled, according to her advertising, 'young ladies . . . in the useful and ornamental branches of education . . . an English education with the addition of the French language, if required, and including music and drawing'.

Business, education, Christianity and improving the lot of the poor and needy were the foundations of Kilner and Maria Waller's life, and when they had children, they raised them as they themselves had been raised, according to the Holy Gospel.

The Wallers had the courage of their charitable convictions. They defied polite society, and the law, by continuing to employ in their home Agnes Jones, a convict who had worked in the home of Maria's brother, Henry, after she fell pregnant to Henry's cook.

Then, it seems, Kilner grew homesick for England. He wrote that while he enjoyed living and raising his family in Australia, 'desolation was felt by many a heart once happy in its British home'.

Perhaps that is why in 1853, after eleven years of marriage, the Wallers decided to leave Launceston and live in England. They sold their luxurious John Street property and their belongings, which included four poster beds, dining tables, a damask-covered lounge and chairs, pistols in a case, an Oriental bookcase with escritoire and chiffonier, a spinning wheel, pianos and a twelve-key flutina (a predecessor to the accordion), scores of paintings, a library of leather-bound books including John Bunyan's *The Pilgrim's Progress* and the complete works of Sir Walter Scott, Hogarth and Shakespeare, a Wedgwood dessert service, a wheelbarrow and a magic lantern.

The family boarded the auxiliary sail and steam vessel *Great Britain* in December 1853. By then, Maria and Kilner had five children; John would be born in August 1854. With them was a servant to help Maria with the youngsters. In England, the Wallers lived in central London and at Spring Grove House, 13 kilometres from London, a substantial estate that was once home to Captain James Cook's botanist Sir Joseph Banks. They travelled throughout rural England, visiting Maria's relatives in Gloucester and Colchester in Essex where Maria, wrote Kilner, had been 'born within the sound of its cheerful bells' and played within the castle and abbey walls. The family spent time with Kilner's stepmother, Sarah Waller, who had cared for the young man after his parents died. A highlight of the Wallers' trip was their visit to Kilner's ancestral home in Ireland, Castle Waller, near Newport, County Tipperary. The occasion was delightfully recorded in a local newsletter.

A very marked instance has just been communicated to us of the undying attachment of the Irish people to the old soil and its ancient lords. Mr Kilner Waller, who has passed all his life in India and Australia, and who but recently returned to his native land, paid a visit on Monday last to his old home of his fathers; and although his incognito was most rigidly preserved, the keen sense of the Celtic adherents and tenants of the Waller family soon divined who the visitor was, and before long the castle walls [sic] bonfires were lit, and many a merry jig was lilted to the sweet sounds of the Irish pipes. Altogether it was one of those occasions famous in story, and once common enough in the history of our islanders, but now rare as angel's [sic] visits, the result of the solemn visitations of Divine Providence over our land. The old castle is hastening to decay, for it is now over 700 years old, and sustained a bombardment in the days of Cromwell, but its ivy grown battlements will long be an object of local and family interest.

Just as they had in Australia, in Britain Kilner and Maria moved in formidable circles. They hobnobbed with the Duke of Wellington, the Earl of Shaftesbury, the lords Grosvenor and Goderich and the Lord Mayor of London, proposing and conducting campaigns to raise money to subsidise the expenses of emigrants to Australia. In 1841, Maria's brother, Henry, had been in England encouraging emigration to the colonies and selecting servants for Tasmanian farmers. He also lobbied to end the transportation of convicts to Australia. Kilner Waller continued this work. In Britain in the 1850s, for every person with a job, many, many more were unemployed, homeless and starving. At the same time, Australia's potential was being hobbled by a dearth of skilled and unskilled workers. Kilner's solution to both problems was to increase the number of industrious but poor Britons emigrating to Australian cities and towns, notably Launceston, where there were opportunities to earn a good living. To this end, in 1857 he argued his case in a series of letters to newspapers in England and Australia. 'It is quite obvious,' he wrote,

that we have room and callings for vast numbers of unemployed persons from Great Britain, male and female, those that have health and strength and willingness to proceed to the bush as useful men and women on farms and stations and otherwise . . . Gentlemen, on finding men willing to learn the occupation for which they are intended are frequently too glad to accept their services at remunerative prices; and ladies have often told me the same. It would not be amiss, however, to pay great attention to the sort of candidates who are proposed and accepted to take their passages to this colony, for very much depends upon this . . . It must be borne in mind that Australia is not a manufacturing country of any great extent where we can occupy girls on spinning jennies, looms and all sorts of light manufactured articles; but a country of wool, tallow, gold and other natural products . . . shepherds are more required than manufacturers, ploughmen than weavers, manual labourers than landscape gardeners, girls at the milking pail than ladies' maids, laundresses than dressmakers.

By 1857, the Wallers had decided that, after all, their home was in Australia, but in Sydney rather than Launceston. In July 1857, John Gough Waller, on his brother's behalf, placed an advertisement in the Sydney press: 'WANTED, a House, containing eight or nine rooms, suitable for a respectable family; must have garden, stables, and coach-house; neighbourhood of Woolloomooloo or Darling-hurst preferred. Apply to JG WALLER and CO, Wynyard-square.'

Having heard positive reports about the *Dunbar* and its master, James Green, Kilner Waller purchased eight cabin-class tickets and an intermediate berth for their servant on the clipper for a May 1857 departure.

Suddenly Maria had qualms, perhaps a premonition, that she would die on the voyage home. Her brother, Henry Dowling, later told how, 'on a very recent occasion, writing to a Christian friend here, Maria expressed an apprehension that she should not live to reach her adopted country; and gave utterance to some desires in the event of her husband and children being deprived of her maternal care'. These thoughts of impending death moved Maria to express her fears in a letter to a friend in Launceston, but, as if to tell her friend that she didn't fear death and welcomed the heavenly glory that she was sure lay beyond, she tucked into the envelope a copy of the words of the hymn 'Nearer, My God, to Thee', composed by the British actress Sarah Flower Adams in 1841, with its vivid images of death, angels and ascending to heaven.

After the two Waller adults, their six children and a servant boarded the *Dunbar* and their belongings were stowed, Kilner Waller approached Captain Green and asked permission to give daily Bible readings on the voyage. His offer was accepted.

It's possible that Waller was having his own thoughts about mortality. In his final days in England, he added a codicil to his will, naming his beneficiaries should the ship sink. Yet Waller's faith in the *Dunbar* and Captain Green to deliver him and his family safely to Sydney Cove was such that he chose his English friend Charles C. Troughton to be a signatory to and administrator of the codicil; Troughton had also booked passage on the *Dunbar* so would hardly be in a position to ensure that Waller's wishes were met if the ship did go down. That aside, in choosing Charles Troughton as a signatory, Waller was typically judicious, for Troughton was a man after his own heart.

The 30-year-old Troughton was a partner in the Shoreditch banking house of Messrs R. Davies & Co. It was written of him in the *Newcastle Journal* that 'he showed punctuality, integrity, kindness and business habits'. Yet, more than that, he was admired for his 'affectionate interest in the poor . . . [and] loving regard for children. This induced him to devote his energies, time and talents for their benefit and Christian training.' As he prospered as a banker, he gave financial support to the Shoreditch Sunday and National schools, where he served as honorary treasurer. 'He encouraged the deserving children with rewards of clothing and books as well as by words of cheering and kindness,' noted the *Journal*. 'In the distress which prevailed so widely in the winters of 1854-5, when 12,800 bread and coal tickets, besides blankets and relief in many shapes, were distributed mainly through his agency, he was most zealous and indefatigable in visiting the poor from house to house, in relieving their wants and sufferings, soothing their anxieties, and, above all, by stimulating others by his influence and example to do likewise.' It's likely that Kilner and Maria Waller persuaded Troughton to travel with them to Australia, but when someone asked him why he was taking a break from Shoreditch, the bank and his good works to sail to Sydney, Troughton replied that he was going for his health.

Marian Egan and her children, Gertrude and Henry, and Henry's much-admired new pet, the Russian wolfhound rescued from the Crimean battlefield, were returning home to Sydney on the *Dunbar*. They had been away a year, during which Marian, 39, had introduced Gertrude, eighteen, and Henry, twenty, to their paternal grandparents and travelled in Britain and Europe. As the three watched the southern English coast disappear and looked out at the open sea ahead, there was just one small cloud on their horizon. While they had been touring Rome, marvelling at the Colosseum, the Forum and the Trevi Fountain, they had sat for a portrait to take back to Sydney with them, but the artist had not been able to complete it before the *Dunbar* sailed. The artist undertook to package up the painting and send it out on the next ship, the *La Hogue*, the *Dunbar*'s sister clipper, addressed to Marian's husband, Daniel Egan. Not ideal, as they had hoped to present it to Daniel themselves to mark their homecoming after so long apart, but short of cancelling their booking on the *Dunbar* and accompanying the painting on the *La Hogue*, this arrangement had to suffice.

There's little doubt that Marian's, Gertrude's and Henry's disappointment at leaving the portrait behind was assuaged by the *Dunbar*'s first-class trimmings and trappings and the knowledge that there would be much celebrating with Daniel and their large circle of friends once they resumed their privileged and happy existence in Sydney. Although Gertrude and Henry were the children of Marian and her late husband, Henry Cahuac, 56-year-old Egan had welcomed them into his life as if they were his own, and was in the throes of building a fine mansion for his family on Old South Head Road at Watsons Bay as a welcome home surprise. Sadly, by the time the portrait of his loved ones arrived on *La Hogue*—marked '1 package Egan'—and was delivered to Daniel Egan's door, it brought him only sadness, and his half-completed dream home lay abandoned.

Another family luxuriating in a first-class cabin by the *Dunbar*'s poop deck was the Meyer clan of eight. Abraham, 49, Julia, 32, and their children: Lazarus, nine; Hannah, eight; Rachel, six; Lewis, four; and infants Julia and Morris. Their two servants sailed steerage. Abraham Meyer and Julia Hart had been married at the synagogue in York Street, Sydney, in 1845. Giving his daughter away was the colourful Asher Hart, who, despite being a leader of Sydney's Jewish community and a seat holder at the synagogue, had a hot temper and was handy with his fists. Just two months before Julia's wedding, he was charged with assaulting one James Butler who, Hart believed, was being overly familiar with one of Hart's other daughters, Rachel. The court heard that Hart and his son, Lazarus, 'promised to knock Butler into next Christmas and commenced the abbreviation of the intervening period by taking at least a week's growth out of him by the violence of their behaviour'. Also in the congregation at Abraham and Julia's wedding was Abraham's brother, Solomon Meyer, who had been arrested for 'sly grog selling on a large scale and in the most impudent manner'. Unlike their relatives, Abraham and Julia worked hard and lived quietly and within the law.

Abraham Meyer profitably managed general stores in Goulburn and Queanbeyan, then in 1848, the year his and Julia's first child, Lazarus, was born, he opened his own Railway Store in Queanbeyan. To attract customers, Abraham published an advertisement in the local paper: 'Mr Meyer feels confident that his stock of linen and woollen drapery, hosiery, haberdashery, grocery, ironmongery, wines, spirits, &c, &c is not to be equalled in any other store in the colony for either quality or prices, therefore defies all competition, and trusts that he will receive a portion of the public patronage.' Perhaps, though, his confidence was misplaced because just three years later he published another advertisement:

Selling Out. A Meyer, proprietor of the above establishment, shortly intends removing to Wide Bay, and takes this opportunity of acquainting the public generally, that he is selling off his extensive stock of Drapery, Hosiery, Haberdashery, Clothing, Ironmongery, and Grocery, at greatly reduced astoundingly low prices, for Cash only . . . All parties indebted to the above establishment are requested to settle their accounts forthwith: any outstanding debts not paid on or before the 31st August next, will be placed in the hands of my Solicitor for recovery without further notice . . . He must ensure a total clearance of stock in a very short time.

Although chastened after the Railway Store failure, Meyer went on to involve himself in other more successful enterprises in and around Queanbeyan. By 1854, he and Julia were wealthy. They lived in a grand house and gave to charity and supported the York Street Synagogue's 1854 fund-raising campaign for 'the starving Jews of Palestine'. Two years later, the Meyer family and servants holidayed in England. When it was time to go home, in mid-1857, Abraham Meyer saw no reason not to return on the *Dunbar*.

The Meyers already knew some of their fellow passengers, such as Thomas Hyacinth Macquoid, who was the owner of the Tuggeranong homestead, Waniassa, 16 kilometres from Queanbeyan. Macquoid was the son of the third sheriff of New South Wales, and had been publicly congratulated when he repaid the debts of his spendthrift father. Macquoid was travelling with his friend and near-neighbour, grazier Edward Severne, whose property was Gudgenby. Macquoid and Severne had sailed to England in January 1855 on the Dunbar line clipper *Vimeira* whose master was Henry Neatby and its first officer James Green who, as a reward for his sterling service under Neatby, was placed in command of the *Vimeira* when it returned to Sydney early in 1856.

As well as socialising with Macquoid and Severne, Abraham and Julia Meyer likely acquainted themselves with another cabin-class passenger, Isaac Simmons, who, like them, was a mainstay of Sydney's Jewish community. Simmons' father, James, had arrived in Sydney as a convict in 1815—his death sentence for burglary having been commuted to fourteen years in the colony. On emancipation after four years, James Simmons founded the Emu Warehouse on the corner of George and King streets, and then the Jerusalem Warehouse clothing store on George and Barrack streets. He expanded into money-changing and selling groceries, then became the City of Sydney's first Jewish alderman. Son Isaac was born in 1836 and seemed destined to emulate his father's business success. After finishing school in Sydney, he completed his education in England and drummed up import opportunities on behalf of his uncle, Joseph, who owned a Sydney auction house and grocery store. Isaac's studies and work completed, he paid for a ticket to Sydney on the *Dunbar*, determined to return home in style and then live up to the high expectations his father and uncle had for him.

Dublin-born Maria Logan and her husband, Charles, had emigrated to Hobart in 1835. She, a librarian, music teacher, pianist and organist, composer of sacred music and transcriber of indigenous songs, and Charles, Hobart's town surveyor, had nine children together. In 1855, Maria and Ida, sixteen years old, Charles, nine, and Arthur, seven, sailed to England on the *Vimeira* for a holiday and to stay with relatives in Dublin. Maria returned to Hobart in January 1856 on the *La Hogue*, leaving her children to live with her relatives and attend school in Dublin. Young Ida, known as 'a most accomplished girl', Charles and Arthur would return on the *Dunbar* in May 1857 to be reunited with their parents and siblings in Sydney, where the family had moved after Charles was sacked from his job and made bankrupt.

It was a novelty for Captain John Steane RN, who, after a long and illustrious career serving on British warships in famous victories, for once had nothing to do on board but relax. Steane, born on the Isle of Wight in 1795, joined the Royal Navy at age twelve and served on the frigate *Nemesis* off the coast of North America and in 1809, as a midshipman, fought in the siege of Flushing when the British attacked and claimed the French-held Dutch harbour. He also bore arms in the British and Spanish defence of Spain's Cadiz against Napoleon's forces in 1810–11.

Marriage to Ann Yelf in 1818 did not keep Steane dry docked. In the following years, he was on a number of warships, his reputation as a maritime warrior growing with each new charge. He spent much time in the West Indies on the *Venerable*, *Spider*, *Valorous* and *Beaver*—before in 1833 commanding the cruiser *Sprightly* and later the merchant steamers *Hydra* in the Mediterranean, and the *Shearwater* and the *Blazer* off North America and in the West Indies.

John Steane had many maritime passions. In 1827, he was a proponent of inventor John Dennett's controversial rocket to carry a rescue line from one ship to a stricken vessel. Steane praised the rocket's portability, accuracy, range and its bright light that illuminated the area around the ship so its position could be determined by rescuers. Dennett's rocket was duly commissioned by the Royal Navy. Steane's advocacy for it led to him being presented with a gold medal by the Royal National Lifeboat Institution. The medal was 'awarded to persons whose humane and intrepid exertions in saving lives from shipwreck have been deemed sufficiently conspicuous to merit that honourable distinction'.

On retiring in 1841 with the rank of commander, John, with Ann and their children, Thomas and Elizabeth, lived in Sydney, where he was an official with the Australia Station, the Royal Navy's East Indies naval squadron base in Port Jackson. The Steanes' marriage ended because, it was rumoured, of John's 1856 affair with Hannah Watson, wife of Thomas Watson, former Macquarie Light keeper and a chief pilot, now a wealthy man through commercial shipping and trading. It has also been reported, though, like the affair, never substantiated, that Thomas Watson placed a curse on his wife and her lover. Cursed or not, Hannah Watson died soon after. When she was breathing her last, Steane, who had been in England, was sailing to Sydney on the *Dunbar*. It's probable, considering his naval exploits, that Steane—who wore his uniform, heavy with braid and brass, on special occasions during the voyage—and Captain Green swapped stories of their lives at sea.

In steerage quarters on the *Dunbar* were Daniel and Elizabeth Healing, both 30 and a decade married, who were emigrating to

Sydney from Cheltenham in Gloucestershire with children Frederick, eight, George, six, and Louisa, three. Daniel had been an assistant to a linen draper named Staples in Cheltenham and his diligence and bravery led to the arrest of John and Mary Jones after they stole an umbrella and a length of printed linen from Staples' store. Healing shadowed the thieves to the local churchyard and summoned police, who nabbed them. Hoping for a new start for his family, and perhaps a quieter life for himself, Daniel arranged employment as a linen draper in Sydney in what the *Gloucester Chronicle* described as 'a large establishment'.

The Healings' neighbours in steerage were Martha Brown, 33, and her three-year-old son Henry. Martha's husband of six years, William, had sailed earlier to establish a home in Sydney and work as a draper with Messrs Thompson and Simmons & Co. Sailing to Sydney on the *Dunbar*, Martha imagined joyous times ahead when the ship arrived at Sydney Cove and there waiting for her and Henry would be William.

The Misses Hunt, Sarah and Emily, eighteen and twenty respectively, were returning to Sydney after attending finishing school in Bordeaux, France. They, like so many others on the *Dunbar*, had much to look forward to: falling in love and starting a family and, more immediately, reuniting with their older brother, Robert Hunt. Robert had emigrated to Sydney from England in 1854, aged 24, after being educated in France and studying at London's Government School of Mines. Soon after arrival, he was appointed first clerk in the Sydney Bullion Office at the Mint in Macquarie Street. A scientist and chemist, he became deputy master of the Mint, directing its smelting and refining processes, and advising on separating gold from various ores. Robert's hobby was the new technique of wet-plate photography. He would set out in his sailing dinghy the *Terror* to photograph harbour scenes with his Mint colleague and friend William Stanley Jevons who, when younger, had written about housing in the colony. While now in the upper strata of the Sydney establishment, the Hunt siblings came from rebel stock. Their grandfather, John Hunt, was a social reformer in London who, with his brother Leigh, published the liberal newspaper *The Examiner* and served two years' gaol for seditious libel. The poet Lord Byron and the philosopher Jeremy Bentham visited the brothers in their prison cell, where they conducted a literary and political salon.

Robert left Jevons in no doubt that he would be a loving brother to his returning sisters. Jevons wrote to his sister, Lucy:

> After remaining [at school in Bordeaux] it was arranged that [Sarah and Emily] should come out to him here by the ship *Dunbar*, and in the shipping intelligence by the last mail their names were duly inserted in the list of passengers. In Sydney, Hunt had long expected them with pleasure. Very lately he had been busy choosing a small house on the North Shore, furnishing it, and even engaging servants, and was only waiting for the telegraph to announce the arrival of the ship. He was continually coming into my room, which commands a good view of the [signal station] flagstaff and, when disappointed by the flags, always discovering that the ship was not quite due yet.

Adrian de Jongh James was born in Sydney in 1841, the son of H. Kerrison James, secretary of the Bishop of Sydney, William Broughton. Like a number of other young Australians sailing home on the *Dunbar*, the sixteen-year-old had been, reported the *Sydney Morning Herald*, 'benefiting by the educational advantages of the Mother Country'. James' heart was set on being a Church of England minister. The *Herald* said of him that he was 'about to enter, with every promise of success, upon a career of enviable distinction'. James had gone to England, aged thirteen, in 1854, and attended Stockwell Grammar School in London's Lambeth, which was associated with prestigious King's College. 'There,' continued the *Herald*:

> he was enabled to pursue a liberal and successful course of study, and with such application and exercise of high and independent

principles, that, though removed from direct parental restraint, he voluntarily abjured many inviting pleasures and innocent gratifications, and in the laudable ambition of acquiring knowledge, gave up his leisure to the pursuits of learning, and to acquaintance with the numerous channels of intellectual refinement opened to the enquiring. Thus, having attained an honourable position in the first form of the school, and incited by expectation of welcome recognition in Australia, as well as by a desire to complete his studies in the University of his native land, he took his departure on *Dunbar*.

James had chosen the vessel because his friend Thomas Hyacinth Macquoid had also booked a cabin-class passage.

Cabin-class passenger Patrick Downey was a well-known Sydney architect and businessman who, by hard work and good fortune, had resurrected his career and reputation after an early setback and a controversy. He was born in Ballinasloe in County Galway, Ireland, in 1820 and emigrated to Sydney in 1841 on the *Gilbert Henderson* with his parents and four siblings. Downey's talents as a carpenter and his dependability won him steady work. Soon after arriving he fell in love with a countrywoman, Belinda Clune, from County Clare. They married at St Mary's Cathedral in 1842 and lived in a cottage at the corner of William and Palmer streets, East Sydney. By the following year, Downey had established a building company in Goulburn Street in partnership with Daniel McCloskey, but within months the company was insolvent. Downey now teamed with an architect named Clark and they hung out their shingle, Downey and Clark, Architects, Surveyors and Civil Engineers, in William Street, and the firm fared better than his previous enterprise. In 1852, Downey successfully stood for election to Sydney City Council, but then he refused to take his seat. There was a furore and questions were asked of Downey that he refused to answer. He was fined £25, and warned that if he did not pay promptly, legal proceedings would be commenced to recover the money. In 1855, Downey was made deputy chairman of David Jones's store on the corner of George and

Barrack streets, and he and founder Jones set about selling 'the best and most exclusive' clothing and fabrics, 'stock that embraces the everyday wants of mankind at large'. Jones was also chairman of the Metropolitan Building Society, and in 1855 Downey was appointed a director. His other responsibilities did not prevent Downey continuing as one of Sydney's most in-demand architects. He designed major commercial buildings and private dwellings in George, Pitt, Barrack, Elizabeth and William streets and in Darling Point for the city's wealthiest citizens. In late 1856, shortly before he and his wife, Belinda, sailed to England and the Continent for a holiday, Downey invited stonemasons to tender for the job of building a large store opposite the police station in George Street, Circular Quay, not far from the city morgue, or Dead House. Downey would announce the successful tenderer on his return from England on the *Dunbar* in the winter of 1857. As one accustomed to, and able to afford, the best that life could offer, for Patrick Downey, the magnificent Duncan Dunbar clipper was the obvious choice. Belinda was to sail home with her husband, but changed her mind and decided to return on the *City of Sydney* with her friend and relative Eleanor Carmichael. Their ship was delayed in Galle, Ceylon (today Sri Lanka), and the pair took the opportunity to tour the tropical paradise before boarding the *Victoria*. That vessel did not reach Sydney Cove until February 1858 by which time she was six months a widow.

The Peeks, Samuel and Caroline, would have been right at home on the *Dunbar*'s poop deck with their fellow first-class passengers, Captain Green and his officers. Sam Peek's ability to spot a business opportunity and his ruthlessness in making it pay had made him one of New South Wales' richest and most formidable businessmen. The firstborn of thirteen children of Samuel and Hannah Peek of Devonshire, 24-year-old Sam married Caroline Webb of Gloucestershire on Christmas Day, 1831, and four years later they emigrated to Sydney on the *Richard Walker*. Fresh off the ship, Peek bought land in Sydney Town, Balmain and on the coast to the north. When he first travelled to East Gosford, 80 kilometres north of Sydney, around a hundred people lived rough in the bush there on the estuary around a magnificent waterway, today Brisbane Water. Peek immediately saw potential for a township and bought 220 hectares of land whose cheapness belied its natural beauty. To provide quick access from Sydney, there being no road, he built a wharf and founded a steamer service. Peek then had a surveyor lay out plots, which he sold at a profit. An advertisement placed by Peek assured prospective settlers in East Gosford that there were few better places to live and raise a family. It offered to the industrious tradesman

> [inducements] rarely to be met with, the district abounding with timber of every description. Here he can follow his occupation with the benefit of fresh air; and by rearing poultry and cultivating, with very little trouble he can support his family, besides being able, through the medium of the steamer, which plies regularly once a week, to send the over-surplus of his produce to Sydney; but, indeed the consumption of the township is so very great that he would be very sure to dispose of it on the spot, East Gosford being already the fashionable resort for visitors from Sydney and must eventually become the Brighton [England] of Australia.

Though the advertisement had been well greased with snake oil, it worked. By 1841, nearly 200 people lived in Sam Peek's township that comprised dwellings, many of them two-storeyed, public facilities, shops, a blacksmith, a courthouse, hotels and two pubs, one with a billiard table. He named two roads after his wife, and a promontory after himself, and Caroline Street, Webb Street and Peeks Point can be visited today.

Meanwhile, land baron Peek had joined with John Webb (possibly a relative of Caroline's) and was operating S Peek & Co., Sydney Tea and Coffee Merchant, in George Street, Sydney. By 1838, he and Webb partnered with Sam's brother Richard, not long arrived in the colony, and Edward Campbell to found one of Sydney's largest and most profitable tea and coffee, imported grocery and wine store businesses. The partners purchased the land between their establishment in George Street all the way through to Pitt Street and set up a steam coffee mill there. Then came the day in 1839 when Sam Peek and John Webb sold their share of the company to Richard Peek and Edward Campbell for £20,000. A proviso of the sale was that any new enterprise of Sam's would be no threat to the established grocery business. Richard was understandably furious when just eighteen months later Sam and Webb opened a grocery store in direct competition. Richard accused Sam of fraud, sued him and won. Sam became insolvent and was forced to relinquish his East Gosford holdings.

Undeterred, Peek did whatever he needed to do to repay his debts and by 1846 S Peek & Co. was back in business on George Street. As well as involving himself in myriad business ventures, Peek stood for City Council and served as a councillor from November 1850 to December 1851. He used his high profile to join Henry Parkes in his radical campaign to improve the lot of everyday working people who were still considered second-class citizens and deprived of privileges by the landed gentry. If ever anyone could testify that those who made their living by hard work and perseverance deserved more respect than those who'd prospered through climbing the boughs of an illustrious family tree, it was Peek.

With more money now than he and Caroline could spend, the Peeks, who had no children, enjoyed the fruits of Sam's snakes-and-ladders career. They had many friends, were regulars at concerts and theatre, and lived in Richmond Villa, a substantial sandstone home in the Domain. (The Peeks had the house dismantled stone by stone and rebuilt in Kent Street. It is today the Australian Genealogical Society's headquarters.) In 1854 or '55, they sailed to England on an extended holiday to revisit old haunts and tell relatives in Devon and Gloucester about their Australian life. For their return voyage, the Peeks bought first-class berths on the *Dunbar*. Before departing, they painstakingly marked all their belongings and clothing with their name, just in case they were lost in transit.

William Bynon had sailed to England in January 1857, leaving behind in Sydney his wife, Augusta, their daughter, and Augusta's young son from a previous marriage. William travelled steerage because he and his wife were on their uppers. The trip was a last-ditch effort to save their struggling millinery business, Suffolk House in George Street. William's mission was to explore export opportunities and try to raise funds to save the business. Meanwhile, Augusta carried on alone in Sydney as a milliner and dressmaker. Augusta and William had married in 1855, after her first husband, Walter Fayers, with whom Augusta founded Suffolk House, died of tuberculosis, leaving Augusta near-destitute when his wealth of £1700 was mired indefinitely in red tape. Adding to Augusta's despair was that her and Walter's one-year-old daughter, Ada, had recently passed away. Enter William Bynon. He courted and married Augusta and took over Suffolk House's advertising and marketing while she continued at her trade. For all their hard work, profits were elusive, and they were reduced to selling freckle remover, toothpaste and hair dye to make ends meet. Augusta and William had a daughter, Kate, in December 1856, just a month before he travelled to England. There he had little success winning new business and to preserve what little money they had, booked a steerage passage home on the *Dunbar*. He could not have known that back in Sydney, in April, despite Augusta's valiant efforts to keep Suffolk House afloat, it had been made bankrupt and all stock auctioned to pay creditors. No doubt Augusta was counting the days until August when the *Dunbar* would drop anchor in Sydney Cove and she and William could rebuild their life from the ruins.

Intermediate passenger John Holl, just fifteen, was sailing on the *Dunbar* to live with his twenty-year-old brother, Robert, in Sydney, where Robert was an apprentice saddler and maker of horse collars. Presumably, Robert had written to John, telling him of the opportunities that existed for industrious young immigrants in Sydney, so John secured a cot on the *Dunbar*. At the opposite end of the social strata to John Holl was first-class passenger Cuthbert Davidson, the eighteen-year-old son of the late Hugh Davidson, 4th Baron of Cantray. After his older brother, Hugh, became the 5th Baron of Cantray, Cuthbert left Cantray House, the family estate on the River Nairn at Inverness, Scotland, to find fame and fortune in Australia. Not wanting to delay his glorious future, he booked passage on the fastest, most reliable clipper available.

It's a sure bet that the long and uneventful weeks at sea on the *Dunbar* were enlivened by the jovial presence of the partying Mylne brothers, John and Thomas, who were returning to the colony with their sisters Letitia (known as Letty) and Anne (or Annie), their servant Mrs Annan and her two children, and a cache of fine furniture and silverware from the family's Scottish estate. The brothers were renowned raconteurs and bon vivants, as the name of their pastoral run on the north bank of the Clarence River, 5 kilometres from Grafton, attests. Many assumed the cattle station's name, Eatonswill, honoured a town or, perhaps, a mansion or castle back at Longforgan in their Scottish homeland. The truth was much more interesting. 'Eatonswill' was a contraction of 'eat and swill', which was what the Mylnes did to excess with their guests. One legendary Eatonswill party lasted twelve days.

John, born in 1819, had joined the Madras Army of the East India Company in 1833, after his father, Thomas, prevailed on company director Henry Shank to accept his son. John rose to the rank of lieutenant. The army's role was to protect the commercial interests of the East India Company in Madras. John's older brother, James, also served in the Indian Army, but his three-years-younger sibling, Thomas, was too young to enlist.

By the late 1830s, the three Mylne brothers had left behind in Scotland their parents, Thomas and Elizabeth, and siblings, Annie, Agnes, William, Charles, Letty and Graham, after having decided to make their pile in Australia. John and Thomas were more than capable of mixing pleasure with hard work and Eatonswill prospered. The cattle raised there were of the highest quality, as were their horses, one of whom, Splendora, mothered successful racehorses.

According to the 1886 and 1888 *Bawden Lectures: The First 50 Years of Settlement on the Clarence*, preserved by the Clarence River Historical Society:

> John Mylne was an excellent judge of stock, and nothing but the very best obtainable, either in cattle or horses, was of any use to him . . . The Rev AE Selwyn placed on record that it was at the instance of John Mylne that the first clergyman, the Rev John McConnell, was sent to the Clarence in 1844. Selwyn had a very high opinion of John and stated in a letter that he was the person upon whom he relied here for aid and counsel in every good work.

But James Mylne may have been more of a hindrance than a help. The *Bawden Lectures* recorded: 'The run was gazetted in the names of John and Thomas only . . . and so it was of some allotments in South Grafton, and freehold portions at Copmanhurst and elsewhere. James' name is not on them.' On 16 April 1851, Frederick Tindal, who with his brothers Charles, Francis and Arthur owned the neighbouring cattle station and horse stud Koreelah, wrote, 'I have a visitor with me, Mr James Mylne, who spends the day in plaiting stockwhips and reading *Waverley* novels [of Sir Walter Scott].'

Frederick Tindal divided his time between running cattle on his nearby property and painting landscapes. Like most in the district, Tindal, and his brothers, prized an invitation to a get-together with the Mylnes at Eatonswill. Tindal recalled:

> The veranda was 50ft [15 metres] long and nearly high enough for battledore and shuttlecock [a game in which a cork with feathers stuck in it was hit from one player to another with wooden bats called battledores]. Five rooms in the house, neatly furnished, one of them kept for visitors; bananas, oranges, lemons, peaches, etc, in the garden. The Mylnes . . . live the most comfortably of any people on the river. [They] give their visitors wine and ale, preserved fruits, etc. They have a good library, and good armchairs.

There was horscracing on the private racecourse (the Mylnes are credited with introducing the sport to northern New South Wales). There were boating, quoits, the aforementioned shuttlecock and swan shooting, when real feathers flew. Every evening there was a sumptuous dinner accompanied by fine wines from Eatonswill's cavernous cellar followed by roistering till dawn and well into the following day, or days.

In 1856, John and Thomas Mylne, bachelors both, spent a holiday year in Scotland to visit their family. While there, they persuaded Letty and Annie to return with them to live for a while at Eatonswill. They would be joined on the *Dunbar* by their neighbour Francis Tindal, who had been in England mourning the drowning deaths of two of his brothers: Arthur in the shipwreck of a schooner en route to the Clarence River from Sydney, and Frederick, the artist and Eatonswill reveller, when he was trying to cross the swollen Paterson River.

When James Mylne learned that his four siblings and Francis Tindal were returning on the *Dunbar* in August or September, he took on extra servants, restocked the pantry and cellar and decorated the homestead in preparation for the wildest welcome home party the district had ever seen.

10

Life on the *Dunbar*

What is known for certain about the second passage to Sydney of the *Dunbar* is that it was a quick 81-day voyage. The ship sailed the North and South Atlantic oceans, across the Southern Ocean, probably at around 42 degrees south, passing between Antarctica and southern Australia, before heading north to carefully thread her way through the islands of Bass Strait—Captain Green negotiated treacherous King Island, graveyard of the *Cataraqui* and scores of other vessels, on 16 August—and along the east coast of the continent towards Port Jackson.

The *Dunbar* probably sailed nonstop, for there is no record of it having put in at any ports.

What is also known is that it was a pleasant and uneventful voyage; nobody died or even fell seriously ill; there were no untoward incidents; and the *Dunbar* sustained no damage to hull or sails as it sped to its destination. There's little doubt that those on board would have endured intense summer heat in the North Atlantic and bitter winter cold in the southern latitudes. There would have been storms at sea. Crockery would have flown and people would have been knocked off balance. Inevitably, there'd have been the odd weevil in the flour and perhaps a mouse or rat in a grain bin or fished from a water barrel. All that came with the territory of the journey, no matter how luxurious the ship.

The skippers of rival clippers the *Vocalist*, with more than 500 on board, the *Zemindar*, and the *Dunbar*'s sister ship, the spanking new *Duncan Dunbar*, all of which had departed Plymouth before her, later confirmed that the *Dunbar* overtook them and that the passing of each ship elicited cheers and good-hearted jeers from the *Dunbar*'s crew and passengers.

Specifics of everyday life on the *Dunbar* can be gleaned from the published regimens of daily routine on Duncan Dunbar's other clippers, and the diaries and letters of these vessels' passengers and crew.

Dunbar ran tight ships. He knew that high standards on his vessels would attract wealthy passengers and solvent exporters and importers. Captain Green was a stickler for enforcing the rules and regulations and code of conduct of the Dunbar line, all of which were ratified by the British government. Early in the voyage, Green would have assembled the passengers and, probably with first officer James Struthers and second officer John Spence at his side, let them know what he expected of them.

Every *Dunbar* passenger who was not unwell or had another valid reason to remain in their bunk had to be up and about by 6 a.m. Ablutions needed to be completed by the time the breakfast bell rang at 8 a.m. Passengers were expected to wash daily and wear clean clothes to reduce the chances of disease breaking out.

Those in steerage and intermediate class cleaned their own berths, washed their clothes and bedding, and scrubbed their utensils and crockery and toilet pots; there were daily inspections by crew and shoddy work had to be done again. They cooked and ate together in their designated mess.

Cabin-class passengers' quarters were cleaned and their washing done by crew. They could eat in their cabin, their food served by stewards, or in a communal dining cabin. Each would have a turn sitting at Captain Green's table.

For all, lunch was at 1 p.m., dinner at 6 p.m. There were Church of England services on deck on Sundays, and Bible readings by Kilner Waller. Passengers were expected to be present for surgeon Alexander Bayne's regular health inspections. There were school lessons for children.

Mornings, afternoons and after dinner, voyagers could promenade on their designated area of the deck, read books and write letters and make entries in their journal. There was probably a *Dunbar* newspaper to which passengers were encouraged to contribute their observations, jokes, cartoons, tips on how to make the hours speed by faster, and perhaps even items for a gossip column, because, on long voyages, there would have been the usual onboard romances and intrigues. The passengers joked and smoked, sang and played musical instruments, dealt hands of cards and tried to best each other at board and deck games such as cricket and quoits. They fished, and shot at skeets and birds that flew within musket range. They enjoyed plays, lectures, literature and poetry readings, and musical performances. Passengers danced on the polished teak poop deck. They gazed out to sea and at passing islands and ports. They dizzied themselves looking up through the sails at the yellow tropical moon and watching its reflection break into a thousand shards when a breeze ruffled the surface of the water. They gasped at gorgeous sunsets, at enormous wandering albatrosses gliding above like pterodactyls and gulls that circled the ship like vultures. They pointed excitedly at shoals of phosphorescent fish and when the fin of a shark scavenging in their wake scythed the swell.

Captain Green allowed passengers to bring alcohol on board, but made them hand it over to the steward 'for safekeeping' until they disembarked. Crew doled out a 'reasonable' daily ration of ale, wine and spirits. Firearms and gunpowder, too, were confiscated on embarkation and returned at the end of the voyage. Smoking below decks was banned, as were naked flames. Passengers were to treat each other, and the crew, with respect and courtesy. There was zero tolerance for drunkenness, lecherous or 'quarrelsome and disputatious' behaviour. Crewmen's quarters were out of bounds for passengers, nor could they speak to the man at the wheel, nor pound nails into the ship's decks, beams or boards or do any other damage. Captain Green's orders, and those of his officers, had to be obeyed at all times. Lights went out at 10 p.m.

Such was life on board the *Dunbar* until, around midnight on 20 August 1857, just shy of its destination, disaster struck.

11

'Breakers ahead!'

Neither Captain James Green nor his senior crew survived to explain, yet it is possible to reconstruct the chain of events that ended with the destruction of the *Dunbar* from evidence provided in the wake of the disaster and at the coronial inquest.

After passing Cape Howe lighthouse on the south-east corner of the continent on the evening of Monday, 17 August, the *Dunbar* proceeded north along the coast towards Sydney. The weather was inclement and a little hazy, but unthreatening.

Late Thursday morning, 20 August, the clipper was just 12 hours from Sydney Heads. Captain Green left the poop deck, where he'd stood vigil with scarcely a break for the past two days, to, according to custom, thank his guests for their company and contributions to the voyage. He wished them well in the colony and hoped that they would again sail on the *Dunbar*. He rewarded his crew for their job well done with their usual noon tankard of grog. Naturally, they would be able to drink as many tankards as they pleased after the *Dunbar* arrived in Sydney Cove.

In the afternoon, the clipper was making good time beating into a 19–21 knot (35–39 kilometres per hour) north-easterly wind. As the *Dunbar* passed the small industrial port of Wollongong, around 90 kilometres south of the Heads, there seemed to be no reason it could not disembark its passengers at Sydney Cove around 10 or 11 p.m.

The dinner bell was rung at six, as it had been for the previous 80 days of the journey. Cabin-class passengers—the eight members of the Waller family and as many Meyers, the Misses Hunt, Marian Egan and her daughter, Gertrude, and son, Henry, Captain Steane, the four Mylne siblings, the Logan youngsters, Sam and Caroline Peek, Charles Troughton and Patrick Downey among them—would have been seated at their dining tables as stewards laid their last supper before them. In the steerage and intermediate messes, Daniel and Elizabeth Healing and their three children, William Bynon, James and Eleanor Clarke and their sons Henry and James, and the servants of the cabin travellers—gathered for their final meal together at sea. Through dinner, all would have been in high spirits, recalling memorable moments on the voyage but glad it was nearing its end. They would have enjoyed their food and drink with family and newfound friends and toasted the prosperity, adventure and love that surely awaited them after the *Dunbar* dropped anchor in Sydney Cove.

Today, technology and advanced communications warn ships' masters of approaching bad weather in time for them to take appropriate action. There was no such warning for Captain Green in 1857.

It was around 7.30 p.m. when, in a heartbeat, the day's steady showers and north-easterly winds transformed into an east-south-easterly gale with lashing rain squalls and 32 knot (60 kilometres per hour) winds generating 5 metre swells that buffeted the *Dunbar*. Torrential rain speared down from growling leaden clouds and beat on the deck and sails. The storm clawed at the *Dunbar*'s stern like a hungry lion chasing down a gazelle. Green ordered the fore and main topsails and the foresails shortened—or double-reefed—to halve the sail area. This lessened the effect of the wind, slowed the ship and gave the helmsmen better control over its direction.

At 8.30 p.m., the *Dunbar* was around 9.7 nautical miles (18 kilometres) out to sea from Botany Bay. Through the blackness and sheeting rain, Captain Green could occasionally make out the revolving beam of Macquarie Light high on the cliff-top 20 kilometres up along the coast from Botany Bay. Having entered Sydney Harbour many times, Green knew that the entrance to the Heads was 2.2 kilometres north of the lighthouse.

At this time, in the lookout at South Head Signal Station, assistant signal master Henry Packer, knowing that the *Zemindar*, the *Vocalist*, the *Duncan Dunbar*, the *Ann and Jane* and the *Dunbar* all were due, strained to see lights from any approaching ships. It was no easy task, for, as Packer would recall, 'the booming wind shook the station', the seas below were 'mountainous' and the stars and moon were hidden by 'dirty, leaden clouds, the kind that mariners dread'. Looking to the south through his telescope, he briefly saw the lights of a vessel out to sea from Botany Bay. The light was shrouded by the storm and Packer did not see it again. The signal station man could not have known that the *Dunbar* had left the other arriving tall ships in her wake and the ship's light he had so briefly seen was either it or the brigantine *Nora Creina* that was making for Sydney Cove from the Shoalhaven River, south of Sydney. There was another vessel in the vicinity, the small coastal steamer *Grafton*, captained by Charles Wiseman, but it was approaching the Heads from the north, from Yamba on the Clarence River. The *Nora Creina* made it into Port Jackson and on to Sydney Cove. Wiseman of the *Grafton* decided it was too risky to try to enter the Heads in such dangerous conditions and remained at sea overnight.

Meanwhile, in the *Dunbar*'s cabins and compartments, passengers' gaiety must have turned to deep concern when at around 9 p.m. the storm, already terrific, worsened. The *Dunbar* pitched and bucked wildly in the mountainous swells and the wind rose to around 43 knots (80 kilometres per hour) and wailed in the rigging. (The Beaufort Scale describes winds at 75–85 kilometres per hour as a strong-to-severe gale.) Yet, they would have reassured each other, they were in one of the sturdiest ships afloat helmed by a fine captain, and continued to prepare for arrival later that night or, possibly, if Captain Green decided it was safer to do so, the day after. To calm their nerves, those with access to alcohol might have poured themselves a fortifying glass, perhaps two. They may have tried to take their mind off the gale by donning their finest clothes so they would look their best when they descended the gangway at Sydney Cove later that night, or played cards or games, or pulled their cot covers up over their heads and prayed for sleep. Or in their terror they might simply have prayed. They would have reminded themselves that their present predicament must surely end and then there would be reunions with loved ones and the familiar streets and pastures of home. How good that would be.

By 10 p.m., the wind, according to later estimations from the weather station, was nearing 53 knots (100 kilometres per hour) and whipping up 10 metre cresting waves. The rain hammered down. This was no ordinary storm. Captain Green ordered the boatswain to summon all hands on deck—'All hands to wear ship!' In oilskins and sou'wester on the weather side of the lurching poop deck, the elements lashing his face, Green, flanked by first officer Struthers and James Johnson, the burly able seaman from Drogheda, grappled with a dilemma.

Should he turn seawards and try to ride out the storm far from the unlit coastline cliffs, then enter the Heads in morning's light? That's what the Port Jackson sailing directions recommended. In extremely rough weather a master 'should wait outside the Heads until daylight or more favourable conditions prevailed' rather than risk colliding with the cliffs. And even if the gale hadn't weakened by morning, at least he would be able to see where he was going. And, although open-decked pilot boats did not normally venture outside the Heads in rough seas at dark, in daylight a pilot boat would surely assist. Certainly some of the crew assumed that the *Dunbar* would remain at sea overnight and, whether arriving at this conclusion themselves or notified by crew members, many of the passengers did too, and undressed and went to bed.

Or, despite the weather and with severely limited visibility, should Captain Green try to enter the Heads that evening and run for Sydney Cove or, once through the Heads, shelter in the protected haven of Watsons Bay until it was safe to proceed to Sydney Cove?

The cautious option would have been to lie-to offshore—and Green was a cautious skipper. Yet he chose the latter option. Why, will never be known. We can only speculate.

Did he fear that the *Dunbar*, which was carrying at least 122 lives and uninsured cargo, was not sturdy enough, despite all its iron and copper reinforcing, to survive the heavy seas outside the Heads in an increasing gale with a dangerous lee shore, and feel there was a better chance of survival if he entered Port Jackson? Even though the *Dunbar* was at least a week ahead of schedule, was Green under pressure from merchants waiting to take delivery of cargo as soon as possible? Did he allow himself to be persuaded to be rash by passengers unwilling to delay their arrival even for a night? That last was unlikely, because James Green was too strong a master to be swayed by others, especially when his ship and reputation, not forgetting his and the others' lives, were at stake. Was his decision influenced by physical and mental fatigue? There would be testimony that the *Dunbar*'s master had 'not been off the deck for two hours since we first made land, some days previously'. There was surely no truth in the newspaper accusations in coming days that Captain Green was prepared to risk all because he had bet money that he would anchor in Sydney Cove on or before 20 August. Or did James Green simply decide that, having entered Sydney Heads without mishap eight times before, there would be nothing the weather gods could throw at him over which he and the *Dunbar* could not prevail?

Whatever his reasons for doing so, Green chose to take his ship through Sydney Heads. That decided, he followed, like every other master of a Duncan Dunbar vessel was expected to do, the advice for those entering Port Jackson contained in *Horsburgh's Standard Sailing Directory of 1855*, the standard navigational text of the day.

In the winter months there is much blowing weather on this coast and as the gales from seaward prevail often between north-east and south-east it is prudent [when sailing from the south] not to approach too close to the shore until in latitude 33 degrees 50' south [that is, level with Macquarie Light]. When in this latitude steer in for the coast. The entrance to the Harbour will show itself when you come nearby the lighthouse tower and by the Heads on each side, which are high, steep, perpendicular cliffs . . . having soundings from 15 to 12 fathoms [27 to 22 metres] between them.

An hour shy of midnight, now around 1 nautical mile (1.8 kilometres) off Ben Buckler headland at the north end of Bondi bay, Green set his course. The *Dunbar* would sail close-hauled on a starboard gybe before the east-south-east gale, on a heading of 034 degrees to gain him the necessary sea-room. Then, when he estimated he was level with Macquarie Light, and around 6 nautical miles (11 kilometres) offshore, he would wear ship to port and take the *Dunbar* north-west. This, Green estimated, would deliver his ship in around 30 minutes into the middle of the fairway between South and North Heads, and into Port Jackson.

It's thought that Captain Green now made a fatal error. Although the *Dunbar* was being propelled by the south-easterly gale at around 6 knots (11 kilometres per hour), it, with sails reefed, was heading directly into a forceful 3 knot (5.5 kilometre per hour) current flowing from the north-east. Sailing virtually blind and with its sails reefed, Green, it's assumed, overestimated the *Dunbar*'s speed because he was oblivious to the current, similar to someone walking the wrong way on a moving footpath. Green may have believed that the *Dunbar*'s speed was 6 knots, when, because of the current retarding his progress and his vessel's shortened sails, it was half that. Leeway may have added to his confusion. The wind was shoving the *Dunbar* sideways and towards the coast at the rate of around 1 nautical mile per hour and Green, in the conditions, may not have factored that in. Therefore, with the current and the leeway, the *Dunbar* was further south and closer to the cliffs than Green calculated.

And, compounding his plight, Green was unable to take his bearings from Macquarie Light, which he had planned to do when it was time to wear ship to port and run north-west towards and through the Heads. The shrouding rain and mist, the massive swells and the swollen clouds that seemed to scrape the top of the *Dunbar*'s mainmast had obliterated his point of reference, allowing only intermittent glimpses of the lighthouse's revolving lantern. Consequently, when Captain Green, having attained sufficient sea-room, ordered his two helmsmen to change course from north-east to north-west, the *Dunbar* was not level with Macquarie Light at all, but 1.2 nautical miles (2.2 kilometres) south of it. He now had the helmsmen turn the wheel to port, swinging the bow towards what he mistakenly thought was the entrance to Port Jackson. Instead, the clipper's bowsprit was now pointing directly at an enormous, unlit cliff face, beyond the view of the ship's lookouts.

Thirty minutes later, Green, unable to see land or landmarks, estimated that the *Dunbar* had passed the northern extremity of South Head and was now in the fairway between South and North Heads. By his reckoning, North Head was around 0.32 nautical miles (600 metres) to the north. So he ordered second officer John Spence and third officer John Pascoe to the top of the forecastle to watch for the massive headland. He shouted to them above the wind, 'Do you see anything of the North Head?' Green was reassured when Pascoe yelled back that he did not; consequently, his calculations must be correct. Then suddenly Spence, who had been straining to see through rudimentary binoculars, or 'opera glasses', cried, '*Broken water ahead! Breakers ahead!*'

Green assumed that the waves that Spence saw breaking were smashing upon North Head. To him, this could only mean that the *Dunbar* had sailed further than he thought across the mouth of Port Jackson and it was now too close, and dangerously so, to the northern headland. He reacted quickly. He called to the helmsmen to turn 'hard a port'. This, he believed, would swing the *Dunbar* to the left, averting a collision with North Head and taking the ship into Port Jackson. A close shave, but all would be well.

Even though there was little chance that a pilot would, or could, assist, it was procedure for chief steward James Ward to light a blue flare and hold it over the port rail to try to attract the attention of anyone on duty at Macquarie Light or in South Head Signal Station who might despatch a pilot crew from Camp Cove. The dim flare was never seen, managing only to prod, not pierce, the rain and the dense salt spray from the breakers, which shot high into the air and engulfed the signal station and the lighthouse, polluting tanks of drinking water, killing vegetable gardens and caking with salt the windows of homes in Watsons Bay. Even if the flare had been seen, even if a pilot boat captain had dared brave the storm, by now the *Dunbar* was beyond help.

It was nearing midnight when, to James Green's horror, the previously obscured beam of Macquarie Lighthouse stabbed through scudding thunderheads on the *Dunbar*'s port side around 500 metres to the south. The sight held a terrible truth. The *Dunbar* was not in the harbour fairway at all; it was still around 1.8 kilometres *short of the tip of South Head*, right upon sheer 60 metre cliffs. Spence's 'Broken water ahead! Breakers ahead!' were not on North Head but on the northern bluff of The Gap.

Captain Green tried to save his ship. He cried to the crew, 'Square away!' meaning to haul up the foresail so the *Dunbar* could run before the wind, and to the helmsmen, 'Port your helm!', a desperate manoeuvre to veer the *Dunbar* violently to starboard away from the cliffs and towards the open sea. ('Port your helm!' is seafarers' vernacular from the days when ships were steered by a tiller and not a wheel.) In normal circumstances, such an order may have averted the disaster that followed. Not this night. Most of the *Dunbar*'s sails were reefed, it was heavily laden with cargo, passengers and crew, at the mercy of the gale and the current and the huge waves powering directly onto the shore, and she could not turn.

The great ship was plucked up by the swell as if by a mighty hand, and flung broadside, bow pointing north, onto the sawtooth rocks around 1.75 kilometres south of the entrance to the Heads, 250 metres north of the signal station and 740 metres north of Macquarie Light.

The *Dunbar* had sailed for 81 days from England without a hitch, only to come to grief 6 nautical miles (11 kilometres) from Sydney Cove.

In the signal station on the cliff-top above, Jane Graham, wife of station superintendent James Graham, sat upright in bed. Telling her story in days to come, she claimed she had woken from a dream in which a ship had run aground below the station, and a sailor was lying on a rock ledge. She had implored her husband to go outside and investigate. 'For God's sake, Jim, there is a poor fellow lying on the rocks below. Help him!' James, she said, grumbled at her to go back to sleep. Jane Graham was having none of that, so sure was she that what she had dreamed was actually happening. She roused assistant signaller Henry Packer who was in his bed nearby. 'For God's sake, Henry, help that man under the cliffs!' Jane told how James had then managed to calm her, explaining that she was only having a nightmare, and she returned to sleep.

In Macquarie Light, superintendent Joseph Siddins heard his black-and-white dog, Jack, barking and tearing about on the cliff-top. Siddins later explained that he wasn't concerned because Jack was always being upset by cows wandering onto the signal station grounds. Besides, 'The weather was so bad I feared for the safety of the lighthouse.' (Joseph's son, R.L. Siddins, would confirm that 'under some bushes on top of the cliff were Jack's footprints, and the scrub on the edge of the precipice showed that the dog had torn off the bark in his efforts to get down'.)

The blunt force impact when the *Dunbar* struck the rocks and then the battering by successive walls of water crumpled the clipper's hull and snapped and toppled its heavy teak masts as if they were twigs—first the mizzen, then the mainmast. The tonnes of teak crushed anyone they fell upon then hung from the ruined hull, a tangled cluster of timber, canvas, rigging and spars. Seawater burst up through the split hull, throwing sailors into the air. Massive breaking rollers surged over the deck, stove in the lifeboats and carried away the disintegrating superstructure. Lying on its beam ends, the *Dunbar* groaned in its death throes as its oak, teak and iron skeleton convulsed. Its vaunted fortifications were no match for the pulverising sea and rocks.

When they heard the sailors' shouts and felt the ship juddering violently, then the collision, Abraham Meyer, who had left his wife and six children in their cabin, and the architect Patrick Downey hurried onto the deck and found bedlam. They were soon joined by other hysterical passengers. That many were naked or in nightwear indicates that Green had such confidence in his ability to reach port that he had felt no need to send crew to warn them to be ready to abandon ship.

Those who remained in their compartments were killed by collapsing timber or drowned as water coursed through the vessel. Maritime historian Basil Lubbock likened their plight to that of 'rats caught in a trap'. In their final moments, when they knew that they would die, did passengers think of people and places they loved, conjure memories of happy times? Did James Green, struggling to stand fast on the poop deck, think of Alice whom he would not embrace again, and their child whom he would never see?

One can imagine heroes trying to rescue others, others sitting quietly on their bunks, exhorting loved ones to be brave and assuring them that God and Captain Green would save them. It would not have been unusual if there were those who trampled family, friends and strangers that they might reach safety first.

In the days that followed, a Sydneysider, impelled to write to a newspaper, tried to imagine the plight of the *Dunbar*'s female passengers, some of whom had pleaded with second officer Spence to tell them that they would survive.

Mr Spence, the second officer, knew there was no possibility of their being saved. Poor girls! What bright prospects a few moments before were spread around them. How had their imagination wandered to those well-known and sunny spots where they had spent so many happy hours? How had they anticipated the embraces of a loving mother, the fond welcome and acclimations of their Australian homes? In the fullest conviction of safety, they had doubtless that night committed themselves to the care of Providence, expecting to occupy their cabins for the last time, and to enter the grand portal of one of the finest Harbours in the world on the approaching morning. What agonising thoughts brushed upon them with the cry of 'Breakers ahead!', and during the moment of terrible suspense between the first notice of danger to the crash under which all their earthly hopes were forever buried. What various expression of human character would appear at that moment! The calm resignation of some and the outburst of passionate grief of others when stricken by the king of terrors; yet even at that dreadful instant there would be one moment for human affection; to utter words of consolation and tenderness; to give a last embrace; even then thoughts, more rapid than lightning, would turn from the yawning deep to the opening Heaven, and from the cold relentless rock to the bosom of Eternal Mercy.

There was pandemonium. A nightmare cacophony of anguished prayers and curses and the screams of parents and children snatched from each other's grasp by the roaring torrent of seawater swamping the vessel, of despairing moans of the injured and trapped, of cracking timber, of crashing cargo and crates, lifeboats, bulwarks and deckhouses splintering, of terrified livestock bucking and bellowing, and above it all thundercracks and the banshee gale. The *Sydney Morning Herald*, in its account, would report, 'the shrieks of 120 [sic] souls were borne to heaven'.

Terrified passengers begged Captain Green and his officers to tell them what was happening. Where were the lifeboats? Were they going to die? Even while knowing the ship was doomed, the deck quivering, the planks creaking under immense water pressure, Green tried to ease their distress, calmly assured them that all would be well. Moments later, James Green was swallowed by a wave and spat overboard. He was never seen again. First officer Struthers, second officer Spence and third officer Pascoe were washed away too.

The officers were followed into the churning sea by other crewmen and passengers. The Irish midshipman James Johnson saw his captain go overboard just before he, too, was knocked flying by the surging sea. Crew and passengers flailed wildly in the waves and tried to cling to floating debris and each other, but as massive breaker upon breaker battered them they soon drowned or, like the ship that had brought them all the way from Plymouth to the very doorstep of Sydney, were dashed to pieces on the razor rocks. Most could not swim, and those who could would not have been able to remain afloat. Around the dying ship was a snarl of bodies, broken wood, ropes and canvas, crates, clothing, animal carcasses and flotsam.

Soon, it was over. The pride of Duncan Dunbar's shipping line lay shattered on its side and, with those who sailed on the *Dunbar* and the cargo it carried, was claimed by the sea. By half-past midnight, the screams had died. All that could now be heard was the keening wind and the rain and the roar of the ravenous waves.

12

Bad tidings

At the same time as the man walking on the beach at George's Head in the early morning of Friday, 21 August, saw the red cow with white spots being savaged by sharks, across the water at Watsons Bay, harbour pilots Hydes, Jenkins and Robson stood on the clifftop high above The Gap. They leaned into the driving rain and wind and looked down into what Hydes called 'the deep, rocky, shelving bight' and saw in the foaming cauldron a sight that chilled their blood. Naked, mutilated corpses tumbled back and forth, like grotesque broken dolls, in the waves that crashed onto the rocks. Tossed along with them were spars and timbers and other flotsam that could only mean that a large ship had been wrecked nearby and that the bodies and debris had been swept up the coast and into The Gap.

Soon, Hydes, Jenkins and Robson were joined on the cliff-top by James Graham and Henry Packer from the signal station. They too were gripped by the grisly sight below. If Jane Graham had really dreamed of a wreck in the night, surely her husband's spine tingled.

The pilots then made their way south along the top of the precipice of Outer South Head towards the signal station and Macquarie

Light and saw below, around 190 metres south of the plunging ravine known as Jacobs Ladder and 250 metres north of the signal station, the broken shell of a ship in the rollers, lying broadside. Bodies floated amid the debris and sharks had gathered. Reported Hydes, 'I discovered about half past 7 on Friday morning . . . the wreck of some large ship. It is situated at the extreme end of a curve of the South Head and human bodies washing about, too truly told the sad tale.'

From what remained of the ship, Hydes surmised that it had been a large vessel 'of around a thousand tons, possibly American-built', with heavy timbers, hooped masts and bowsprits, copper fastenings and internal fittings of unpainted light wood common to those used in the construction of emigrant ships. The timbers had been demolished by the collision with the reef and prolonged battering by waves, and 5 centimetre diameter copper bolts and iron nails had been twisted and bent as if they were wire pipe-cleaners.

Having weathered the gale offshore overnight, the paddle-steamer *Grafton* rounded North Head and entered Port Jackson around 9.30 a.m. Captain Charles Wiseman saw bodies and severed and mangled legs, arms, trunks and heads drifting in the fairway. There were the torn carcasses of cattle. The topmast of a large ship stood surreally straight up out of the water. Timber, bedding, bales and containers were tangled in the steamer's paddles. The distressed Wiseman reported all this to maritime authorities when the *Grafton* docked in Sydney Cove.

Meanwhile, James Graham returned to the signal station where, because the murky weather prevented semaphore signalling and, despite promises by the government, there was still no telegraph line to the city, he penned a letter advising of the wreck. He ran with the letter to Macquarie Light keeper Joseph Siddins, who sent a messenger on horseback along New South Head Road to deliver the bad tidings to Captain Robert Pockley, the 34-year-old superintendent of lights, pilots and navigation, and newly appointed harbour master, at Sydney Cove.

'Kid glove' Pockley, so called because he was a disciplinarian and a stickler for doing things right and promptly, was an experienced man of the sea. He had been born in Greenwich, England, in 1823 and as a boy he had worked alongside men on his father's whaling boat. There was a story that the vessel collided with a whale and sank, and he clung to the back of the whale until rescued. Pockley arrived in Sydney in 1841, aged eighteen, and, already a master mariner, he commanded sailing ships on the dangerous Sydney–Hobart run.

Graham's letter, which reached Pockley at 10.30 a.m., read:

Sir,

I have the honour to state for your information that there has been a vessel wrecked last night under the [signal station] flagstaff supposed to be a sugar vessel by the quantity of sugar bags floating about. The hull of the vessel has all gone to pieces, and there is nothing visible but the spars [sic] . . . I have not been able to ascertain [its] name.

I have the honour to be Your Obedient Servant,

James Graham, signal master

Captain Pockley was driven in a carriage to South Head through what he described as 'thick and violent' weather. Before setting out, Pockley had commissioned the fourteen-year-old 37-metre coal-fired iron paddle-steamer *Washington*, under Captain Williamson, to rush water police and port officials to South Head. The *Washington* had been built in Scotland in 1844 and before steaming to Sydney in 1854 had been a familiar sight on Liverpool's River Mersey. It moored at Watsons Bay beach and police and officials, trailed by reporters who had got wind of the wreck, hurried to the top of The Gap. As it would for those who had been there in the first light of day, what they saw when they looked down would haunt them for the rest of their lives. 'On reaching The Gap,' reported the *Empire* journalist,

a horrible scene presented itself. The sea was rolling in, mountains high, dashing on the rocks fragments of wreck, large and small, and

130

bodies of men, women and children, nearly all in a state of nudity, by which it may be inferred that the catastrophe occurred when the passengers were in their beds. Upwards of 20 human bodies were counted under The Gap—the waves dashing them against the rocks and taking them back in their recoil. Pieces of masts and spars, the half of a studdingsail boom, and part of the ship's flooring, with innumerable torn pieces of cotton and woollen goods, were being dashed ashore by the violence of the sea.

Captain Pockley arrived at the signal station at noon. He craned over the precipice there and looking 400 metres northwards, he knew at once that James Graham had not exaggerated. Pockley would write in his official report to New South Wales treasurer (and former premier) Stuart Donaldson:

I saw the splintered fragments of what appeared to have been a large ship scattered about the base of the precipitous cliffs of the South Head, with many human bodies washing about in the heavy breakers, dashing on the rocks. The gale was blowing heavy at this time from south-east, and knowing that there was no possibility of any part of the wreck having gone to the southward, I despatched the pilots and their crews along the cliffs to make a strict inspection, and ascertain if any survivors were to be seen, or if any bodies were landed upon any accessible spot from whence they could be removed . . . Finding that it was impossible, from the violence of the gale and the fearful sea, to make any scrutiny of the cliffs from a vessel outside, I sent my boat, with the deputy Harbour Master and Harbour Master Assistant, to examine the Harbour as far as it was prudent for their own safety to venture, and ascertain if there were any [more] bodies, or clue to the wreck.

Another who went to The Gap that Friday was William Stanley Jevons of the Mint. The letter he would write to his sister, Lucy, in England was discovered a century later by John Lanser of the Australasian Pioneers' Club.

Last Thursday night a storm began, with heavy rain, black clouds and very strong gales from the east . . . Towards the middle of [Friday] the rumour crept rapidly through the Mint that there was a large wreck somewhere outside the Heads. This was doubtless unpleasant intelligence, but no one saw any reason to believe it was *Dunbar*, and the shipping list contained a number of ships much more likely to arrive than *Dunbar* . . . At daybreak the next morning I got up and started with O'Connell for the Heads. After a 5-mile [8-kilometre] walk through mud and rain, we reached the lighthouse, and soon made our way to a low part of the cliffs where a small number of persons, some from Sydney by cabs and horses, the rest from the neighbourhood, were already collected. The place is called The Gap, being a partial break in the great line of cliffs opposite the part of the Harbour called Watsons Bay . . . Here the cliffs fell to the height of less than 100 feet [30 metres], and beneath was a slight recess where a flat shelf of rocks, just a little above the sea level, ran out to a short distance. On looking down with the rest, nothing was at first sight apparent but the huge waves of the Pacific Ocean regularly rolling in, and each time entirely covering the lower rocks with a boiling sea of pure white foam, or now and then striking the projecting shelf with a loud bursting noise, and throwing out a dense misty spray almost as high as the cliffs on which we stood. But soon there was evidence of the wreck: small fragments of wood mingled with the seaweed; portions of spars or pieces of large timber, already quite rounded off by grinding on the rocks; bits of clothing, some apparently of silk, also long pieces of sheeting or bedding torn into shreds, and other clothing apparently tied up in bundles, were now and then seen. All these things were carried up on the top of one wave, lodged on the shelf of rock and exposed to view for a few moments till the succeeding wave enveloped them again in foam, and thus invisibly removed them. But as you will anticipate, there was now and then mingled with them objects of yet more fearful appearances . . . But to leave descriptions perhaps of needless horror, we then walked along the cliff a few hundred yards to where the hull, or main part at least, of the vessel was yet supposed to lie, marked only by one or two fragments of spars yet attached to the rigging, or by loose rope ends now and then appearing at the surface. The ship appears to have run full-on to the cliff almost below the lighthouse [sic] some time during Thursday night, and to have gone to pieces and sunk almost immediately, unknown to anyone on land, and possibly, we may hope, almost without the consciousness of any on board.

Another ship to remain outside at sea the previous night was the schooner *Ann and Jane*. Mid-morning, it entered Port Jackson, its sails in tatters. The *Washington* towed the *Ann and Jane* into Watsons Bay, with a striped cotton shirt and a piece of a muslin dress snagged on the tow chain. With the *Ann and Jane* at anchor, the *Washington* scoured Port Jackson. By the afternoon, the east-south-easterly storm had swept bodies, wreckage and cargo from the wreck site that had not lodged in the bight at The Gap through the Heads into Sydney Harbour, Middle Harbour and The Spit, North Harbour and Manly Cove.

New South Wales Parliament was in sombre session in Macquarie Street. One member called on premier and colonial secretary Henry Parker to confirm or deny the circulating reports that a ship had foundered outside the Heads the previous night. By now, 3.25 p.m. on Friday afternoon, the premier had read James Graham's and Captain Pockley's reports but the identity of the wreck was still not known. 'I've not received any really authentic information about the subject, and to detail mere rumours might be to agonise feelings for no purpose whatever,' Premier Parker told the House.

However, the government has taken the earliest opportunity, on hearing of the disaster, to procure correct information, and to afford such relief as might be necessary. Owing to the thickness of the weather, the signals at South Head could not be properly understood, and the consequence was that Captain Pockley went down himself to the scene of the wreck; but the only information that has been furnished to the Government was to the effect that a vessel had been wrecked last night on the outside of South Head.

Premier Parker relayed Captain Wiseman of the *Grafton*'s account of seeing bodies and bedding floating between the Heads and the topmast of a large vessel standing out of the water, and said that 'from this it would seem that the first report was correct, and that the wreck seen on the outside of South Head had subsequently drifted into the fairway of the Heads'. Yet, as Wiseman's report had not been officially verified, 'I do not put it forth as being worthy of implicit confidence'.

Meanwhile, word was spreading in the taverns of The Rocks and Paddington, the grand halls of Macquarie Street, the offices, salons and cafés of Hunter, King and George streets, that a tall ship had foundered in the previous night's gale and bodies and debris were piling at outer South Head and in Port Jackson. Questions flew. What ship? Who was travelling on it? Was it a British vessel, an American? An emigrant or a merchant ship, perhaps a sugar carrier out of Manila? The scattergun speculation meant that everyone expecting family and friends on the *Duncan Dunbar*, the *Vocalist*, the *Zemindar* or the *Dunbar* feared the worst. As *The Empire* newspaper reported, 'in the course of the day, as rumours of the fearful reality assumed a consistency, a feeling of consternation took possession of the public mind'.

In the late afternoon, a cask and a ship's mail bag were recovered from Middle Harbour. The cask, which contained tripe, was stamped 'Ship's stores *Dunbar*' and the mail bag 'No. 2, per *Dunbar*, Plymouth, May 29.' 'This, and other articles,' declared Captain Pockley, 'convinced me that the unfortunate ship was *Dunbar*, of and from London.'

Further evidence that it was the *Dunbar* that had gone down accumulated by the hour. When pilot crewmen David Frazer and Tom Clark picked their way gingerly along the bottom of the Outer South Head cliffs, taking care not to be swept into the sea by the waves, they found a large chest on the rocks. Inside were pork, whale-oil candles, boys' cricket bats and an invoice from Sydney company Thompson, Symonds & Co. The invoice was made out to the *Dunbar*.

Searchers found, somehow still intact in the water, a parchment railway luggage label, marked 'Mylne, passenger, Scotland'. The *bon vivants* John and Thomas Mylne, of Eatonswill on the Clarence River, and their sisters Letty and Annie, were known to be *Dunbar* passengers.

On the lid of a floating box was a brass plate, 7.5 centimetres by 5 centimetres, engraved with 'No. 3 S Peek, Esq, Passenger'. Not far away was a tattered pillow case on which was sewn the monogram 'S Peek'. Samuel Peek, the larger-than-life entrepreneur who had created East Gosford and his wife, Caroline, had told their Australian friends and associates that they'd booked home passage on the *Dunbar*.

Another box lid found floating was inscribed 'Mrs Healing . . . milliner &c'. Elizabeth Healing, her husband, Daniel, and their children, Louisa, Frederick and George were listed on the *Dunbar*'s manifest.

A gangway board emblazoned with the rampant lion, symbol of the Duncan Dunbar line, was found bobbing in Middle Harbour.

The *Dunbar*'s famous figurehead, the beautifully carved rampant red lion on the scroll, was located by water police near the site of the wreck.

By now the identity of the wrecked ship was beyond doubt. Captain Pockley advised Premier Parker and Governor Sir William Denison, the *Dunbar*'s shipping agents and the press.

With confirmation of 'this most melancholy event', as Premier Parker termed it, parliament was adjourned. 'Under any circumstances,' he said,

a wreck such as the one that has recently occurred would be most deplorable, since the unfortunate passengers must in many instances have relatives and connections amongst those residents here. But in this instance, it was the more so, since it was known that persons closely connected with a member of this House were passengers on this luckless vessel. Seeing this, he and his friends considered it would be but right that the House should suspend its proceedings.

Daniel Egan, member for Maneroo (later Monaro) in the Legislative Assembly and former mayor of Sydney, had collapsed on learning that his wife, Marian, and her children, Gertrude and Henry Cahuac, were dead.

While maritime officials, police, search parties and politicians now knew that the *Dunbar* had been wrecked, in the early evening there still had been no official public announcement. Distraught people desperate for news clustered outside newspaper offices. In an early evening edition, the *Sydney Morning Herald* reported that there had indeed been a shipwreck by the Heads, but while acknowledging the rumours that it was the *Dunbar*, the publication was not prepared to state that the ship involved was the great clipper. It was as if the editors of the *Herald* were in deep denial: so long as the *Dunbar* was not positively identified, the wreck simply could not be it. The editorialist wrote, unconvincingly, 'We demur, with the present proof, to declare positively that that fine ship, with her greatly respected commander, Captain Green, and a large number of passengers, many of them old and respected colonists, is really lost.'

Then, at last, at around 10.30 p.m., the lingering hopes of those with loved ones on the *Dunbar* were dashed finally when a notice was posted outside *The Empire* office. It advised that the harbour master had recovered a mailbag marked '*Dunbar*, Plymouth, May 29'. Then were published the names of the *Dunbar*'s passengers and crew: the eight Wallers and the eight Meyers, the Mylnes and Francis Tindal, Marian Egan and Gertrude and Henry Cahuac, the Misses Hunt, Captain Steane, Patrick Downey, the three Logan children, the five Healings, the four Clarkes, Captain James Green, his officers Struthers, Spence and Pascoe, Charles Sappie, young Tom Kay, and all the other lost souls . . .

13

'A feeling of intense melancholy'

The grim pall that hung over Sydney Town on Saturday, 22 August, 30 hours after the shipwreck, had nothing to do with the teeming rain and racing leaden clouds. The scarcely imaginable had happened: the mighty *Dunbar* had been destroyed on Outer South Head and no hope was held for survivors. The lead article on the black-bordered front page of the *Sydney Morning Herald* was headlined 'Further Particulars of the Shipwreck at the Heads'. It read, 'The hopes we entertained last night that the wreck would not be the *Dunbar* have proved fallacious. That unfortunate vessel must have struck between The Gap and the Lighthouse, and have instantly been dashed into a thousand pieces, and not a single soul is saved to tell the sad and melancholy story.'

The news that the *Dunbar* had been wrecked and its passengers and crew, officially recorded as 122, but probably more, had perished was a dagger to the heart of Sydney. Never had there been a calamity of this magnitude in the colony. The destruction of the clipper traumatised the nearly 57,000 Sydneysiders because, while other ships had gone down on the voyage to Sydney, foundering, catching fire, hitting an iceberg, simply disappearing, there had never been the loss of such a fine, seemingly unsinkable ship at the very entrance to Port Jackson. And adding to the anguish, among the dead were prominent people whose success and hard work had helped to transform the desperate settlement of Arthur Phillip into a thriving city. The loss of the *Dunbar* was a reminder of how gossamer-fragile was people's hold on life in a fledgling nation so far across the sea from their family, friends and heritage.

Just when New South Wales and its citizens were prospering thanks to gold, wheat, wool, manufacturing and commerce, the *Dunbar*'s demise rammed brutally home that safe passenger and merchant seafaring to and from the Old Country could never be taken for granted. No matter how fast and strong the vessel, or how skilled the master and crew, those who went to sea in sailing ships were always at the mercy of the elements and fate.

Kieran Hosty, head of curatorial and research and maritime archaeologist at the Australian National Maritime Museum, a *Dunbar* authority who has done much to preserve relics from the wreck, summed up the impact of the tragedy on the colony this way, 'Imagine a fully laden jumbo jet crashing into Botany Bay today. The loss of the *Dunbar*, and at least 122 souls on the doorstep of Sydney was catastrophic. It had a profound effect on the city. We have to remember that in the nineteenth century everything came to Australia by sea. The colonists who lived here had either arrived by sea, or were descended from people who had arrived by sea.' What happened to the passengers on the *Dunbar*, Sydneysiders shuddered to think, could have happened to me.

There was another fear, mostly unvoiced, by the people of Sydney, that in this place where pubs far outnumbered churches and crime was still rampant, that God had wrecked the *Dunbar* to punish the colony for its rough and rowdy ways. On the Sunday after the wreck, the churches of Sydney were packed.

At 9 a.m. on Saturday, 22 August, Captain Robert Pockley met the New South Wales commissioner and inspector-general of police, Captain John McLerie, at Sydney Cove where they boarded their

chartered Manly steam ferry, the *Black Swan*, commanded by Captain
Sullivan. Their terrible task was to locate and retrieve the *Dunbar*
bodies for identification and burial. McLerie vowed, 'We will leave
nothing undone to recover the remains of the unfortunate sufferers.'
McLerie was a Scot, born in Ayrshire in 1809, a decorated soldier
in the Fusilier Guards and after emigrating to Australia in 1844 he
fought in the First Maori War in New Zealand from 1845 to 1847.
Appointed Sydney superintendent of police in 1850 and shortly after
inspector-general of police, the urbane and literate but steely McLerie
cleansed the police force of corruption and cowed Sydney's hooligan
mobs and the bushranging gangs that terrorised the outskirts of the
city. Yet perhaps none of this could have prepared him for what he
was about to encounter on the waters of Port Jackson.

Joining Pockley and McLerie on the *Black Swan* were New South
Wales coroner John Skottowe Parker, Port Jackson health officer and
former coroner Dr Haynes Alleyne, water police inspector Samuel
North, and a large complement of police, water police and volunteer searchers with telescopes, hooks and ropes. Also on board were
civilians such as assistant government surveyor and wool-broker
John Valentine Gorman and Jewish businessman Joseph Raphael,
who knew and could identify some of the *Dunbar* victims. Sydney
merchant John Gough Waller, brother and business partner of Kilner
Waller, brother-in-law of Maria and uncle of the six Waller children,
had not shied from joining the searchers. On a separate boat was
Captain Henry Mangles Denham, master of the Royal Navy ship
the *Herald*, and several officers and crew. Denham had charted the
waters of Port Jackson and knew every cove and inlet.

Stacked on the deck of the *Black Swan* were 70 rough wooden
coffins—called 'shells'—that had been hammered together by
carpenters the previous night.

The *Empire* reporter sensed:

A feeling of intense melancholy [pervading] the whole of those
present, and the numerous coffins sent down to the wharf to receive

such bodies as might be picked up added to the general gloom. It was a painful sight to witness the agonising feelings of many who were there, either cognisant of the fact that their friends and relatives were passengers of the ill-fated ship or expecting that to be the case.

To board the *Black Swan*, the officials had to force their way through hundreds of ghouls, women, men and children, who thronged around it, angrily demanding to be allowed to embark so they could see the bodies and the wreckage. There were wild scenes as police battled to hold them at bay so that those author-ised to do so could board. Nevertheless, around 30 members of the mob managed to storm the police barricade and scramble on board. Although Pockley and McLerie worried that the overloaded *Black Swan* could sink, they believed that removing the interlopers might have led to bloodshed, so agreed that the safest thing to do was press on.

The *Black Swan* steamed out through the Heads. The plan was for the vessel to remain at a safe distance from the cliffs of Outer South Head while those on board scanned the base of the cliffs south from the tip of the promontory to Macquarie Light, looking for survivors and bodies floating in the water or wedged in rock indentations and ledges along the way. But crashing waves ensured there was no such thing as a safe distance for the small *Black Swan*, so Pockley and McLerie left the larger and more robust *Washington* to scout Outer South Head while they concentrated their search on North Head and Middle Head. The *Black Swan* could search Outer South Head when the seas and wind abated.

'After passing Bradleys Head,' wrote Pockley in his report to the *Dunbar* coronial inquest, 'I proceeded very close along the port hand shore, examining carefully with good glasses, and despatching the boats to examine more closely those places shewing any indi-cations of the wreck having been deposited there.'

In the *Black Swan*'s wake were water police boats under the command of Inspector Cowell and craft of all types that had been chartered by the public. Newspapers had acquired boats and filled them with reporters and sketch artists.

Port Jackson was littered with the floating remains of the *Dunbar*. One searcher wrote that on the Saturday morning 'it was impossible for a vessel to move a yard without encountering fresh evidence of the extent of the heart-rending tragedy'. The bodies and the volume of debris turning over in the roiling brown spume convinced John McLerie on the *Black Swan* that *two* ships had foundered and he ordered four large steamers to probe the base of the cliffs from The Gap all the way to Coogee to locate the second wreck. They found no second vessel, nor any bodies, south of the *Dunbar* wreck site.

Some of the search party members gingerly edged their way along the cliff-tops of Outer South Head from the northern tip, past The Gap and the wreck site to Macquarie Light, eyes peeled for bodies on the rocks far below for signs of life. By now, nobody expected to come across a survivor, yet they pressed on.

Since early morning an enormous crowd of people, those with connections to the *Dunbar* victims, those who came to mourn, and some to simply ogle, had been gathering atop the cliffs. They travelled by horseback, horse-drawn carriages, cabs and omnibuses, bullock drays and on foot, the still-powerful onshore winds blasting into their faces, to join Watsons Bay locals staring down at the terrible scenes. A large proportion—some reports put the number at from 10,000 to 20,000—of the approximately 57,000 population of Sydney had made their way along the quagmires that were New South Head and Old South Head roads. Reported the *Herald*, 'The spectators were deeply affected. Some running together with eagerness to suggest impossible schemes of active exertion. Some sitting apart, abandoned to their own agonies of sympathy and sorrow.'

One who arrived at The Gap at 11 a.m. recalled, 'I, like most of the spectators, mingled in the general excitement then prevalent, which may be more easily imagined than described; and after walking about for some time, listening to fears here and hopes there, hopes that someone or more might yet be found living to clear up the awful mystery that must ever hang over such a disaster.'

Once on the precipice that afforded a good view, those trying to locate the body of a relative in the waves below or simply rubbernecking resisted relinquishing their prime position, ignoring the pleas of those at the back of the scrum crying out to be let through. 'Hideous fascination seemed to bind [the observers] to the spot,' one reporter wrote, '. . . while at the fearful spectacle of the remains of fellow human beings in so awful a position—immediately before their eyes and yet out of reach—each determination to leave the fatal locality became overpowered by a desire for further knowledge, many dreading lest they should have to recognise the familiar face of friend or relative.'

What at first seemed to be a bale of hay or wool tumbling on the rock shelf of The Gap proved to be the corpses of two women, one middle-aged, the other young. Each held the other tightly in her arms. The bodies were reported as being those of Marian Egan and Gertrude Cahuac. Mother and daughter were swept away and never seen again. There was no sign of Marian's son, Henry, or his Russian wolfhound. Henry's body was never found; the carcass of the wolfhound would wash up in Manly Cove. The magnificent animal had survived the Crimean War only to perish at South Head.

Marine historian Basil Lubbock reported the nightmare spectacle in his 1924 book *The Blackwall Frigates*. He wrote of the 'low cries of anguish [that] ran quivering through knots of people [at The Gap] whose eyes seemed to be glued to that table rock over which the mutilated bodies of their friends and relatives washed to and fro'.

The *Empire* journalist told of the 122 'unhappy beings' who'd been 'swept into eternity with scarcely a moment's warning. Now the mortal remains of those unhappy beings were part of a terrible tableau at The Gap.'

The mayor of Sydney was Alderman George Thornton, a forceful, handsome man with elaborate sandy side-curls. Thornton was born in Sydney in 1819, son of Samuel Thornton and his wife, Sarah, whose death sentence for larceny in England was commuted to transportation to Australia for life. Thornton was a sailor—on his schooner the *Tom Tough*—a merchant, ship-broker and politician. A man of contradictions, when elected mayor he ordered all stocks and pillories removed from public places but continued to allow cock-fighting. At The Gap, Thornton bustled to the front of the crowd to look down. He would write of 'the dreadful disaster . . . the dead and mutilated bodies as they were thrown upon the rocks, the succeeding waves washing off again the naked remains'.

Just after 11 a.m., an excited cry. A fellow named Joseph Palmer looking down over the cliff-top and noticed something fluttering on a rock ledge 10 metres above the wreck site. Surely, thought Palmer, it's a bird or some kind of animal, but then, movement again. Focusing through the hanging mist, he saw a figure on the ledge waving an item of clothing. 'A man on the rocks!' Palmer cried. 'A live man on the rocks! There he is! There he is!'

As the onlookers saw him too, they shouted, 'It's a miracle!' And, considering what the man on the ledge above the raging sea had endured, so it was.

14

A miraculous rescue

There are different versions of how the sole survivor of the wreck of the *Dunbar* was rescued. Although contradicted in years to come by people who claimed the credit, some of whom were actually at Outer South Head that day, the most credible account is that of Alderman George Thornton, mayor of Sydney. Thornton was front and centre at the scene and his version of events, on which the following is closely based, was supported by eyewitnesses.

Onlookers' initial elation that the man on the ledge had survived the shipwreck turned quickly to disquiet with the realisation that the thunderous waves and the jagged rocks of the shoreline prevented access to the ledge from a boat, so the rescue would have to be performed from the cliff-top. After some deliberation, police inspector Mortimer and a sergeant named Healy decided that the survivor would have to be desperately weak and traumatised after 33 hours' exposure to the cold, the wind and the rain, without food and water, and within sight of his shipmates' mangled bodies in the waves below. He would be in no condition to climb a rope or a rope ladder to the cliff-top. The only way he could be rescued was for someone to descend 60 metres into Jacobs Ladder ravine, around

190 metres north of the ledge, climbing part-way down the ravine and then being lowered on a rope to the bottom of the cliff face, try to scramble among the exposed rocks to the survivor without being knocked into the sea, then, at the ledge, signal to those above to lower a rope with a harness or bosun's chair attached, strap the survivor in and motion to them to heave him up. Should the rescuer slip on his way down Jacobs Ladder in the wet and wild conditions, he would fall to his death or be dashed against the cliff face and become yet another *Dunbar* victim.

No surprise, then, that among the sightseers and even police or searchers there was no stampede to volunteer to be lowered over the edge.

Then, according to Alderman George Thornton and others who were there, up stepped an unlikely Samaritan. Arni Olafsson Thorlacius was born on a farm called Innri-Fagridalur on the west coast of Iceland, in 1836, and had recently arrived in Sydney where, for reasons he never publicly explained, he changed his name to Antonio Woolier. The twenty-year-old was employed as an apprentice watchmaker by an Elizabeth Street jeweller named Flower. After learning that the *Dunbar* had been wrecked on Saturday, Woolier, Flower and another apprentice, Dick Jenkins, had set off before daylight and walked the 11 kilometres to join the crowd at Outer South Head. When the call was made for a volunteer to rescue the survivor, Woolier, sandy-haired, 167 centimetres and stocky, whose favourite pastime in Iceland was scaling rock faces to collect birds' eggs, cried, 'I'll go!'

No doubt relieved that it was he and not them who would be going down, those in the crowd gave the young Icelander three cheers. Flower later told how Woolier shed his hat, coat and boots and left them with Dick Jenkins then strung a hemp rope around his waist and descended into the chasm of Jacobs Ladder. Down he went, lashed by the wind, until he reached a precipice and could go no further. He motioned to those above holding the other end of his rope to pull him back up. Once more atop the cliff, Woolier composed himself and tried again. This time he cleared the precipice and was lowered to the base of the cliff and, timing his progress to avoid the crashing waves, made his way to the survivor on the ledge. Flower wrote, 'In that perilous work many times he had to wedge and jam himself between rocks to prevent being washed away.'

Reaching the ledge, Woolier found himself face to face with a burly young man with thick black hair and beard. His only clothing was a shredded and sopping blue shirt, a drenched singlet and torn light cotton pants, no shoes. He was exhausted and disoriented, his face was wind-burned red raw, but his only visible wound was a cut on his knee.

Woolier strapped the man into the leather harness, or bosun's chair, that had been lowered 60 metres onto the ledge by the men directly above. The rope attached to the harness was itself fixed to a makeshift derrick comprising a block and tackle and a wooden spar that extended 3 metres out from the cliff. (It was later claimed that the rope, which was in poor condition and beginning to fray, was unstrung from the flagstaff at the signal station when no other rope was handy.) At Woolier's wave, the men at the derrick began pulling the survivor up the cliff face. It could not have been an easy haul. The man was heavily built and at least 187 centimetres tall.

Twenty minutes later on the cliff-top, while Woolier remained below conducting a fruitless 45-minute search for other survivors, the dazed and staggering survivor was dragged over the lip of the cliff and mobbed by a back-slapping crowd. 'What's your name?' they cried. The answer came in a thick Irish brogue. 'James Johnson, able seaman, *Dunbar*.'

That established, people beseeched Johnson to tell them if their loved ones had also survived, but, even if he had known, in his confusion and weariness Johnson was incapable of responding. It's said that among that crowd was Jane Graham, the signal master's wife, who had dreamed that a shipwreck survivor was on a ledge below the signal station and pleaded with her husband to try to rescue him. When she saw Johnson she reportedly gasped, 'My

God! That's him! That's the man I saw on the rocks.' 'Who? What man?' someone nearby wanted to know. 'Oh, never mind,' said Jane Graham, 'no one would believe me.'

Johnson was given brandy and wrapped in blankets, then carried by pilot Robert Hutchinson of Captain John Hawkes' crew, retired policeman James Smith and others down the hill to the Marine Hotel in Watsons Bay (today, Dunbar House in Robertson Park). There he was greeted by Premier Henry Parker and examined by doctors West and Duigan who prescribed a hot bath, a nourishing meal and a good sleep in a warm bed.

Back at the cliff-top, Alderman Thornton and others had lowered the harness to Woolier and pulled him up and over. Thornton and Captain William Loring of the Royal Navy ship *Iris* exhorted bystanders to applaud the young hero and reward him with coins. A hat was passed around and a sum reported as being from £10 to £14 (about as much as an unskilled labourer would earn in three months) was raised.

'We adjourned to a hotel nearly opposite,' recounted the jeweller Flower, 'where the host found warmth and comfort for Woolier, Mr Thornton presenting him with the £10 [sic] in a most enthusiastic manner. Woolier said, "I did not do it for money, but for the feelings of my heart." [Thornton] then advised me to take him home after such excitement, and so we both walked home again to Elizabeth Street, to that little house next to the Great Synagogue.'

In days to come, Antonio Woolier denied an *Empire* report that claimed that during his first descent on Jacobs Ladder, he had become 'frightened and desired to be drawn up'. Now Woolier wanted it known that he had never been frightened, and had only returned to the top because the men at the derrick were paying out the rope, explained the *Empire*, 'with such rapidity as to make him apprehensive that it was not properly attended to . . . He then motioned with his hand for them not to lower him so precipitately. We make this explanation at Woolier's request, as we should be exceedingly sorry to be the means of misrepresenting conduct so meritorious and praiseworthy as his has been in connexion with the late wreck.'

After leaving Woolier, Alderman Thornton hurried down the hill to the Marine Hotel to join reporters anxiously waiting for the sole survivor of Sydney's worst marine tragedy to wake and tell his story.

When James Johnson opened his eyes after only a couple of hours' sleep, the doctors allowed him to face the milling pressmen. Johnson confirmed his name and his ship, told his interrogators his age, twenty, and that his home was Drogheda in Ireland. He had been at sea for eleven years and, while he had once sailed from England to Melbourne and back, this was his first voyage to Sydney.

Thornton waited while the newspapermen bombarded their miracle man with questions, scribbled down his answers then raced each other back to the city to file their story. In the reporters' fevered haste to scoop each other, they failed to scrape the surface of Johnson's experience, and much of what appeared in the rushed reports in that evening's and next day's newspapers was wrong. The *Dunbar* did *not* strike The Gap, and the body of Captain Green had *not* been recovered, all of which had been reported. Too, in telling the craning scribes that a packed lifeboat had been lowered, Johnson was not thinking clearly. The Irishman was also quoted as saying there were two other survivors on ledges above the wreck site. It would take days before the papers checked their facts and offered readers a more accurate account of the disaster. What most reporters did get right was Johnson's opinion of his shipmates as 'steady men', and his respect for Captain James Green.

Finally alone in the late afternoon with Johnson in his room at the Marine Hotel, Alderman Thornton, with no deadline to meet and a maritime background, asked salient questions and drew from Johnson a more comprehensive and coherent account of the *Dunbar*'s last hours than Johnson had garbled to the reporters, and he spoke at length about his escape from the wreck and ordeal on the ledge. Thornton filed Johnson's statement to the Sydney press as a letter to the editor. The letter ran prominently on Monday, 24 August, and dominated the initial coverage of the disaster.

Thornton began:

I have been all day down at the scene of the wreck of the *Dunbar* and had a long interview with Johnson, the man who was saved. If the statement he made to me, and which I carefully noted, be of any service to you, as information of a correct character for the public, who all feel a deep interest in this melancholy event, I shall be glad that I have taken this course to forward it.

Johnson, despite his weakened condition and the mental trauma he'd suffered, had responded to Thornton's gentle and empathetic questioning and was able to tell his story, wrote Thornton, 'without affectation or braggadocio, and with the straightforward simplicity of the sailor'.

After Thornton established that, as an able seaman, Johnson was a comparatively lowly member of the *Dunbar*'s crew and could only surmise Captain Green's thoughts and motivations, Johnson had described to Thornton the clipper's last hours to the best of his knowledge, from what he witnessed on the night and in replaying the calamity over and over in his mind while on his ledge hoping for rescue.

Because nobody else lived to tell the tale, James Johnson's interview with Alderman Thornton and the evidence he gave two days later to the coronial inquest are the most credible means of understanding why and how the *Dunbar* foundered.

Johnson said he had not been privy to Captain Green's decision to make for Sydney Cove and when advised of it he had been taken aback. The weather being so terrible, Johnson and other seamen had fully expected Green to remain at sea until morning, but the crew trusted their captain's judgement and did not express their qualms to Green. Johnson explained that he had understood that Green's plan was to sail north-east to gain sea-room and then, when level with Macquarie Light, change course to the north-west towards the coast and so deliver the *Dunbar* through the Heads. But, Johnson believed, Green had mistaken his position. Green, assuming that the *Dunbar* had cleared South Head and was in the harbour fairway, ordered the helmsmen to veer left to, as he thought, enter the Heads into Port Jackson. But, of course, continued Johnson, the waves were not breaking upon North Head but on The Gap. Green's hard-a-port command had put the *Dunbar* on a collision course with the cliffs 1.75 kilometres short of the Heads. When the beam of Macquarie Light pierced the clouds overhead, said Johnson, Green had realised his predicament and cried, 'Port your helm' to turn to starboard away from the cliff and towards the sea. All too late. The heavily laden clipper's reefed sails and the immense power of the onshore swell and wind had conspired to thwart Green's last-moment manoeuvre and the *Dunbar* had smashed broadside onto the rocks.

Johnson then told an awed George Thornton what he had not told the reporters: how he had miraculously saved himself and avoided sharing the fate of the others. He had been part of the chief officer's watch on the poop deck when the *Dunbar* struck the rocks. 'The first sea that breached over the vessel knocked me down.' Realising he would have to abandon ship and swim for his life, 'I stripped off my pea jacket and boots and clung to the mizzen mast chains to stop myself being swept overboard.' Then he had waded through the rushing torrent and scrambled below into a cabin where passengers cowered. The cabin was immediately inundated. Now Johnson climbed up and through the cabin's skylight and onto the lee side deck. 'The vessel kept breaking up aft . . .' He had clung to the chain plates of the fore-rigging until they gave way when that section of the ship also broke up. 'I, the chain-plates and four attached planks were pitched into the sea.' He had grasped a floating plank and held on for dear life, then, he told Thornton, he was joined on the plank by the tattooed boatswain and former Sydney water policeman, Charles Sappie, and two 'Dutch seamen'. (There were no registered Dutch crew members onboard, according to the *Dunbar*'s manifest, so perhaps Johnson mistook two of the German, Swedish or Finnish crewmen for Dutchmen.) The 'Dutchmen' had been quickly knocked from the plank and swept to their death, leaving only Johnson and Sappie clinging to the plank. Moments later, said Johnson, 'a huge sea threw me and the boatswain on shore amongst some pieces of timber, from which I scrambled to a higher shelving rock to avoid the next sea . . . but the poor old boatswain, less active, was carried away, and perished.' Sappie's last words to Johnson had been, 'We shall have a watery grave.' Johnson had somehow squeezed himself into a crevice on the ledge 'and I laid down and slept'.

When Thornton asked were there any other survivors, Johnson replied, 'I believe all the others are lost. I have seen no others alive, only their dead bodies.'

The first thing Johnson saw when he regained consciousness on the Friday morning 'was dead bodies floating in the sea. I saw that I was the only person there. I was about 10 yards above the level of the sea. The spray washed the rocks upon which I was sitting, but it was not slippery. I was not in any danger of being washed away.'

Johnson saw a steamer—it was the *Grafton*—about to enter the Heads. He had waved frantically; he had shouted—but the storm drowned his cries. The *Grafton* had continued past and on through the Heads. His attempts to attract the attention of someone on board the passing schooner *Ann and Jane* were as futile. At midday another ship—the search vessel *Washington*—came into Johnson's view. He had waved, again to no avail.

The Irishman spent Friday and Friday night on the ledge wet, cold, starving and parched. On Saturday morning, he told Thornton, 'I endeavoured to get along the rocks. I could see people on the cliffs above, but could not make myself seen.'

Or so he thought.

15

Beyond belief

Leaving James Johnson at the Marine Hotel, Alderman Thornton returned to The Gap. Having been there earlier in the day, he had no illusions about what awaited him.

At The Gap, a brave fellow, whose name I have not yet learned [it was local man Francis Osborne], volunteered to go down to collect some of the corpses now and then lodged on the rocks beneath us; now a trunk of a female from the waist upwards, then the legs of a male, the body of an infant, the right arm, shoulder and head of a female, the bleached arm and extended hand, with the wash of the receding water, almost as t'were in life, beckoning for help; then a leg and thigh, a human head would be hurled along; the sea dashing most furiously, as if in angry derision of our efforts to rescue its prey. One figure, a female, nude, and tightly clasping an infant to her breast, both locked in the firm embrace of death, was for a moment seen, then the legs of some trunkless body would leap from the foaming cataract, caused by the returning sea, leaping wildly with feet seen plainly upwards up in the air . . . to be again and again tossed up to the gaze of the sorrowing throng above.

We procured a rope, lowered the man, with some brave stout hearts holding on to the rope above, and in this manner several portions of the mutilated remains were hauled up to the top of the cliff until a huge sea suddenly came and nearly smothered those on the cliff, wetting them all to the skin. I caused the man to be hauled up, thinking it was too dangerous to continue. It was a heart-rending scene, and I was glad to leave it, which I did soon after, and returned to Sydney about dark.

The bodies retrieved from The Gap by Francis Osborne were placed in coffin shells and loaded onto the *Black Swan*.

All that Saturday morning and afternoon, while Thornton and the reporters scribbled in their pads trying to chronicle Johnson's Lazarus-like return from the dead, and to convey the ghastly scenes at The Gap and the wreck site, the search continued for bodies in Port Jackson.

The *Black Swan* and the steamer *Pelican* patrolled the shores of North Harbour, Middle Harbour and Sydney Harbour, searching the water, beaches and rocks for bodies and, everyone hoped against hope, more survivors. There were none of the latter but many of the former—most of them damaged in the collision, gashed by sharp rocks or mauled by sharks—and many body parts.

Sydney businessman John Gough Waller on the *Black Swan* had come to identify his brother Kilner and his family of seven.

Harbour pilot John Robson recorded his account of the body hunt.

After an early breakfast I went in my boat round Middle Harbour, and then walked across the neck of land to the inner Middle Head Battery, where I saw a portion of two sides of the ill-fated vessel, and on proceeding one hundred yards [90 metres] further to the south, I observed a hind portion of her wholes and upper-works; near the latter a female was entangled, but, with the assistance of two men who were on the beach, we succeeded in extricating her from the wreck, and laid her alongside a little boy who had also been picked up previously; he appeared to be about three years of age—he was quite perfect, except a slight graze on the left side of the forehead. The lady, I had forgotten to mention, had her scull [sic] entirely taken off, as well as her left leg much broken, but the foot was still attached, which was remarkable for its smallness, as well as the hands. I cut off a lock of her hair, which was light brown intermixed with a few grey hairs . . . Nothing else came under my notice particular that day, except the distressing sight of mutilated bodies which could not be recovered.

Eleven corpses had been washed under a sandstone ledge by the beach just north of Hillery's sandspit at Middle Head (today The Spit). The next day they would be placed in coffin shells to be collected by a steamer crew and taken to the morgue, or Dead House, at water police headquarters in The Rocks.

The boat chartered by *The Empire* anchored at the ledge where the corpses lay. Among the dead were the flamboyant Sydney architect and real estate developer Patrick Downey who was identified by his father, Julia Meyer and one of her six children who were identified by Joseph Raphael, and the retired Royal Navy man, veteran of the Napoleonic Wars, Captain John Steane, whose linen underwear bore his name. The *Empire* reporter noted that Steane's face 'was not much disfigured, but his clothing was considerably torn . . . Downey's face and legs were badly bruised. A young lady, about 13 years of age, was next found, who had not suffered much from contusions . . .'

John Gough Waller was asked if he could identify any of the bodies and was aghast to recognise his sister-in-law, Maria Waller, the teacher and daughter of the pastor of Launceston's York Street Baptist Chapel, and his beautiful and talented niece, Mary, known to all as Polly. He also believed the damaged body of a girl was eight-year-old Kate Waller, but the corpse was later found to be that of a young woman unrelated to the family. He would write to a friend, 'I discovered my darling Maria thrown up in one of the bays of the Harbour, about three miles [5 kilometres] from the scene of the disaster. She was decently clad in her night dress, and having all the appearance of a placid death, and a cheerful and confiding submission to the will of a wise and never-erring God. Poor Polly lying close beside her.'

The *Empire* reporter described the body of a seaman whose face had severe contusions and was swollen grotesquely and whose right foot was broken at the ankle. He was subsequently identified by James Johnson at the Dead House as sixteen-year-old midshipman William Butler Williams from Newport in Wales. 'It was evident,' Johnson said, 'that when the ship struck he was on deck upon watch, for he was fully dressed and had on a monkey jacket [a waist-length coat with a tapered tail at back] and comforter. [His] linen was marked "WBW, 24".'

Some of the other bodies under the ledge, including that of an adolescent girl with gold earrings, would be identified later by friends and family at the morgue. Others' disfigured features defied recognition.

A member of the search party named Isaac Moore recovered the scarcely marked and well-dressed bodies of a woman and two men floating together in the waters by The Spit.

Off Middle Head, a fellow named Crawford came upon bodies. 'One had his shirt and drawers on and was of a slight-built frame, apparently 30 years of age. The other was a tall, fine-built man, dressed in a dark brown pea coat and black trousers, with neither boots nor stockings, about 30 years of age. Another body floated up without a head, and another man was washed up a small creek a short distance from Hillery's Spit.'

The carcasses of three cows or bulls eddied nearby.

There was the corpse of a woman, recalled Captain Robert Pockley, 'very large . . . very stout. The features too much mutilated to allow me to make any identification.'

At Manly Cove, Philip Cohen, manager of the Pier Hotel near the ferry wharf, told Captain Pockley that he had entered the water at the cove to recover two bodies in the surf, and as he approached he saw sharks savaging the corpses. Cohen said he had tried to prise one body from the jaws of a shark. 'This shark was a huge monster and he was determined not to let go of his victim. I tried to take the poor man away from the shark, but the shark won and disappeared with him into the deep water.' Cohen told Pockley that he had been 'astounded by the ferocity with which [the sharks] fought for their prey'. Cohen added, with some hyperbole, 'This is a dreadful disaster, filling the sea around here with more than a hundred corpses, [it] has attracted every shark in the Pacific Ocean.'

Cohen's bravery was lauded by many, but not by Manly locals George Birch and Benjamin Skinner who called him a liar.

On reading the *Herald* of Tuesday, the 25th, we were astonished to find an account of Mr P Cohen's terrific combat with a shark; also that he, unassisted, rescued several bodies. We can positively state that it is a mistake, as there were other persons engaged in finding and carrying them up on the beach, Mr Cohen never having laid a finger on them. We merely state this to remove the imputation that has been cast on the other inhabitants of Manly Beach, of inhumanity towards the unfortunate.

Off Manly, five more bodies were taken aboard the *Black Swan*. One, that of a second Meyer child, was identified by Joseph Raphael. There was a sailor, and a large man whose face, reported *The Empire*, was 'frightfully battered and disfigured, and whose body was also greatly bruised'.

On the beach off North Head Quarantine Station, the HMS *Herald* located three corpses. One, identified by a name tag on his clothing, was 21-year-old Isaac Simmons, returning to take his place in his father's world of politics and business. Sharks had ensured that the other two corpses were unrecognisable. Some recovered arms were tattooed with anchors and ships and other designs favoured by sailors. On one arm, between the elbow and wrist, the letters 'GM' were inked within an anchor, perhaps to honour a lover or a family member, for there was nobody with these initials in the *Dunbar*'s manifest.

By Saturday afternoon, the waters and beaches of Port Jackson were strewn with broken timber, canvas and rigging, boots, bedding, gloves, hats, heavy coats and waistcoats, a lounge suite, hams and corned beef, cattle, chickens and dogs, beer casks branded 'Tooth', tubs of pickles and crates of brandy and red wine. Thousands of white candles littered a beach, giving the appearance from a distance of a blanket of snow. There were children's toys, a piece of crochet still pierced by a needle attached to a cotton reel that, read one account, 'seems as if it were only just laid aside by the fair fingers that but a few moments later were motionless in death', sweets and silks, a lady's glove, musical instruments including a piano, a package of paintings, letters and poetry books.

Two volunteers named Chapman and Hayes found 15 metres of the *Dunbar*'s keel, deck planking and copper-fastened hull timber drifting off Edwards Beach (today the northern end of Balmoral Beach).

A wooden door with green shutters, numbered 68, floated in the fairway of the Heads.

A Bible washed up on Forty Baskets Beach, near Manly Cove, was recovered by two boys, William and Daniel Whealey, and remained in their family's keeping for a century.

Thomas Sullivan stumbled on a package on the shore at Middle Harbour. Inside, somehow undamaged, were eighteen collodiotype (an early type of photography) portraits, two letters and a book of religious poetry. The address on the package was legible: Rev. John Gale, c/o Mr Wheatley's, Gunning, Yass. Gale, just 27 then, was a Methodist missionary three years in the colony, who would become a journalist and founder of the *Queanbeyan Age*, a coroner, magistrate—and friend of the bushranger Ben Hall before Hall turned to crime. One day, seven years after the *Dunbar* went down, John Gale rode to the top of a hill and, looking down on the wide brown plains, declared this would be a fine site for a city and worked hard to create Canberra. He lived to age 98, long enough to see the Prince of Wales lay the foundation stone of Australia's capital 63 years later, in 1927.

Three more bodies drifted off the beach at Watsons Bay. 'One with the exception of the top of the scull [sic], and the loss of part of the left arm, was entirely whole, and seems to have been a fine man,' reported the *Sydney Morning Herald*. 'The other two [corpses] were only trunks, the mutilated remains of unfortunate sailors.' The bodies of a woman and three children bobbed in the fairway of the Heads. Nearby were two teak planks marked *Dunbar*.

One volunteer searcher came upon the corpse of a woman, apparently about 25. She wore a wedding ring,

[and had] small ears and apparently good features, but the skull and upper part of the forehead being destroyed, it will not be easy to identify the face. The limbs were much bruised and presented a most shocking appearance. We trust someone will be able to identify the body as it will be very gratifying to us to learn that our trip has been the means of restoring the body of some dear friend to her sorrowing relatives.

Drifting ethereally off a Middle Harbour beach was a nightdress marked 'MA Dobell'. Floating nearby was a handkerchief with 'Mrs Howell 1856' stitched on it, and two rings, each inscribed with 'WD', were on the fingers of a female victim. An item of women's clothing bore the name 'I' or 'J' Logan'. If 'I Logan', the garment was probably that of eighteen-year-old first-class passenger Ida Logan, who was sailing to Sydney with her eleven- and nine-year-old brothers Charles and Arthur. The *Dunbar*'s manifest has no Dobell or Howell or person with the initials W.D. A tattered linen shirt was collected from rocks. It had a label: 'CJ Troughton': Charles Troughton, the big-hearted English friend of Kilner Waller who witnessed the last-minute adjustment to Waller's will, and was travelling to Australia for his health.

After hearing Philip Cohen's harrowing (though, according to George Birch and Benjamin Skinner, apocryphal) tale at Manly, at around 11 a.m. Captain Pockley off-loaded from the *Black Swan* all who were surplus to the mission 'and thus lightened and less encumbered' and with the seas calmer today than the day before, the ferry steamed out of the Heads to Outer South Head. There, with the *Black Swan*, both vessels around 100 metres offshore, Pockley and his men used telescopes and

opera glasses [to examine] minutely every crevice capable of holding a living being, to a long distance beyond where the vessel had struck. Having reached sufficiently far south, I returned equally close to the shore, and again repeating the same strict scrutiny of the cliffs, proceeded to Watsons Bay, convinced that there were no survivors then on the crags outside. Upon arrival in Watsons Bay, I learned that a man had been rescued from the cliffs.

As the day's light faded, Captain Pockley supervised the removal of bodies from where they had been stacked on the bluff at The Gap. There was neither time nor capacity for niceties. The corpses and body parts were crammed into coffin shells on the deck of the *Black Swan* alongside other shells already occupied. The *Black Swan* then sped its sad cargo to Circular Quay and the Dead House. The coffin shells were received by Coroner John Skottowe Parker and water police supervisor and magistrate Samuel North. After such a day, the task of trying to identify the contents of the shells could wait till morning.

* * * *

Robert Pockley attended church with his family regularly each Sunday. Not on 23 August. As he made his way by carriage from his home to Circular Quay, it was cold with occasional showers but the heavy rain and roaring winds had lessened considerably and for the first time in four days there were patches of blue sky over the harbour city. Yet after Captain Pockley's harrowing Saturday, and the certainty of more distressing experiences that day, he could have taken no comfort in the improving weather.

At the quay, Captain Sullivan had the *Black Swan*, with the harbour master's boat cabled to its stern, fired up and ready to receive Pockley and his assistant harbour master, Police Inspector-General Captain John McLerie, and detachments of city and water police. There were more coffin shells on deck, for the *Black Swan* and the police and privately chartered and press craft would again be looking for bodies in every cove of Port Jackson. At points, police went ashore to explore crevices in which a body, or bodies, might have lodged. Midday found Pockley leaving the police to their work and steaming in the *Black Swan* to Watsons Bay to collect three more corpses from The Gap recovered by pilot Hydes and an unlikely volunteer search squad comprising a solicitor named Moffitt, labourer George Cox, bowling alley proprietor Charles Rodgers and McMahon the local postman. One body, on whose forearm was tattooed 'HB', was largely unmarked. As was the second body hauled up the cliff on a rope, which also had a tattooed arm with 'GB' inked beside an anchor. The third body could hardly be described as such, comprising only a trunk and an arm. At the end of the day, Pockley would ferry them to a Dead House that was becoming congested.

James Johnson was waiting for Pockley and McLerie that afternoon when they docked in the *Black Swan* at Watsons Bay jetty. They plied the harbour as the afternoon withered, finding no more corpses, only body parts, personal effects and *Dunbar* wreckage and cargo. Shortly before the chartered steamship returned at sunset to the Dead House in The Rocks to start the task of identifying the corpses, someone onboard fished a child's straw hat with a feather in its band from the water. Pockley asked Johnson if it was familiar. It was. 'It's the hat of a young girl who wore it in the tropics to protect her from the sun.'

16

The Dead House

On Saturday and Sunday, while Pockley and McLerie, city police and water police were combing Port Jackson, nineteen identifiable *Dunbar* victims, as well as many unidentifiable corpses and body parts, were in shell coffins and being ferried to the Dead House. The city morgue sat like an ugly sore by the police station near Cadman's Cottage, the Sailors' Home and the Mariners' Church and among the taverns, cheap lodgings and dance halls at Campbell's Wharf on George Street North on the western edge of Sydney Cove.

The deceased deserved better, for the Dead House, the city's only official morgue in 1857, was a blight on Sydney. Although only three years old, it was a dirty and decrepit charnel house, built of brick on a stone foundation with a slate roof and boarded-up windows to prevent passers-by peeping at the macabre sights within. The lack of ventilation meant it stank perpetually of decomposing flesh, a smell that defied the most vigorous scrubbing and fumigating. At less busy times than 23 August 1857, it doubled as a police lockup for drunken sailors and other law-breakers.

One doctor named Mackellar flat-out refused to conduct a post-mortem examination at the Dead House because the place was in such a 'filthy and horrible condition that he determined never again to enter it until some alteration had been affected. There was not even water there for him to wash his hands and he was compelled to go out to the waterside to wash them before he returned home.'

To Sydneysider George Atkinson, the Dead House's 'poisonous stench posed a risk to the health of the living' and the building needed to be demolished.

> While obsolete and ruinous old buildings and other nuisances are opportunely disappearing from our city for the sanitary relief of the public, why not condemn that scandalous outrage upon the inhabitants of George Street North by immediately condemning the existing morgue at the Circular Quay? It is situated between the Mariners' Church and reading room and the Sailor's [sic] Home. The former is visited by thousands periodically, and the Sailors' Home boards and lodges numerous sailors, who must be sufferers from the stench so close to them, more particularly when putrid bodies are brought there for post-mortem examinations. Only those who have to endure the poisonous effluvium extending, say, 150 yards [135 metres] around the morgue, can fully describe the sensation to the nostrils of the neighbours as well as the numerous passengers, and many lady visitors, arriving at the Australian Steam Navigation and Peninsular and Oriental Companies' wharves. I trust therefore you will use your all-powerful influence to have the subject of my just and truthful complaint at once removed to where it will no longer poison the atmosphere of thickly peopled quarters. By doing so you will confer a favour on the public.

The Dead House would continue to offend for another half-century, until demolished in 1906.

Lists of known *Dunbar* passengers and crew, which had arrived from England on a mail ship days earlier, were posted all over the city and published in newspapers on the Saturday. Those with relatives or friends on the ship were urged to come to the Dead House early on Sunday morning to try to identify the corpses and—perhaps by recognising a ring, a scar, a birthmark, a tattoo—the body parts. There was no time to let the dead lie in state because, there being no refrigeration, the bodies needed to be buried the following day.

Just as church bells rang in Plymouth on the Sunday in May when the *Dunbar* slipped out of the port on its final journey, so too, all day and into the evening this Sunday in Sydney Town, bells pealed to mourn the ship and its passengers and crew. There were sermons dedicated to the wreck, the precariousness of life and how we must all accept unquestioningly that 'God moves in a mysterious way/ His wonders to perform/He plants his footsteps in the sea/And rides upon the storm'. A number of the *Dunbar* dead were parishioners at the great colonial chapels, St James' Church and St Mary's Cathedral in Macquarie Street, where a solemn dirge was sung and a mass for the deceased conducted. The congregations at St John's Anglican Church in Darlinghurst, the Free Church, Sydney Synagogue (where *Dunbar* victim Isaac Simmons was known by all), the Presbyterian Church and the places of worship in outlying areas were packed to bursting. At Sydney's Congregational Church, where James Johnson's rescuer, Antonio Woolier, worshipped, people spilled out onto Pitt Street as the Reverend W. Cuthbertson delivered 'an eloquent sermon' about the tragedy. Two hundred kilometres west of Sydney, at All Saints' Church in the goldmining town of Bathurst, Reverend T. Sharp delivered an 'impressive and eloquent' sermon on how life held no guarantees. At nearby St Stephen's, Reverend J.B. Laughton drew his discourse from Amos 4:12, 'Prepare to meet thy God', and, according to one who was there, his sermon was 'characterised by the same fervid eloquence which usually accompanies the reverend preacher's addresses'.

Family and friends who came to the Dead House on Sunday morning had to force their way through a large crowd of people who had gathered outside on the street to express their sympathies, try to snatch glimpses of the bodies inside as the door opened and closed, or just be part of the event. Some ghouls gained entry by claiming to have known the deceased, but, when they saw what was inside the Dead House, they may have wished they'd remained in the street.

Once inside, people were confronted by, according to one victim's family member, 'truly a mournful sight, and one which will not readily leave the mind. The father claimed the son, the brother his brother, and the friend his friend. Even those who had not so painful an interest in this heart-rending scene were affected even to tears.'

Among the bodies were those of Maria and Polly Waller and their female servant (whose name is unrecorded). They, for the second time, were identified by John Gough Waller. The corpse of Isaac Simmons was confirmed by his uncles Joseph and Isaac Simmons. Three of Julia and Abraham Meyer's children—Rachel, aged six; Lewis, four, and baby Morris—were identified once more by Joseph Raphael and a Mr Jacobs. The body of six-year-old George Healing was the only one of the five Healings to be recovered. Maria and Charles Logan were inconsolable when they viewed the corpses of their children: Ida, eighteen, Charles, eleven, and Arthur, nine. Captain John Steane was recognised by a number of people. Everyone, it seems, knew Captain Steane.

When James Johnson arrived at the Dead House with Captain Pockley that Sunday evening he remained composed and passed calmly by the bodies giving names to those passengers and crew whom he recognised.

Johnson is not known to have ever mentioned suffering what would nowadays be known as post-traumatic stress and survivor guilt. In his day, to admit to such was considered a display of weakness. Dr James Hanson, James Johnson's brother Henry's great-great-great-great-grandson, told this author that it would be unusual if his ancestor didn't have to deal with both, whether the conditions had a name or not.

Apparently he kept a brave face, but enduring the wreck of his ship, being marooned on the ledge, seeing people he'd come to know well on the 81-day voyage drowning and their bodies smashed repeatedly on the rocks and being attacked by sharks . . . Then he had to identify their bodies at the morgue. All that would have an impact on him. He was a simple lad and suddenly he had gone through a terrible ordeal and then found himself the centre of attention. I think James after *Dunbar* was a troubled person. The photographs of him when he was old . . . there's a look in his eyes that tells me he's seen things that others haven't.

Coroner John Skottowe Parker walked alongside Johnson, jotting down the names and the numbers on the deceaseds' coffins to check them off against the *Dunbar*'s manifest and so that they could be marshalled for the afternoon funeral procession the next day. Johnson identified first officer James Struthers of the prodigious strength, apprentice seaman John Gavin, midshipman and former London tea dealer John Ridley Jerram and chief steward James Ward—who had lit the futile blue light just before the *Dunbar* struck the cliffs. Perhaps Johnson paused to gaze at the face of the *Dunbar*'s boatswain, Charles Sappie, who had clung to the wreckage alongside him and whose final words to Johnson, just before he went under, proved to be half-true: 'We shall have a watery grave.' The sixteen-year-old midshipman William Butler Williams was identified by Johnson and by his aunt, Mary Biss, of Sydney, who could only recognise him by his long blond hair.

An *Empire* reporter gained entry and wrote of:

The perfect body [though we know his face was bruised] of a fine young man (entirely clothed) identified as Mr J [sic] Downey, the architect, identified by the father and brother of the deceased. The scenes at the examination of the bodies were heartrending, but in deference to the feelings of the survivors we forbear to enlarge upon this painful theme. We cannot help here once more noticing the inconvenience arising from the smallness of the Dead House. The scene otherwise shocking was rendered far more so by the confusion resulting no less from the confined space than the morbid desire of a number of people to see, solely out of curiosity, a spectacle which most persons, one would suppose, would desire to avoid.

Coroner Parker had sworn in a jury of eminent men to hear testimony and pass judgment at the coronial inquest into the tragedy that would take place on Sunday evening and Monday. But first, the coroner and the jury were required to view the contents of the coffin shells. All were moved, some to tears, and at least one fainted. Nobody involved was in a state to start the inquest after that, so it was agreed to reconvene on Monday morning.

By nightfall on Sunday, any corpse in a condition to be recognised, had been. After the jurors had completed their grim due diligence and left for the day, the identified colonists' corpses were borne away in hearses by their families to be buried privately. The crew members and unidentifiable bodies and the body parts would be interred in a mass tomb at Camperdown Cemetery the next day.

Jury foreman was John Valentine Gorman, the assistant government surveyor who co-founded the wool-broking company that in 1888 became known as Goldsbrough Mort & Company Limited. He and another appointed juror, Joseph Raphael (an irascible Jewish businessman, politician and philanthropist with a reputation as 'the foulest-mouthed man in Sydney'), had spent Saturday looking for bodies. The other members of the jury were Walter Hamilton, Henry Ferris, Joseph Marchant, Henry Doyle, baker and ship provedore Alexander Smail, John Glasson, John Spearin, Howard Capper, John Hampton, Alexander Dickman, and none other than the hell-raising clipper master James Nicol 'Bully' Forbes, who had cheerfully risked the *Marco Polo* and the lives of his crew and passengers during his record 68-day voyage from Liverpool to Port Phillip Heads in 1852. If anyone understood clipper ships and the dangers of the sea, it was Bully Forbes.

After his work at the Dead House was done, James Johnson spent the night in Sydney, probably with his brother Henry and Henry's wife, Mary-Anne. Henry was a seaman and sailmaker recently arrived in the colony from Ireland, who, after meeting and marrying his compatriot Mary-Anne in Sydney, became a lighthouse assistant keeper and later keeper. James had endured so much, and having to recount the events all over again at the coronial inquest and then be chief mourner at the funeral would surely take its toll.

* * * *

Reporters and journalists, artists and typesetters worked through the night to publish the latest news and conjecture about the *Dunbar* tragedy in Monday's newspapers. The *Sydney Morning Herald* opined:

> No sadder event has for a long time past excited the sympathy of the citizens of Sydney than the loss of the *Dunbar*. The destruction of a fine ship and a valuable cargo, although in itself not insignificant, is a trifle compared to the loss of more than a hundred lives. Whole families are plunged into mourning. Reunions, fondly anticipated and momentarily expected to be realised, have been abruptly hindered, and hindered forever. Instead of the warm and loving welcome come tidings of a terrible catastrophe and then the cold, mutilated, half-unrecognisable forms of those who will never cheer the social circle more. Almost at the threshold of their own homes they perished—so near once more to their friends and relatives—and yet so far.

The newspaper remarked that while wrecks of flimsy vessels near dangerous ports and with incompetent masters were not uncommon:

> here was a vessel built as strongly as teak timber and honest English ship-wrighting could make her, entering one of the finest Harbours in the world, commanded by a cautious, vigilant and experienced sailor, who, both as mate and master, had frequently entered the port before and knew it well. Yet, after a successful voyage it has

been flung onshore almost in sight of the anchorage at the very base of the lighthouse [sic] and with the loss of every soul onboard except one. So fallible are the calculations of mortals!'

The *Herald* imagined the voyagers excitedly anticipating arriving in Sydney, but, 'Alas no! One frightful crash, one sudden waking in terror, one bewildering consciousness of the awful fact, one hopeless struggle with the boiling surge and all their earthly experiences alike of joy and sorrow were closed forever.'

Then the writer turned to the 'opinion often expressed by nautical men that the entrance to Port Jackson is not properly lighted'. He cited a recent inquiry in Melbourne into the lighting of the Australian coast, and specifically the Sydney coast, which found what seasoned sailors already knew: there should be a light on North Head and one at the northern tip of Outer South Head.

The public's lust for more details of the wreck was insatiable. On the Saturday that James Johnson was rescued and the search for bodies began, the *Empire* and the *Herald* published special *Dunbar* editions. In a city of around 57,000 inhabitants, a remarkable 38,000 newspapers were sold. As many papers would be sold again on Monday and Tuesday. In a small community, such as Sydney was then, everyone was affected by the loss of the *Dunbar*.

Contrary to some published reports, Captain James Green's body was not among those found in Port Jackson and delivered to the Dead House. The captain's corpse was never located. At first, it was believed that Green's wife, Alice, had died with him, although James Johnson was sure Alice Green had not been on board. The cause of the confusion was a letter that Captain Green had posted in April to the *Dunbar*'s Australian agents Messrs Smith, Campbell & Co., saying that Alice would be accompanying him to Sydney. James Green's friends were relieved when a letter post-marked London addressed to Captain Green care of the agent's Sydney office arrived in Sydney on the *La Hogue* a week after the *Dunbar* was wrecked. The back of the envelope was signed 'Mrs Alice Green' and dated 13 June, which was thirteen days after the *Dunbar* had set sail. Alice Green clearly was not on the *Dunbar*, having remained in England to give birth to her and James's baby. Because in those days there were no electronic communications, Alice did not learn that she was a widow until early November, three months after James Green perished, and shortly before she went into labour. Alice James Green was born on 14 November, but died eighteen months later of brain disease.

17

How and why

The King's Arms ale house in The Rocks was known as a convivial place. Patrons drank deeply and spun yarns of the sea, and their raucous hubbub exploded from the confines of the pub and blended with the workaday din in Lower George Street. Conviviality, however, was in short supply this Monday, 24 August, the day of the New South Wales Government Coronial Inquest into the 'Death of the Passengers and Crew of the Ship *Dunbar*, Lost at South Head on the Night of Thursday Last, the 20th Instant'. As those who were to hear and give testimony assembled at the King's Arms, the ale stayed untapped and the tavern was sombre. The only yarns spun were horror stories. The fire blazing on the dining-room hearth could not warm the chill.

At 11 a.m., Coroner John Skottowe Parker, the jurors, Inspector-General Captain John McLerie and inspectors North and Cowell of the water police, Dr Haynes Alleyne, maritime officials, seamen and police, relatives and friends of victims and those members of the public who arrived early enough to squeeze inside, took their seats or stood around the walls.

Flinty Coroner Parker in his black frock-coat reminded the jurors:

[of the] solemn nature of your duty . . . You are called together to perform a public duty; to investigate the causes which resulted in so dreadful a catastrophe as that of the loss of the ship *Dunbar*, with all hands—only one excepted—on the coast and within a short distance of the Heads. No matter how kind or excellent a man the captain might have been, you . . . should declare, having heard the evidence, and calmly considered all the circumstances which might be submitted to you, whether the captain of the ill-fated ship was, or was not, to blame in having pursued the course which led to such tragic results. No stone should be left unturned to arrive at the truth. If you cannot arrive at the truth after one day's investigation, then you must adjourn to a second and so on until you have thoroughly sifted the evidence. It is the more necessary that the fullest inquiry should be made in order that the friends and relatives of the deceased should see that the owners were not at all to blame; and, on the other hand, that owners of vessels in England might be made aware that their property was fully protected in this country.

Parker's directions suggested that it would be less problematic, and better for business, if Captain James Green was found to have been solely responsible for the wreck. The dead can be blamed, but not prosecuted or sued—unlike governments, ship-owners and brokers.

Having gathered the previous day and studied James Johnson's statements to the press and Alderman Thornton, the jurors had a broad grasp of the events that likely led to the *Dunbar* foundering. And, of course, Raphael and Gorman had searched for bodies with Captain Pockley and Inspector-General Captain McLerie.

Now before them stood Johnson, the first to testify. All eyes were on this bear-like man who took his oath on the Holy Gospel and spoke for nearly an hour. He reiterated what he had told Thornton two days before, and the jurors drew new details from him. The inquest was as stunned by Johnson's story—told in his sailor's vernacular rather than as interpreted by George Thornton—as Thornton himself and his readers had been. Johnson's testimony and that of others who followed him onto the stand was transcribed in the *Coroner's Inquest Register, 1857*.

Johnson began by confirming that the *Dunbar* had left Plymouth on 31 May and that it was a fine ship 'in good discipline; we found the ship always worked well, and kept good headway . . . it was not a leaky one'. Although he did not know Captain Green's christian name, he wanted it understood that Green and first officer James Struthers were experienced and excellent seamen. He was unsure how many passengers were on board, but believed the crew numbered 59. It had been a

> prosperous voyage up to the time of the wreck; in fact, no accident or mishap had occurred . . . there were not any deaths or births during the voyage. The crew and passengers were all healthy. The ship was well-manned and disciplined; there was a sufficient number of able-bodied seamen as well as boys . . . everything passed in a very satisfactory manner up to the time of the ship's striking.

Sailing up the east coast of Australia, Johnson continued, the weather had been rainy and hazy with the wind gusting from the north. By the time the *Dunbar* had 'made' Botany Bay, the weather had deteriorated. The wind was now blowing hard from the east-south-east and the rain was heavy.

> The sails were reefed and we were close-hauled . . . we shortened sail after making the land off Botany; there were three reefs in the main-topsail, and the fore-topsail was close-reefed; the mizzen-topsail was stowed; the spanker was brailed up; we took the second jib in, and also the main-topmast staysail . . . The vessel was then laying her course about north-east and by north; she had not plenty of room for she was making too much lee-way because she had not enough sail upon her.

Green and James Struthers had manned the poop deck from 8 p.m., alongside the wheel-man, after which the rain intensified further and 'the lighthouse was seen only at intervals . . . The night was very dark; we could not see a hand before our face.'

According to Johnson, because of the current driving down from the north-east and slowing her progress, the close-hauled ship was sailing at around 3 knots an hour. He had assumed Captain Green was aware of that.

I remained on deck because I belonged to the chief officer's watch. The captain remained on deck notwithstanding that the watch was relieved, and he gave the orders as usual; everything was properly attended to as usual. All orders were strictly obeyed, and there was nothing whatever to show that there was any dissatisfaction or disobedience on the part of the crew . . . [the] ship was not labouring heavily; she obeyed her helm readily. There was one man at the wheel until the orders were given by the captain to square away [square the sails so the ship sailed before the wind] . . . The captain was walking upon the weather side of the poop.

At around 11 p.m., testified Johnson, Green had ordered all hands on deck. Had, one juror interrupted, any of those hands been drinking? 'I am sure there had been no drinking aboard,' retorted Johnson. 'The men were all very steady. We were allowed only one glass of grog daily [which they had consumed at lunchtime]. I am quite sure that all the men were sober and steady.'

Johnson continued:

When we got the yards squared the order was given to haul the foresail up; the order was immediately obeyed . . . the light was distinctly visible, but only at times . . . There was a look-out upon the forecastle, an able seaman had been placed for the purpose of keeping a look-out for the land. The second and third mates [John Spence and John Pascoe] had also been sent to keep a look-out on the forecastle.

My own impression was that in going along the coast we carried too little canvas; the ship, too, was making much leeway.

Captain Green called out to the men on the forecastle, 'Can you see anything of the North Head?'

The forecastle watch had cried out that he could not. To that moment, said Johnson, he had seen no cause for alarm.

Moments later, 'the second mate called out, "Breakers ahead!"'
Johnson continued:

I think when the captain gave the order to square away he was under the impression that he was entering the Heads until he heard the second mate cry out, 'Breakers ahead!' but that is only my own surmise. The officers did not tell him that they saw North Head. Nor did anyone else say so, because it was not to be seen. There was no opening to be seen that I could detect; in fact, I could see nothing ahead at all. I was not apprehensive of danger; and just before we struck, I thought we were going straight into the harbour.

Then, directly above, the lantern of Macquarie Light broke through the clouds. 'The captain did all in his power to save the vessel and neglected nothing so far as I saw . . . We could see the light. It was right over us.'

Interrupted juror Gorman, 'How did you know it was the Sydney light that you could see?'

Johnson replied:

I only knew it was the Sydney light from what men on board the ship said. They told me it was the Sydney light because they had been here before. We [had] expected to go in the next morning at daylight. Nobody ever thought the captain would have tried to get in that night.

About two minutes afterwards we bumped . . . port bow first . . . broadside onto the rocks. At the time of striking, we were endeavouring to stretch out to the eastward. Her head was lying to the northward, and she was drifting with the rise and fall of the sea . . . it was somewhere about the port bow we struck the rocks first. There was no order given to lower the [life]boats. They were washed away by the first sea; the lashings were off and were hanging to the davits ready to be launched at a moment's notice; there was no Clifford's lifeboat onboard. There were four lifebuoys, two astern and two on deck. As she bumped, she fell over and then it was impossible to lower a boat. The sea did not make a clear breach over at first. We had four boats, two upon each side. There is not the least truth in the report that the longboat had been launched, or that any passengers had got into it.

At this time the passengers had come from between decks, and were running about the main deck imploring mercy, and uttering piercing and heart-rending cries for succour. The ship was lying broadside on in the heavy surf . . . When the vessel struck I did not observe any of the passengers throwing off their clothing; I saw some of the young ladies, when going into the cabin, running about in their chemises, screaming, screeching, and crying, and calling on Mr Spence to know if there was any possibility of being saved . . . The captain was standing upon the poop, cool and collected.

Johnson told how Captain Green had tried to calm panic-stricken passengers by telling them 'The *Dunbar* cannot break up. She'll last until morning.'

The survivor continued, 'I could hear no orders given after the ship struck. The foremast stood a long time; she was in the surf about five minutes before she began breaking up and then went with a great crash. There was great confusion . . .'

There was pin-drop silence in the room as Johnson told how he survived when no one else did; how he had escaped the broken ship, seized the floating plank with the three others who lost their grip and then was thrown by a wave onto a rock and fell unconscious. 'After I found myself upon the rock my senses returned, but I could hear nothing except the noise of the sea. The first thing I saw in the morning was the dead bodies floating in the sea. I saw that I was the only person there. I was about 10 yards [9 metres] above the level of the sea. The sprays washed the rock upon which I was sitting.'

Juror Raphael asked Johnson if dropping the anchors could have saved the *Dunbar* from crashing into the cliff. Johnson replied that that would have been futile. 'She would have veered on.'

Now the survivor named those whose bodies he'd identified in the Dead House the previous day.

Young Mr Williams, midshipman. Charles Sappie, I believe formerly in the water police here, the boatswain; also, John Gavin, seaman. The servant girl of Mr Waller, one of the cabin passengers, also Mr Waller's eldest daughter [Mary or 'Polly'], and I think one of Mr Meyer's children, a girl; among the passengers I knew an old captain of the navy, Captain Steane, and I identified his body. Miss Logan was a passenger, about 20 or 21 years of age [Ida Logan was eighteen]. Also, two Masters Logan . . . they used to dress in a kind of French uniform.

When asked could he recall any of the other passengers and crew, he told the inquest:

There was a Master Weiss onboard. He was an apprentice. Doctor Bayne was the doctor of the ship; and the third officer's name was Pascoe. The second officer's name was Spence. One of the midshipmen was named De Verd [there is no record of a crewman of this name on *Dunbar*; Johnson probably meant a midshipman named variously in crew lists as Au Verne or De Veruel]. There were six midshipmen on board. The captain's steward's name was [James] Ward. We had four life-buoys on board. The chief cuddy steward was named Sam [Samuel Simper]. We had four bulls and two milch cows, some sheep, and pigs on board. There were three Finlanders among the able seamen, and about eight Dutchmen [this, too, is at odds with the—admittedly unreliable—crew lists, which show that the only non-British or -Irish crew members were Swedes Manson and Woodworth, the Germans Hoyne and Bey, and the Finn Amar or Aman]. The men in my watch were Alexander Munro [in the crew list as Luke Munroe], William Miller, John Lewis, Thomas Chapman [or Chappell], John Douglass [or James or Henry Douglas], John Couleston [Colstone], George Lenan [or Lemor], Henry Cumming, John Guy. These men were all in the starboard watch. There were three apprentices, [Thomas] Horne, [James] McGuffy [or McGuffie], and [John] Allen. Among the steerage passengers I knew Mr and Mrs Healing and their three children, Mrs [Martha] Brown and one child [Henry], Mr [James] Clarke, wife [Eleanor], and two children [Henry and James]; also a Mr [William] Bynon, whose wife I think I heard was out here [in Australia]. Mr Bynon, I think, went home [to England] in *Dunbar* last voyage . . . There was a gentleman on board in the habit of reading prayers to passengers and crew. I think it was Mr [Kilner] Waller. There was a Mr [Charles] Troughton among the passengers. This Mr Troughton told me during the voyage that he had a brother drowned off Cape Horn.

If Coroner Parker wanted James Johnson to take this opportunity to incriminate his captain, he was disappointed. Johnson finished his testimony by stressing again how composed James Green had been in the crisis, how staunchly he had held his post and done everything he could to prevent the collision, and adding, 'The captain was universally respected in the ship.'

Charles Wiseman, master of the steamer *Grafton* that had remained safely outside the Heads on the night and entered next morning through a sea strewn with bodies and debris, also vouched for the *Dunbar*'s master when he followed Johnson onto the stand. 'I do not think any blame can be attached to Captain Green for the loss of *Dunbar*,' he declared. When quizzed by a juror as to whether a captain of a large vessel approaching the Heads from the south on such a night should run for Sydney Cove or ride out the storm at sea, Wiseman replied that while the best course of action for a sturdy steamer such as the *Grafton* was to remain outside the Heads, if he had been in Captain Green's situation on a sailing clipper, 'I would certainly have preferred running in to risking the danger of such a gale as blew on August 20, especially on a lee coast . . . I have heard the evidence as to the position of *Dunbar*, and under the circumstances, I would not have hesitated in endeavouring to run into the harbour.'

Wiseman agreed that Green mistook the waves breaking on The Gap for North Head. 'The Gap is very apt to lead captains of vessels astray as to the proper position; I have frequently mistaken it myself . . . there was no doubt but the [sic] Gap was taken for the entrance into the harbour.'

Wiseman now raised a topic that would be aired at length in the homes and meeting places of Sydney and in parliament in the weeks to come. Indisputably, playing its part in the disaster was the far from ideal location of Macquarie Light, atop the cliffs 2.2 kilometres south of the harbour entrance, which left the northern section of South Head and the entrance to Port Jackson cloaked in darkness. Had there been a low-level lighthouse on the point of South Head, it would have been seen by the *Dunbar*'s crew and guided the clipper through the Heads. Wiseman said, 'At present you have to pass [Macquarie Light] for a mile [sic] before you can round the harbour.'

After Wiseman, it was the turn of Archibald Fletcher, master of the steamer *Nora Creina*. He told the inquest that when returning to Sydney from the Shoalhaven River last Thursday night he had sighted at around 10 p.m. the lights of 'a large ship about two miles [3 kilometres] off [Macquarie Light]'. He did not know the identity of the ship. He had then steamed through the Heads and into Sydney Cove before the storm reached its height. Captain Fletcher said that although conditions were heavy and getting worse, 'There was no signal of distress of any kind [from the *Dunbar*]. When I saw her, she was perfectly safe.'

Fletcher testified that when the *Nora Creina* passed the ship, his vessel was much closer to the coast and he could see Macquarie Light now and then. Fletcher surmised that the captain of the ship, which he had later learned was the *Dunbar*, battered by 'sudden gusts of wind and torrents of rain, with very heavy sea, would have had trouble seeing the lighthouse and the Heads'.

Coroner Parker reminded Fletcher that the law of the sea required an able vessel to act as a pilot to any ship in trouble, and demanded to know why the *Nora Creina* offered no assistance to the *Dunbar*. Fletcher retorted, 'Had I seen a signal of distress, or been called upon to render assistance, I could have piloted the vessel into port, and would have done so.' But he had not, so did not.

Captain Fletcher joined Wiseman in criticising the location of Macquarie Light too far south of the Heads to be a guide into the harbour on a night of poor visibility and too high on the cliff to be seen by a vessel close in.

And Fletcher had harsh words for the pilot boat service, which had not been available when the *Dunbar* needed assistance. He did not consider the existing, easily swamped open-decked pilot boats 'adequate to rendering [help to] vessels in distress . . . in very heavy weather'. It was little wonder that pilot crews were reluctant to risk them in dangerous times when they were most needed. 'If this port was provided with decked pilot vessels similar to those in Melbourne, Liverpool and other ports, assistance might have been rendered, and *Dunbar* might then have been saved. She could then have had a pilot on board before dark. Considering the trade of this port, I do think the Government ought to have proper decked pilot vessels provided.'

Captain Robert Pockley was scheduled to give evidence, but sent his apologies because 'my first duty' was to be out in Port Jackson and at Outer South Head continuing the search for survivors and corpses. Pockley was rebuked in absentia by Coroner Parker. 'I think that on such an occasion, Captain Pockley ought to have attended as requested. I do not think he is acting rightly in failing to come.'

In the following days when the search for bodies had been scaled down, Pockley did make a statement that was appended to the inquest's transcript. In it he detailed all that he had done in the days after the tragedy, and defended the efficiency of those manning the signal station and Macquarie Light, both establishments being his responsibility as harbour master.

> I found that five men were stationed, as usual, in the Signal Tower, and that they kept a strict watch of two hours each from sunset to sunrise. [If Jane Graham is to be believed, her husband James, the signal master, and his assistant Henry Packer were both asleep. There may have been others on duty.] The night was intensely dark and rainy, with a heavy gale blowing dead on shore. At midnight the dog at the lighthouse aroused the superintendent by his furious barking. The superintendent then went up to the lantern, and found the keeper at his post, in the act of trimming the lights. About this time the gale was blowing most furiously . . . It was impossible to see any object a few yards distant, and the roar of wind and sea rendered their own voices almost inaudible; the wind was so fear-fully violent as to alarm the keepers for the safety of the lighthouse. Under these circumstances it would have been impossible for them to have become acquainted with the dreadful tragedy that was being enacted at their very feet. The first intimation of the wreck was observed by the pilot at The Gap when daylight broke and he discovered the fragments of the ship beneath him . . . I cannot attach any blame to any person in my department, or attribute any neglect of duty by which the awful event would have been prevented.

Testifying in Pockley's stead at the coronial inquest was the jury foreman, John Valentine Gorman. Having helped recover bodies, he had earned the right to speak. When he learned on the Friday that a ship had been wrecked, Gorman had gone to The Gap at 3 p.m.:

> during the half-hour that I remained there I saw several human bodies tossed about on the surf, being washed on the rocks and off again with each succeeding sea. I returned to Sydney at dusk and shortly after-wards went down to the office of the *Sydney Morning Herald* to learn

if any positive information had been received of the name of the vessel that was wrecked; during the day it had been variously rumoured about the town that it was the *Vocalist*, the old *Ann [and Jane]*, [or] *Zemindar*, but having friends on board *Dunbar*, and having heard that some imported bulls had been washed ashore, I was anxious to learn the truth; shortly after I got to the *Herald* office, Captain Pockley came there; from him I learned that it *was* the *Dunbar*, that a mail bag had been found, and a cask of provisions, both marked per *Dunbar*, and that some fittings had been cast up with a mounting of a lion, the crest of *Dunbar*. On the following morning, having ascertained that a steamer [*Black Swan*] was going down the Harbour in search of bodies, and to investigate the matter, I went in her. I found Captain Pockley in command of her; he was accompanied by Mr McLerie, and several of the police, also Dr Alleyne and the Coroner, and there were police boats and the doctor's boat in attendance.

The *Black Swan*, continued Gorman, had spent the day searching Port Jackson, and he had assisted in the recovery of bodies, 'including those of Hannah Waller, Captain Steane, William Williams and one of the Meyer children, as well as unidentifiable body parts'.

Gorman praised 'the exertions of Mr McLerie, Captain Pockley, Dr Alleyne and Coroner Parker, in fact everyone connected with the expedition. We found the police stationed at the various points, and I was told that Inspector Cowell and his party had even been without provisions for an entire day; all seemed to be doing their best to aid and assist in recovering the bodies of the unfortunate victims.'

Coroner Parker adjourned the inquest at 4.30 p.m., so those involved could join the funeral procession of the *Dunbar* victims from the Dead House to Camperdown Cemetery in Newtown. The cortege had been supposed to get underway at three o'clock, but was delayed until five when the inquest ran overtime. James Johnson, Coroner Parker, the jurors and the victims' friends and families were to ride in the lead coaches.

* * * *

It was mid-evening when the inquest reconvened at the King's Arms after the funeral. The final witness was juror Joseph George Raphael, a friend of victims Julia and Abraham Meyer and Isaac Simmons.

> I was with the expedition on Saturday for the purpose of seeking out and identifying any of the family of Mr Meyer and Mr Simmons. After viewing the different bays, and entering Middle Harbour, I there identified one of the children of Mr Meyer. I also was present when several other bodies were identified from the marks on their linen. After leaving Middle Harbour, the steamer proceeded to Manly Beach, where we were informed there were three bodies on shore, one of which I identified as that of a son of Mr Meyer.

Coroner Parker now summarised the evidence given that day and directed the jurors to retire to consider the testimony they had heard and return with a finding.

Just 45 minutes later the jury was back and foreman Gorman faced Coroner Parker.

> The jury finds that the bodies viewed are those of some of the passengers and crew of the ship *Dunbar*, out of London, commanded by Captain Green, and bound to this port, and that the said ship *Dunbar* was wrecked outside of the Sydney Heads, close to the Gap, on the night of Thursday the 20th August, causing the death of the said parties. There may have been an error of judgment in the vessel being so close to the shore at night in such bad weather, but the jury do not attach any blame to Captain Green or his officers for the loss of *Dunbar*.

Gorman finished by requesting that the following statement be appended to the finding. 'The jury consider it their duty to put on record their opinion that the present pilot arrangements for this port are most inadequate, and desire to draw the attention of the Government to this matter.'

Coroner Parker made no comment on the finding. He echoed Gorman's congratulations of all who had recovered bodies, and the water policemen who had prevented the looting of the *Dunbar*'s timbers, canvas, metal and cargo. He then discharged the jury and ordered the room cleared. The inquest concluded shortly after 11 p.m.

The finding seemed perfunctory and much too brief to do justice to such a calamity. It stated the obvious and skirted serious issues. The jury's decision that there 'may have been an error of judgment in the vessel being so close to the shore at night in such bad weather' but clearing Captain Green and his officers of any culpability for that error was a contradiction in terms. The jurors condemned the pilot boat service as inadequate, but failed to acknowledge the unsuitable location of Macquarie Light or the lack of any other lights on the headland as factors contributing to the disaster. James Johnson was not subjected to cross-examination by the coroner or jurors, and was allowed to deliver much of his testimony jumping haphazardly from one observation to another.

Although Coroner Parker had cautioned that the verdict should not be rushed, the entire inquest and delivery of its findings was conducted in a single day, including a five-hour adjournment for the funeral. Yes, the bodies needed to be arrayed and identified on the Sunday as there was no refrigeration at the Dead House and the corpses were deteriorating, but the identification and burial could have been conducted, and then further and more detailed testimony heard after the funeral.

Perhaps the once-over-lightly inquest can be explained by the fact that just the day before, James Johnson, Coroner Parker, Inspector-General Captain McLerie, Dr Alleyne, jury members Gorman and Raphael and most likely Bully Forbes and other jurors as well had been key participants in the aftermath of a horrific event. It's almost understandable that they wanted to get the inquest over and done with so they could get some rest.

18

The city weeps

The wreck of the *Dunbar* was a defining moment for the city of around 57,000 inhabitants on the edge of a vast inhospitable continent at the bottom of the world. It united Sydneysiders in grief and adversity, just as Gallipoli, the Great Depression and the Covid-19 pandemic would in years to come.

So many of the dead were from Sydney. The colony mourned its own. Uniting in the face of this tragedy hardened the young city's resolve to stand on its own feet and helped forge its identity. Suddenly, because of the events of 20 August 1857, and the days that followed, the populace came to understand that Australia was a land apart and they were a people apart, isolated and separated by distance and circumstance from the old world. The future was in their hands.

Undertakers Messrs Stewart and Dixon had been busy at the Dead House since the first corpses of those who'd been 'thrust out on that wide and unknown sea that tolls round all the world—Eternity' were delivered in their shell coffins. They laid the identified bodies, such as those of Maria Waller and her daughter Polly, Julia Meyer and three of her children, Patrick Downey and Isaac Simmons in polished timber caskets adorned with native flowers and released them to their relatives. Stewart and Dixon placed the bodies that had not been claimed or that were too mutilated to be recognised, along with the recovered body parts, in communal coffins.

At midday on a cold, rainy Monday, as the coronial inquest was conducted nearby, a funeral procession of seven horse-drawn hearses, four mourning coaches and more than 70 carriages, with a troop of mounted police in the vanguard, assembled in the rain-slicked street outside the Dead House. Marking time, stamping their feet and blowing into their hands to keep warm, were the uniformed members of the band of the Royal Artillery who would play the 'Dead March' from Handel's oratorio *Saul* to accompany the sad parade.

In Sydney Cove the ensigns of as many as 40 sailing ships and steamers flew at half-mast. At half-mast, too, were the flags on the buildings of Sydney. The city was said by one to have a 'dismal aspect', while another sensed a 'mournful sublimity'.

The funeral procession from the Dead House to Camperdown Cemetery, a distance of 7.2 kilometres, began its stately crawl just before 5 p.m. It rumbled down George Street to the tollgate at Pitt Street, which marked the western edge of the city. From there, where George Street became Parramatta Street (today's Broadway), the hearses and carriages continued west along Parramatta Street to the intersection of Cooks River Road (today City Road). Then it proceeded 2.6 kilometres south-west along Cooks River Road and King Street to seven-year-old Camperdown Cemetery, which would be the *Dunbar* victims' final resting place.

Camperdown Cemetery and St Stephen's Church are on 5.2 hectares that was granted to William Bligh during his governorship of New South Wales. Bligh called the immediate vicinity of the cemetery O'Connell Town, after Sir Maurice O'Connell, the husband of his daughter, Mary. Sir Maurice was the first to be buried there, in May 1848. At its inception, the cemetery was a scrubby field studded with oak and gum trees. A fig tree was planted by the church and stands there, magnificent, today. Bligh named the cemetery Camperdown to mark the Battle of Kamperduin, waged in 1797 off the coast of Holland, in which he played his part in an English victory over the Dutch and the French. Bishop William Grant Broughton consecrated the cemetery on 16 January 1849.

Lining the route to the burial ground in the grim twilight were more than 20,000 Sydneysiders, 35 per cent of the city's population, their faces pinched by cold and grief.

The greatest concentration of mourners was along George Street and Parramatta Street, with their shops and offices—grand sandstone and brick and clapboard with tattered canvas awnings alike—and factories, all of which had closed their doors at 1 p.m. to allow employees to attend the procession. No government building was allowed to conduct business after 2 p.m. People stood with heads bowed, shoulder to shoulder, three- and four-deep outside Paxton's post office, the late merchant Mary Reibey's house, E. Curtiss House Decorator, the London Hat Shop, the Clapham House Boot and Shoe Mart, the fruit markets on Market Street, the Colonial Sugar Refinery, Tooth's Kent Brewery, Christ Church St Laurence, the Stonemason's Arms and the many other ale houses along the way— some of which, anticipating mourners' need to drown their sorrows, quietly remained open for business.

It was written of that day: 'The footpaths through the streets of the city were literally walled with people. In proportion to the number of inhabitants, never can we recollect a scene where the feelings of the people were so keenly and manifestly exhibited.'

There was heard weeping and mournful sighs from the crowd. Hats were doffed as each hearse passed. There was the snorting and snuffling of the horses and the sound of their hooves, the jingle of bridles, the clatter and splash of carriage wheels on the muddy, rutted ground, the strains of the 'Dead March' and for the second successive day the tolling of church bells from St James' and St Mary's, the Syna-gogue, the Congregational and Presbyterian churches in the city and St John's at Darlinghurst. From Circular Quay and the Paddington barracks came the boom and crack of cannon and rifles fired at one-minute intervals, as was military tradition on such occasions.

The procession was headed by the mounted police, then, on foot, the Royal Artillery band, then the seven closed hearses. One contained the body of the *Dunbar*'s boatswain Charles Sappie. In other coffins, it was reported:

[were] a boy aged 3 or 4 years, name unknown . . . parts of human bodies picked up at the Heads on Sunday by Mr Offutt and Mr McMahon . . . the trunk of a female unknown . . . A young female unknown . . . the body of *Dunbar* apprentice seaman John Gavin . . . the remains of an unnamed seaman . . . a boy supposed to be Master Healing . . . parts of a human body . . . a male supposed to be John [sic] Struthers . . . a female unknown . . . portions of human bodies . . . the trunk of a boy unknown . . .

The seventh hearse carried the Union Jack–draped coffin of Captain John Steane. The carriage was escorted by officers and seamen of Royal Navy vessels the HMS *Herald* and the HMS *Isis*. Steane's hearse was open and his casket was swathed in a Union Jack. A reporter wrote, '"The flag that braved a thousand years the battle and the breeze" covered his coffin, and those who had braved all dangers under its folds were now mourning the untimely fate of him who lay mute beneath it.'

Each hearse was flanked by two mounted policemen. The tragic sight, it was reported, '[diffused] in its simplicity a sad and melancholy feeling through the beholders'.

Then followed the chief mourners in the official mourning coaches, shiny black with gleaming headlamps shining through the descending dusk. In the first was James Johnson. Alongside him were Coroner Parker, Captain Pockley and Inspector-General Captain McLerie. Other mourning coaches, also escorted by mounted police, were occupied by the mayor, Alderman George Thornton (who had cancelled the annual gala mayoral ball as a gesture of respect to the dead); L.H. Scott, who was aide-de-camp to Governor William Thomas Denison; members of parliament; military officers; and senior police. Behind them, stretching back more than a kilometre, were private cabs, buggies and wagons.

The procession was forced to halt for around fifteen minutes when a mourning coach's wheels lodged in a pothole widened and deepened by days of rain. The impeded vehicle was freed and wobbled on.

Earlier in the day, hearses carrying the remains of victims who had been identified and claimed by their families had made their own way to Camperdown Cemetery. The bodies of Maria and Polly Waller and their servant had departed the York Street office of John Gough Waller at 2.45 p.m. They were followed by carriages hired by the Waller family's friends and associates.

The remains of Patrick Downey had been taken from the Forbes Street, Woolloomooloo, home of his friend Thomas Martin at 3 p.m. The Downey cortege, bound not for Camperdown but for Devonshire Street Cemetery, numbered three mourning coaches and around 40 private carriages. Also going to Devonshire Street were the coffins of Isaac Simmons, and Julia Meyer and her children— Rachel, Lewis and Morris—who were all interred at the 'Jews' Burial Ground' there.

After snaking slowly down George Street and along Cooks River Road past Sydney University to Newtown, the procession arrived at the eastern edge of Camperdown Cemetery at 7 p.m. an hour after sunset. A large number of mourners had taken their position earlier in the day at a respectful distance from the fresh-dug gravesite.

The unidentified dead were laid together in the large square pit lined with wooden boards as funeral rites were read by the rector of St Stephen's, Reverend Charles Campbell Kemp. James Johnson and the dignitaries, standing in their heavy coats above the pit, and the hundreds lining the cemetery wall joined in the prayers and the hymns.

Light rain fell from clouds that broke apart now and then to reveal a dim half-moon. The scene was lit by guttering candles and lanterns, which, said one mourner, 'gave the melancholy proceeding a very weird and ghostly aspect'.

At the end, as the gravediggers shovelled earth into the pit, the mourners took a last look at the tomb and quietly dispersed. Coroner Parker, James Johnson, Captain John McLerie and the others involved in the coronial inquest hurried in their carriages back to the King's Arms tavern where Parker would sum up the earlier testimony and the jurors would deliver their findings.

* * * *

All that bleak Monday, while the coronial inquest and the funerals were in progress, the search of Port Jackson and its shores for the *Dunbar* victims, remnants and cargo continued. Insurance agent J.E. Graham led the reconnaissance around Middle Head aboard the steamer *Premier*. He saw 'immense pieces of this noble ship lying high and dry among the rocks; her strong and well-made timber torn to atoms, scattered all over the shore. What a miserable salvage out of so much, broken bales, empty casks, nothing worth saving.'

Graham came upon a body wedged among rocks at Spring Cove, Manly. '[The] deceased,' he noted, 'was a young woman, from 25 to 30 years of age. She was measured, and was found to be 5 feet 6 inches high. She is a beautifully formed woman . . . She had a wedding-ring on her finger, with a plain keeper.' The body was taken to the Dead House where it was soon joined by the headless and handless body of a woman found in the harbour fairway by a fisherman named Joseph Silver.

Another body would be found, thought by Dr Redfern who examined it, to be that of a young man about eighteen, stout of build, around 162 centimetres, with long, fine, light-auburn hair and a fair complexion. The doctor's report continued, 'most of the bones of the neck were gone; the scalp with hair and face remaining; the legs are almost denuded of flesh; the left arm gone, and the right much mutilated . . . the mouth and teeth are perfect, with the exception of the lower jaw, which is fractured'. Because the deceased was found among portions of *Dunbar* wreckage Dr Redfern believed it was safe to assume he was another victim.

The woman with the wedding ring, the young man with the light-auburn hair and the remains of the woman were duly interred in the mass tomb at Camperdown Cemetery. The colony wondered if the horror would ever end.

With the dead needing to be buried speedily, there had been no time for stonemasons to fashion the marble and sandstone head-stones and plaques in time for the mass burial in the tomb and the separate funerals of the Waller family members, Captain Steane, Patrick Downey, Isaac Simmons, little George Healing, and the Logan and Meyer children, John Ridley Jerram and William Butler Williams. When the work was completed, the headstones were taken by horse-drawn carts and mounted on the graves.

Those in the mass grave would lie beneath the inscription: 'Within this tomb were deposited by direction of the Government of New South Wales such remains as could be discovered of the passengers and crew who perished in the ship *Dunbar* . . . which was driven ashore and foundered when approaching the entrance to Port Jackson on the night of the 20th August . . . 1857'. The *Sydney Morning Herald* eulogised that, although these victims' names were unknown, they would be 'regretted with equal sorrow. The fine young men and lads—officers and midshipmen of the *Dunbar*—and many a hardy seaman found a last home beneath the waters of Port Jackson. By their wives, their mothers, and their sisters, they are yet to be lamented with kindred tears, and it must be the universal wish and prayer these sorrows may be softened by resignation to the will of Heaven.'

Although only the bodies of Maria and Polly Waller and their servant were buried beneath the marble Waller family memorial at Camperdown Cemetery, the names of all eight family members, Hannah, Mary, Kilner, Kate, Arthur, Edward, Maria and John, were inscribed upon an imposing monument depicting the *Dunbar* being tossed on stormy seas. The inscription reads:

Beneath this monument rest the mortal remains of Hannah Maria Waller and her eldest daughter Mary Dowling Waller which were found on the extreme shore of Middle Harbour having been washed and drifted there from the wreck of the *Dunbar* which occurred immediately under the signal staff [sic] at the South Head on the night of the 20th August 1857 ... Both Hannah Maria and her husband Kilner Waller (who perished with her and his entire family in the *Dunbar*), were members of the Baptist Church at Launceston, Tasmania, under the pastorate of her father the Rev Henry Dowling.

On the base are the words: 'And here may they rest until the Resurrection Morn when the dead shall be raised and the Son of Man shall send His Angels to gather together his Elect from the four winds, from the uttermost parts of the earth, to the uttermost part of Heaven'.

Captain Steane's headstone, just a metre or two from the mass tomb, reads: 'In memory of John Steane, Esq, post-captain in the Royal Navy, a native of Newport, Isle of Wight, one of the unfortunate sufferers in the *Dunbar*'.

The day after the funeral, 25 August, the *Herald* reflected upon the effect on the colony of the *Dunbar* wreck and tried, and failed, to understand why God would allow such a calamity to occur.

The funeral rites of those who by some accident, doubtless ordained by a higher power, have perished under circumstances which might beset us all, engage our higher interests, and are invested with a solemnity which nothing else can give ... Sad indeed has been every phase of the catastrophe—heart-rending not only to those into whose domestic affections it has brought desolation, but to all who have been compelled to witness the ruthless work of destruction which a hand higher and more powerful than Man's permitted and ordained doubtless for His own appointed purposes ... It is really all too painful now to revert to the circumstances of the case, to believe that a vessel leaving our father-land, crowded principally with colonists who had friends, associations, and sympathies, to greet them on these shores, should have gone down, when the haven of their hope was in their sight, without the possibility of a helping hand being held out to them . . . It is useless to harp on the universality of the sympathy expressed. Nothing else but this calamity has been talked of or thought of for the last three days . . . The city has been involved in a shroud of misery and regret.

But we return to the subject more immediately before us—the funeral rites. It makes little matter how the dead remains were committed to the earth. The rugged sailor, the blooming maiden, the playful child and the aged man—whether recognised or not—will all have their graves hallowed by the prayers of those who now, high in hope for their future welfare, will hold their memory sweet and fragrant. Sad, sad, again we say, to see the miserable remains of this catastrophe. On the beach, in the steamers, in the icy charnelhouse in which they were collected, it was sad and solemn enough to see them.

The article closed with a quote from Samuel Taylor Coleridge's epic poem *The Rime of the Ancient Mariner*: 'The many men so beautiful/ And they all dead did lie'. Women and children, too.

* * * *

Alice Green, at home and pregnant in London's Hackney, did not know that she had been widowed until mid-November when, just as she was about to enter labour, the screw-steamer *Emen* arrived in Marseilles, France, from Australia with the news of the *Dunbar*'s fate and that Captain James Green's body was among those lost at sea, and the news was relayed to London.

It was left to James Green's brother, Malcolm, of whom it was said that he never really recovered all his long life from James' death, and his friends to raise the money for a memorial plaque. Alice, now a widow with a new baby, could not afford a marble tablet. Her husband had bequeathed to her his one-eighth share in the

Duncan Dunbar clipper *Vimeira* and his one-sixteenth share in the *Dunbar*, which of course was now worthless. (Green left his father, Malcolm, £500, and £100 to his brother, Malcolm, and sister, Margaret.)

A meeting of around twenty of James Green's companions, admirers, crew and passengers was held at the Lyons Buildings in Sydney's George Street. The agenda was to 'express their approbation of the acts and conduct which marked the lifetime of the late Captain Green. The gentleman was a credit to his profession, and it was with the deepest regret that all who knew him heard of his death and the loss of his ship.' It was resolved to raise money for a marble plaque honouring Captain Green and in so doing 'console his widow by showing that at a distance of 16,000 miles [sic] they could appreciate all that was good and noble in the deceased'.

The plaque was mounted prominently on the west wall of St James' Church. 'In memory of James Green, commander of the ship *Dunbar*, who perished with all of his passengers and crew save one by the wreck of that vessel at the Sydney Heads in a fearful gale on the night of the 20th of August 1857. This tablet is erected by his former passengers and friends as a token of their respect and esteem.'

In time, there would be a second tribute to Captain Green in the form of a white marble monument with an anchor resting upon a cross. It was installed at South Head Cemetery, in sight of the forbidding cliffs that took his life, his ship and—or so it seemed at the time—his reputation.

19

Recriminations

Nowadays, when satellites and sophisticated communications can beam events as they happen into lounge rooms all over the world, it's startling to realise that news of the *Dunbar* did not reach other parts of Australia for many days. And it was November before anybody in Britain knew, and that includes loved ones of the dead, such as Alice Green, the families of other victims, and the *Dunbar*'s owner, Duncan Dunbar.

Steven Waller, a descendant of the Waller family, says that first news of the tragedy reached Colchester, England, in a telegraph message from a passenger in a ship just arrived in Marseilles from Sydney. It was likely sent via Paris and London to the Reverend Dr Messach Seaman, a Church of England clergyman and educator in Colchester and Essex. The message read: 'The ship *Dunbar*, from London to Sydney, has been totally lost. The crew and passengers, 140 [sic] in number, all perished, except one seaman, Johnson. The cargo was valued at 70,000 pounds.' Seaman notified the editor of the Essex *Standard*:

I am induced to ask the insertion of the above notification in the *Standard*, believing that it will be read with painful interest by many in this town and neighbourhood of Colchester; and to whose recollection it will be brought that among the passengers of the *Dunbar* were Mr Kilner Waller, his wife (a native of this town), six children, as fine a family as eye ever saw; and two female servants. Six of their number were on a visit to me only a short time [ago]. How distressing to reflect that parents, children and servants all perished at the same moment, and have now but their one watery grave. How inscrutable are the ways of Providence. With adoring wonder we add: 'Thy way, O God, is in the sea, and Thy path in the great waters, and Thy footsteps are not known.' Psalms lxxvii.

> Yours, & c., Greenstead Rectory, 17th Nov, 1857.
>
> M Seaman.

Three days later Reverend Dr Seaman sent a postscript to the newspaper: 'From later particulars I learn that there had been between 30 and 40 bodies washed ashore, among which was recognised that of Mrs Kilner Waller, with her daughter clasped in her arms.'

Most British newspapers reprinted sections of Seaman's letter and, as soon as the colonial newspapers docked, the articles that had appeared in the Sydney press in the days after the *Dunbar* was lost, including George Thornton's interview with James Johnson, were published. Obituaries of Captain Green and British passengers, such as the three members of the Healing family from Cheltenham, and crew members were published widely. The Bedfordshire *Mercury*'s journalist ended his report with the words, 'Here then is a tragedy; not the creation of the poet's pen, but alas, a reality.'

The *Standard* accompanied Seaman's letter with an editorial that must have made painful reading for Alice Green and the late captain's family.

After the evidence of [James] Johnson, we cannot help offering the non-nautical, but not, therefore, necessarily un-nautical, opinion that if the *Dunbar* had only taken, for safety's sake, one tack of three or four hours off land an hour after sighting it, this direful calamity would not have happened. Time is of value, but life is of more value. The preservation of the lives of more than a hundred of our fellow-creatures (nay, of one) is of incomparably more importance than the arrival of a clipper six hours sooner than, with prudence, she would have done. This awful calamity involves the loss of lives of 120 [sic] human beings, a fine large and costly ship, and cargo worth about £73,000.

In Sunderland where the *Dunbar* had been built, the ports where she'd anchored, and the towns where victims had lived, there was mourning. Duncan Dunbar himself, though he had lost other ships, was inconsolable. The *Dunbar* and its master were close to his heart. Yet with the tears, there were more bitter recriminations. Taking the *Standard*'s lead, *The Times* of London flayed James Green, accusing him of 'gross carelessness and mismanagement'. Green, 'a man of great experience . . . probably had too much confidence in his own conception of his ship's position. A stranger would have used more caution.'

* * * *

While it took some months for the British media to learn about the *Dunbar* and gang up on James Green, their Australian counterparts had been figuratively keelhauling him since the day after his own and the other victims' funerals.

In the early shock of the disaster, there were kind words for Green and expressions of sadness that such a fine skipper had perished. In those first days with the wound still raw, it would have seemed in bad taste to question his captaincy and apportion blame. And the coronial inquest had attached no blame to Captain Green.

But after the funeral, some in the colony felt a need to find a scapegoat for the loss of life and the ship and, being unable to defend himself, Captain Green who, after all, had chosen to brave the Heads in appalling weather and then miscalculated his position, was a convenient and obvious target.

In parliament, Premier Henry Parker denounced Green's decisions and his confusion on the fatal night. In turn, and with some justification, the Opposition accused Parker of attacking the defenceless captain to divert attention from his government's long-term failure to make Port Jackson safer for shipping by building more light-houses in strategic locations, upgrading the pilot boat service and establishing a telegraph line from the signal station and Macquarie Light to Sydney to replace the unreliable semaphore flags.

In its scathing editorial of Tuesday, 25 August, the *Sydney Morning Herald*, a friend of the Parker government, piled on. The editorial began gently, stating that 'No generous man will refuse a tear to the memory of Captain Green' and praising his 'intrepidity, fortitude, self-reliance', then turned nasty. 'His career was fortunate, until it became fatal. [Green must not] escape the reproach of putting into obvious peril the invaluable interests at his disposal.' The paper claimed, as far as is known without evidence, that Green's decision to enter the Heads may have been motivated by 'a determination to anchor within a given hour', intimating he had made a bet on his arrival date and was determined to win it. Green had tried to enter Port Jackson:

> when prudence and the commonest nautical experience would have made retirement imperative. With the same wind and weather, others stood out to sea, whilst he madly approached a coast where a false manoeuvre or miscalculation would leave no chance of recovery or retreat. The commentary on this sad instance of rashness and folly is a dark and full one . . . We have seen on the shore the fragments of fellow-beings which reproach this cruelty; we have collected from every rock the items of this awful indictment.

Seldom, the editorial continued, did a ship 'bring so many whose loss would be more deeply felt, or felt so long. Who without dry eyes can recall their fate? What a map did time open before them but a few hours ago! So cheerfully did they confide in the commander that although within sight of the coast they retired to rest.'

That Green went down with his ship in no way absolved him of blame. In fact, the newspaper supposed, it was a good thing that Green had died because, 'Had he survived, he would have been haunted with the distressing remembrance of sights and scenes which those who had no share in producing cannot look upon without horror.'

The *Herald*, naturally, stated all the foregoing 'with reluctance and sadness. Captain Green is beyond the reach of human reproach. Those who died with him had no time for complaint. In that agonising instant, other thoughts, we may suppose, occupied their minds. Could we imagine that every cry of anguish and despair fell on the ear of the unfortunate commander as an accusation, he paid a fearful penalty—far more bitter than the bitterness of death.'

The searing editorial infuriated the masters of 35 vessels currently in Port Jackson and they rallied to defend one of their own. In a joint statement, the captains rebuked Captain Green's critics. Green's decision to 'bear up for the port was a judicious one and the verdict found by the jury in the inquest was borne out by the evidence'. Each of them would have done the same thing.

One former captain, calling himself 'Nautilus', said it was unthinkable that Green would ever have risked life, ship and cargo trying to win a bet. Further:

> From all we can learn, Captain Green did all that man could do under the circumstances [to save his ship]. It is unmanly and cruel in the extreme to assail his memory, and perhaps by adding to the already overflowing cup of sorrow, send his young widow broken-hearted to an untimely grave. May she find many kind friends and supporters who will make amends for those who (perhaps thoughtlessly) have driven their fangs deep into her heart.

Happily, Alice Green remarried in 1862, had five more children and lived till 1911.

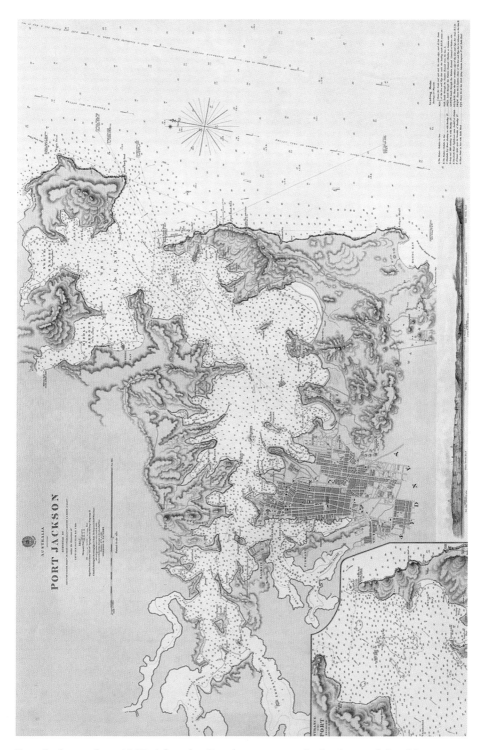

Port Jackson circa 1857. After the *Dunbar* was wrecked, pieces of the ship, cargo and bodies were swept into the waterway and onto the beaches. This chart was created under the supervision of Captain Henry Denham—one of those charged with the grim task of collecting the *Dunbar*'s dead bodies from around Port Jackson. He knew every cove and inlet of the waterway. *National Library of Australia*

Watsons Bay and the Heads circa 1824, as depicted in Joseph Lycett's painting *View of the Heads at the Entrance to Port Jackson*. The flagstaff of the early signal station is at right. *State Library of NSW*

In 1826, artist Augustus Earle completed a lithograph of South Head signal station. Thirty one years later, when the *Dunbar* foundered, more buildings had been added to the signal station site. In the distance to the south is Macquarie Light. *State Library of NSW*

The Gap on a turbulent day. It is believed that the *Dunbar*'s captain James Green mistook the northern bluff of The Gap for North Head. It was on the shelf of the bight, around 850 metres north of where the *Dunbar* smashed into the cliffs, that bodies of victims, cargo and pieces of the ship were washed up. *Larry Writer*

Macquarie Lighthouse was a rendezvous for fashionable nineteenth-century Sydneysiders. Its beam pierced the storm too late to warn Captain Green that his ship was on a fatal collision course with the cliffs of South Head. *Sydney Harbour Trust*

Clippers and steamers on Sydney Harbour in the mid-nineteenth century. The harbour was the beating heart of the colony. *Unknown*

The *Dunbar*, renowned as the safest, fastest and most luxurious clipper in the golden age of sail, offered voyagers a first-class passage from the old world to the new. *State Library Victoria*

David Little's painting captures the sleek, serene beauty of the *Dunbar* in its glory days. The wreck of such a seemingly indestructible ship at the doorstep of Port Jackson and the loss of its passengers, many well-known and much-admired, traumatised Sydney and were catalysts for urgent safety measures to prevent further calamities. *David Little/State Library Victoria*

Dunbar victims Marian Egan (centre), daughter Gertrude and son Henry, sat for this haunting and poignant portrait by an unknown artist shortly before returning home to Sydney. Unfinished when they sailed on the *Dunbar*, the painting arrived safely on the next clipper. *National Portrait Gallery of Australia (purchased with funds provided by the Liangis family, 2014)*

Duncan Dunbar II, photographed in his final year, 1862, reigned over the largest fleet of three-masted clippers on earth, but the *Dunbar* was the millionaire merchant prince's pride and joy. He was shattered by its loss. *Camille Silvy/National Portrait Gallery, London*

The year after it was launched, in 1854 during the Crimean War, the *Dunbar* was requisitioned by the Royal Navy as a troop transport and hospital ship. The clipper is depicted—bottom panel, third from right—among the fleet embarking British troops at Varna. *Illustrated London News*

James Johnson's rescuer, the Icelandic youth Antonio Woolier, descended Jacob's Ladder, a plunging ravine 190 metres north of where the *Dunbar* foundered, and clambered along the wave-smashed rocks to the ledge where the Irish survivor clung. *Larry Writer*

Burly Irishman James Johnson, photographed in Sydney days after his rescue. His natural mental and physical strength helped him survive his 36-hour ordeal on the ledge exposed to the elements and witnessing his shipmates' mutilated bodies below, when others would have surely perished. *Freeman Brothers/Caroline Simpson Library*

Survivor James Johnson in his later years. After a tumultuous life as both rescued and rescuer, he raised a family and found peace and anonymity in Newcastle and then suburban Sydney. To the end, he could hold listeners of all ages spellbound with his tales of the sea. *Australian National Maritime Museum*

The wreck site. At left is the ledge where James Johnson was thrown when the *Dunbar* struck the rocks. At right is Jacob's Ladder ravine, down which Johnson's rescuer Antonio Woolier descended. *Larry Writer*

In the days following the shipwreck, illustrators and writers feverishly turned out booklets and images of the calamity that were snapped up by an insatiable public. These are two artists' imaginings of James Johnson's rescue. *Unknown; James Fryer/* Wreck of the Dunbar

John Pascoe, third officer of the *Dunbar*, was photographed before departing for Sydney. Captain Green, in his confusion, ordered the eighteen-year-old to the top of the forecastle to keep a lookout for North Head in the *Dunbar*'s last minutes before foundering on South Head. *Museum of Applied Arts and Sciences*

Mayor of Sydney George Thornton, politician, businessman and sailor, was prominent on the South Head cliff-top when James Johnson was rescued. Later that day, after witnessing the carnage at the wreck site and The Gap, Thornton conducted the most authoritative interview with the 'miracle survivor'. Eight years later, in 1865, Thornton was the hero when another Dunbar Line clipper, the *Duncan Dunbar*, ran aground off the coast of Brazil. *City of Sydney Archives*

Captain Robert Pockley rose mightily to his grim task. The superintendent of lights, pilots and navigation, and Sydney Cove harbour master, scoured Port Jackson for *Dunbar* victims, and organised the transportation of bodies to the Dead House for identification and subsequent burial.
State Library of NSW

Days after the shipwreck, an unknown person carved this inscription into the cliff-top at the exact point where *Dunbar* sole survivor James Johnson was hauled to safety. In 1906, 49 years to the day after the clipper was destroyed, the weather-beaten markings were reinscribed by local identity Edwin Sautelle. *Unknown*

THE KEEL OF THE DUNBAR AT HUNTER'S BAY, MIDDLE HARBOUR.

As depicted in this illustration that graced one of the commemorative booklets, a section of the *Dunbar*'s keel washed up on a Middle Harbour beach. Other wreckage, cargo and bodies littered Port Jackson. *James Fryer*/Wreck of the Dunbar

In the months after *Dunbar* foundered, deputy master of Sydney Mint and photography pioneer Robert Hunt searched the waters of Port Jackson in his skiff for the belongings of his sisters, *Dunbar* victims Sarah and Emily. On 13 December 1857, Hunt photographed *Dunbar* timbers that had been salvaged and stacked at a Lavender Bay boatshed. *Chau Chak Wing Museum*

Hornby Lighthouse on a rough and stormy day. The light was constructed on the northern tip of South Head in the aftermath of the *Dunbar*'s demise to guide approaching ships to and through Sydney Heads. North Head is in the distance.
Larry Writer

While the body of *Dunbar* captain James Green was never recovered, he and his seafarer brother Malcolm are memorialised at South Head Cemetery, a short distance from where his ship collided with the cliffs.
Larry Writer

(Top) Watsons Bay locals salvaged one of the *Dunbar*'s anchors from the wreck site in 1910. The anchor was displayed in the *Dunbar* Relics museum (centre) at Watsons Bay until 1930 when it was mounted at the south end of The Gap to form part of the *Dunbar* memorial (below).

The *Dunbar*'s bell now resides in the vestibule of St John's Anglican Church, Darlinghurst. A number of the victims' loved ones and friends were parishioners at St John's, which was built the year after the ship was wrecked. *Larry Writer*

A *Dunbar* passenger's denture plate was recovered from the ocean floor by divers. *Australian National Maritime Museum*

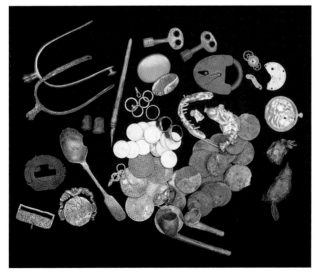

Relics from the wreck site were plundered by scuba divers, but later acquired by the Australian National Maritime Museum for cataloguing and preservation. *Australian National Maritime Museum*

A chest belonging to *Dunbar* victim Captain John Steane, the Royal Navy commander, was found in the days after the wreck. Remarkably, it was in good condition, except the final 'e' of the captain's name on the chest had been dislodged. Today its home is St John's, Darlinghurst. *Larry Writer*

Australasian Pioneers' Club past president John Lanser at the handsome round table fashioned from salvaged *Dunbar* timber that holds pride of place at the club's Sydney premises. *Larry Writer*

Charles and Mary Logan's memorial in St John's Anglican Church, Darlinghurst, to their children Ida, Charles and Arthur who died on the *Dunbar*.
Larry Writer

The mass grave at Camperdown Cemetery where unidentified *Dunbar* victims and recovered body parts were interred on the Monday after the shipwreck, 24 August, after a funeral procession attended by 20,000, 35 per cent of Sydney's population. Another of the ship's anchors lies beside the tomb. *Larry Writer*

'Nautilus' finished:

Had a man by any such motive, as imputed to him, brought about such a dreadful sacrifice of life, do you think he could have looked on so cool and collected as he did in the moment of death? No! To me this is the most conclusive evidence that he acted as any prudent and skilful seaman would have done under the circumstances, and after much deliberation chose what he considered the lesser of two evils; viz, attempted to get into port and thereby save life, rather than attempt to keep to sea and perhaps thereby lose all. After she struck, with death before his eyes, the appalling and indescribable scene which must have followed, the shrieks, groans and prayers of men, women and children, all about to be launched into eternity—if this, I say, were brought about by his wanton recklessness, do you imagine he could have been cool and collected? No, his conscience would have smote him, nothing but the fullest conviction of having to the very fullest extent and utmost of his ability performed his duty to God and man, could have consoled him in such a moment and made him meet his doom with that Christian fortitude which we may well admire and be proud of as the noblest attribute of a British seaman.

A more measured rebuke of Captain Green's critics came from Captain J.C. Tucker, of Lower Fort Street, who had observed Captain Green's expertise, good judgement and 'untiring energy' when he, Tucker, had been a passenger on the *Dunbar* on its maiden voyage to Sydney in 1856.

I feel bound, in justice to the memory of Captain Green, to say that I for one acquit him of all blame; and further, that had I been situated as he was on that ill-fated night, I should most assuredly have run for port, as he attempted to do, rather than risk the chance of working a heavy ship off a dead lee shore, against an increasing gale . . . There was he with a tight and stanch [water-tight] ship, and with possibly an able crew, with a valuable freight also of lives and cargo, and a ship uninsured; there was also a safe port under his lee within an hour's sail. He saw the darkness of the night, he knew also that there was some degree of danger in entering the port in such tempestuous weather.

Captain Green had weighed the situation, did what he thought was best, but had 'failed and was lost'.

Captain Williamson, master of the paddle-steamer *Washington*, made the point:

[that] Captain Green had the choice of two dangers, namely, that of carrying on [with] as much sail as possible on the starboard tack, and endeavouring to keep to sea, and that of running with a fair wind for the Harbour; and, to a person acquainted as he was, there could be no hesitation as to which was the least . . . [but] by losing sight of the light, he lost the only guide to his position. That Captain Green mistook his distance from the lighthouse there can be no doubt; but it is easy to find fault, especially by those who are incapable of decided action themselves.

Captain Bloomfield had been in a similar predicament to James Green.

On my last voyage from London in the *Asa Packer* . . . I made Sydney Light at night in a heavy south east gale . . . and I had the greatest difficulty in making out the entrance [to Port Jackson], in consequence of the driving rain, and I had actually turned the ship's head towards The Gap when I chanced to see its outline in relief against a light cloud which showed me my error only in time to prevent total shipwreck.

The *Dunbar*'s Sydney agent, Smith, Campbell & Co., stood to lose much money when the ship and its cargo were lost, but, emboldened by the captains' defence of James Green, announced: 'Not any remarks of ours could add to the weight of [the captains'] quiet, but insuperable, defence of Captain Green's last act. We shall simply say that we have never heard any master of a vessel more highly spoken of by passengers, officers, or men; or more admired for considerate care, calm courage, upright and faithful conduct, and gentlemanly courtesy.'

Suddenly, on Thursday, 27 August, the *Sydney Morning Herald* changed tack. The newspaper, having, its editorialist wrote, now pored through the coronial inquest testimony and the finding of the jury, revised its opinion. The inquest's exoneration of Captain Green was, after all, 'correct'. The *Herald* now rose above its earlier lambasting of Green by disingenuously claiming, against every journalistic tenet, that its role was not to print facts but to reflect prevailing public opinion—'the pulsation of the day . . . the feelings of the general mind under the present aspect of affairs; which had turned against James Green'. But now that readers, it seemed, believed the pillorying of the *Dunbar*'s captain was unfair, the *Herald* sang another song. Its condemnation of James Green of only days ago should not be taken seriously, it was 'open to contradiction and correction; it can affix no stigma if exaggerated or passionate which a few days will not remove'. Then the *Herald* hypocritically attacked its own correspondents who had 'stigmatise[d] the navigation of the ship with great severity, [those] persons [with] but slender pretensions to professional knowledge to pronounce . . . censure on the unfortunate deceased [captain]'—all offences of which the newspaper itself had been guilty.

Many skippers who had been in similar situations to Captain Green and had to make life or death decisions under extreme duress, and those who had sailed with Green and knew his strengths, thought the *Herald*'s volte-face too glib and too late, and that the damage the newspapers had done—and that the government was still doing—to James Green's reputation was irreparable.

20

Disorder in the house

The *Dunbar* was gone—its remnants lost at sea, lodged in crevices of the harbour foreshores, salvaged or scavenged—but the controversy over how it foundered sailed on. Conflicting opinions about causes and culpability were aired through Sydney, and there were heated scenes in parliament. The 121 crew and passengers who died were not the only victims of the wreck. The conservative New South Wales government of Henry Parker was one more casualty.

Once the funeral and the coronial inquest were over, Opposition leader Charles Cowper, sensing a different kind of blood in the water, attacked the government over its inaction on port safety.

On the morning of 26 August, the Speaker, Sir Daniel Cooper, ignoring the elephant in the room whose name was *Dunbar*, began parliamentary proceedings by announcing that impediments to the government's purchase of Crown Land had been removed. Cowper cut him short. The purchase of Crown Land, he thundered, was 'an inconsequentiality in comparison to the melancholy event at South Head'.

Cowper then demanded that Premier Parker answer questions about the *Dunbar*'s demise without notice. Questions such as: had the government conducted an investigation into whether employees at the signal station had performed their role competently on the night of 20 August? Cowper then asked whether, in light of 'The Coronial jury's verdict expressing a desire that the pilot service should be placed on a better footing,' could a more efficient pilot service, with decked instead of open boats, have saved the *Dunbar*? 'I would like to know whether the honourable member would be prepared to state, without notice, whether anything has been done about it.'

If the answer was 'No', and the government refused to remedy the situation, threatened Cowper, 'it might become the duty of some member on this side of the House to do so'—the implication being that the public demanded immediate action to prevent another disaster and, if Premier Parker was not up to the task, a new government, a Cowper government, would be. Finally, although he well knew the answer was no, Cowper asked whether the government had made any progress on its pledge to establish an electric telegraph line between South Head and Sydney.

Responding, Parker declared that nothing could have saved the *Dunbar*. 'From all I could learn, and so far as I could form an opinion,' he told the House, no blame could be attributed to the staff of the signal station. 'There was no possibility at any time of rendering assistance to the unhappy vessel . . . The night was so thick and so obscured by storms of rain that the light in the lighthouse was at times invisible and at other times it was scarcely possible to distinguish it. From the vessel being so near under the land, I am assured that no human contrivance could have saved her.' All of which was undeniable.

The premier agreed that there was a need for another light at the harbour entrance, but on North Head. As for the adequacy of the pilot service, Parker could see no room for improvement:

I cannot conceive that having decked pilot boats would have been of any use in this case. In fact, I have been informed by people well-acquainted with vessels and their management that this unfortunate ship could have received no assistance in the position in which she was placed and I would beg at once, to allay any such feeling, to say that nothing under any circumstances could have been done for the unfortunate sufferers.

Premier Parker finished by repeating that Captain Green's recklessness, more than any other factor, was responsible for the wreck. 'I am sorry to have to say that the conduct of Captain Green was somewhat rash.' Cowper would not accept that. He rose from his seat and accused Parker of trying to cover up his government's ineptitude by blaming 'one who cannot defend himself'.

Treasurer Stuart Donaldson threw a lifeline to his floundering leader. 'I have been in constant communication with the senior warden of the Light, Pilot and Navigation Board [Captain Pockley],' Donaldson declared, 'and he assures me that everything was done, every means used, if not to save the vessel—for it was too late to do that—to recover the bodies of the unfortunate sufferers, and it is a satisfaction, melancholy as it may be, that no preparation of pilot boats, steam tugs or aught else that could be devised would have saved one single life.'

Donaldson said the signal station staff were beyond reproach. 'With the exception of the dog belonging to Mr Siddins at the Signal Station, not one living creature was aware of the fearful tragedy being enacted down on the water.' True, although Donaldson should have known that Joseph Siddins was the keeper of Macquarie Light, not the signal station, an error that was raucously corrected by his political opponents.

Donaldson was at odds with his leader over the culpability of Captain Green, who, he said, had been neither rash nor incompetent. Considering the storm, and the terrible position he had found himself in, the *Dunbar*'s master had done all that he could to save his ship. The wreck of the *Dunbar*, Donaldson believed, was an unavoidable accident. With the death of James Green, 'No one has lost a nearer or dearer friend than me . . . Captain Green was an intimate friend of mine, and I am perfectly convinced that he must have been in a perfect agony.' When Green realised he was not off North Head but almost under Macquarie Light, 'He must have seen his position and must have well weighed all [the *Dunbar*'s] chances.' He had tried to avert a collision with the cliffs, 'but had failed . . . This was his last hope.'

Donaldson asserted:

no lighthouse on South or North Head, no pilot boat, or electric telegraph system could have prevented the tragedy. It might be some sort of a melancholy satisfaction now to know that . . . no human contrivance could have saved a single life. The very instant she struck the rocks, she went to pieces. The very first blow scattered everything in the shape of hope. The only man saved—a strong, powerfully built man—who escaped by chance, had to dive through the cabin to ensure his safety. What chance, then, had weak women and children? There was not a hope within five minutes after her striking of saving one single life by any means . . .

It had pleased God to place them in that position, and to demand that sacrifice of life, and nothing human could have saved them. There had not ever been the chance of scrambling up the masts, with a last hope of escape, for the vessel fell outwards owing to the steepness of the coast, and not inwards as vessels ordinarily fall with the washing of the sea.

Then it was the turn of Treasurer Donaldson to be contradicted. Opposition member Clark Irving believed that an efficient pilot boat system *could* have brought the *Dunbar* safely through the Heads. He suggested that future shipwrecks off and within Port Jackson may be averted if the pilot station was relocated from Watsons Bay to Botany Bay, 'in which case foreign and British ships would be boarded [by a pilot] before they came to Sydney Heads. Had a pilot been aboard *Dunbar*, she might have been saved.'

Irving had a raft of points to make but was called to order by the Speaker who realised that the government was ill prepared for a debate that day. Irving sat down, but his colleague John Robertson, rising above a speech impediment caused by a cleft palate, shouted to the Speaker that *he* would not be silenced. Robertson, blunt, profane, a heavy drinker who affected bushman's clothes and a full beard, who would be a five-time premier of New South Wales and have the park in Watsons Bay named after him, bellowed across the floor that it was a disgrace that it had taken so long for rescue and reconnaissance vessels to arrive at the site of the wreck on the Saturday, and that the ropes supplied to haul the bodies out of the water were 'totally unsuitable for the purpose'. Moreover, 'After the bodies *were* pulled up—naked men, women and children—there they lay without even a blanket to cover them, exposed to the gaze of the crowd. The whole affair was most disgraceful to the country.'

What all protagonists did agree on was that safety measures protecting, as far as possible, the lives of voyagers and maritime commerce had to be decided upon and put into practice without further delay. Those who died on the *Dunbar* must not have lost their lives in vain.

* * * *

A letter to the press from an old-time seaman calling himself 'DP' summed up exactly what needed to be done and was widely read and heeded by decision-makers. DP began by stating that entering Sydney Heads at night was not for the inexperienced master.

With the wind off the land, smooth water, moon, stars and all other assistances of that kind, it may be well enough, but even then it is fit to shake the nerves of a man coming off a long voyage when he gets fairly in the entrance—for the light is then lost—and sees nothing but the towers of black rock in one unbroken line frowning defiance at him. If such be the coast when a weather-shore [that is, when the wind is a westerly], what must it be when a lee one [when the wind was from the east-south-east, as on 20 August]? The Harbour is well enough to make, no one can contradict that, but with a strong wind blowing on the land, the ship scudding, and thick sudden showers of rain, the characteristic of our east winds, making the darkness impenetrable; there perhaps is not another port in the world more terribly confusing to a seaman to *enter* than the loudly lauded one of Sydney. In most other ports, or estuaries, many mistakes may be made, and yet with little or no loss of life; here there can be only one made, but that is the final and the fatal one. An error of a little half-mile [800 metres], as in the case of the poor *Dunbar*, and all is lost; a single look from the most inexperienced eye reads on that rampart of cliffs nothing but rude and mangled death.

What needed to be done, continued DP, was obvious.

Prevention the first: More lights. Had I, or any other, a twelvemonth ago, written as much, we would have been pooh-poohed for our pains. Had we been able to advance the matter in the House of Parliament, we should have been told by the Government . . . 'that the country could not afford more lights.' But the country can't, and the people won't, afford any more losses like the last one, and therefore now it can be both boldly said and written that something must and shall be done in the matter.

The best location for a new lighthouse to safely guide ships into Port Jackson, maintained DP,

[was] where the turning point of the [Port Jackson] entrance takes place—in this case the *low point* of the South Reef—a red light visible eight miles [13 kilometres] . . . Every seaman knows that a light on a high cliff in thick rain squalls, which is the weather we have here to dread, is not so easily seen as a light placed a moderate distance above the water's edge. And perhaps it would not be at all amiss to say in the *Sailing Directions for the Port of Sydney* that unless such leading light

is seen, no sailing vessel with an east wind at night should attempt the entrance without a pilot, as long as she can keep to sea.

The second way to make sailing into the port of Sydney safer was

> to have a more effective system of pilotage at Port Jackson Heads . . . I do not for a moment throw blame or slur upon the pilots now at the Heads, but I think it disgraceful to the Government of New South Wales that such a paltry system should be kept alive when I see the way they manage things in Melbourne. It strikes me very forcibly that a pilot cutter—one of those craft that can keep the sea in any weather, would be very beneficial in preventing any more wrecks like that of the *Dunbar* . . . Had such a vessel with six or any other number of good men and true in her been cruising off the Sydney Heads, we should not now have to lament the loss of the *Dunbar*.

With the Opposition, the press and the public clamouring for action, the government wasted no time. Treasurer Donaldson announced that Captain Pockley's Light, Pilot and Navigation Board would investigate measures to prevent similar accidents. The board's findings would be tabled in parliament at the earliest opportunity and then put into effect.

If those on the Light, Pilot and Navigation Board welcomed input, well, the people of Sydney were happy to provide it. While the board was deliberating, there were public meetings in Hyde Park and the Domain and petitions listing solutions were delivered to politicians' doors. Many newspaper pages were devoted to editorials and letters from veteran seafarers weighing in with their theories on making Port Jackson safe. The *Herald* prefaced a swag of readers' letters, safety proposals, eulogies to victims and ever-more-graphic retellings of the *Dunbar*'s demise with the observation that while the sun was now shining on Sydney, 'as if she sought to efface by her smiles the dark recollections of last week', no sunshine could mend the broken hearts of Sydneysiders.

The wreck of the *Dunbar* is still in everybody's mouth, still knots of idlers gather at the corners of streets to comment upon the fatal event, still in clubs and coffee-houses does the ill-fated vessel form the topic of conversation, and still does the heartburning tear in the quiet retirement of the chamber, bear witness to the extent of the calamity. *Dunbar*'s fate is the all-engrossing, saddening topic in town and country.

21

Keepsakes and chronicles

While politicians bickered and the Light, Pilot and Navigation Board pondered and costed ways to make entering Port Jackson safer, others were cashing in. Capitalising on the obsession with the *Dunbar*, enterprising entrepreneurs, newspaper editors, writers of lurid and sentimental booklets, artists, poets and makers of mementoes were realising that the public was prepared to buy anything related to the *Dunbar*.

Day after day, the *Herald* and *The Empire* broke circulation records slaking readers' thirst with black-bordered special editions. Boasting about how it had sold 15,000 copies on the Saturday after the wreck, *The Empire* reported that, 'On no occasion during the late [Crimean] war did the exciting intelligence brought by the English mails produce so general a feeling of anxious enquiry as was manifested, to learn the truth concerning the ill-fated *Dunbar*, and never have we witnessed such widespread visible grief pervading the public mind of any community as might be seen in the faces of our citizens during the last three days.'

The chronicles were not just read, but stored in desks and on sideboards as mementoes. One of Sydney's most prolific and opinionated social commentators in the mid-1800s was an English emigrant named Richard Rowe, who used the pseudonym 'Peter Possum'. His ripe eulogy, 'The Wreck of the *Dunbar*', was clipped from newspapers and treasured by the Sydneysiders it touched.

> Such a catastrophe as the wreck of the *Dunbar* shows man his little-ness. That 'oak leviathan' melted 'like the snowy flake into the yeast of waves'—crushed, almost literally, into powder, in a moment, by the ruthless sea! All the attendant circumstances, moreover, are so harrow-ing. The time—the place—peaceful slumber in the ship, sweet dreams of friendly hands to be clasped upon the morrow, proud dreams of coming fame and fortune; and then at the very entrance of the port, on the threshold, as it were, of home, the death the weary wanderers have dodged for 16,000 miles stands grinning horribly to think it has them yet, and seizes, at one fell swoop, its prey. As I write, I see the waters brightly blue, and hear their low ripple on the shore; and I feel as I should towards a smooth-faced, soft-spoken, human traitor. For I hear, also, the thunder of the billow as it dashes the proud ship on the rocks, and the wild despairing shriek that rises above the fury of the storm; and I see the sharks at their bloody banquet, and corpses floating thick as seaweed on the surge. May God have received the dead, and comfort those who mourn them.

It took only a day or two after the *Dunbar* went down for objects recovered by salvors and scavengers from the waters and beaches of Port Jackson to begin turning up in Sydney's shops. Prices charged by the profiteers were exorbitant—and some of the relics may even have been authentic. Those not interested in, or unable to afford, a box or toy, a piece of clothing or a chunk of timber purportedly from the *Dunbar* could purchase any of a plethora of other souvenirs.

Printing presses cranked out thousands of copies of George Bradshaw's threepenny booklet *The Wreck of the* Dunbar, which was published just five days after the tragedy. The text was illus-trated with sketches of the *Dunbar* under sail 'from a painting by

Foster of London, the celebrated marine painter': 'The Entrance to the Heads', 'The Morning After the Wreck', 'Bodies Washing Ashore at Middle Harbour', the 'Dreadful Gap' and 'The intrepid James Johnson'.

Four days after Bradshaw's publication, on 29 August, James Fryer's *A Narrative of the Melancholy Wreck of the* Dunbar, *Merchant Ship, on the South Head of Port Jackson, August 20th, 1857 with Illustrations of the Principal Localities*, price one shilling, went on sale. It was illustrated with drawings by artists George French Angas and Edmund Thomas, who sketched the view of The Gap from Jacobs Ladder, the keel of the ship lying on the shore in Middle Harbour, the crowds at The Gap on the Saturday, the rescue of James Johnson, and a map of South Head. *A Narrative of the Melancholy Wreck of the* Dunbar sold out its 6000-copy print run in days and a reprint was hastily ordered.

James Fryer began his booklet by explaining that his aim was to satisfy the public's 'eager, restless craving' for information about the *Dunbar*, and to tell the tale clearly and calmly, in contrast to, he sniffed, so many of his competitors who offered only 'vague, hurried and contradictory' accounts. Fryer wanted it known that he had been careful not to 'give offence to the most fastidious delicacy, or to trespass in any way upon the sorrows of our afflicted fellow citizens, for whom we feel such a sincere but unavailing sympathy'—which did not prevent him reeling off in gaudy detail the horrors of the wreck.

On the heels of Bradford and Fryer came seven editions of the sixpenny *Illustrated Authentic Narrative of the Loss of the* Dunbar *With a List of Passengers and Crew* by H. Bancroft, *The* Dunbar *Letter Paper* by J.R. Clarke, and *The Scene of the Wreck of the* Dunbar. Even a pamphlet of the sermon delivered by Reverend Kemp at the mass burial at Camperdown Cemetery was a bestseller.

The publishers of these booklets suggested that they might be an ideal gift for friends and relatives in England. James Fryer made it known that eight copies of his 'work possessing the greatest possible interest to home readers on receiving news of this awful catastrophe' could be shipped to London on the next available clipper for just eight pence.

J.R. Clarke followed up his *The* Dunbar *Letter Paper* with a commemorative print. He advertised that:

> [he had] just published an excellent view of the locality of the late wreck. The engraving is printed on fine letter paper with fly-leaf, for correspondence. Persons will thus have the opportunity of sending with their letters home by the next mail a truthful picture of the scene of the late disaster, with the sad details of which many a pen will be busy during the next few days. The opportunity, we have no doubt, will be extensively availed of. The engraving, which is finely executed on wood, is by Mr WG Mason, after a drawing by Mr E Thomas.

Paintings, some with artistic merit, others crude affairs dashed off in an hour or two, were exhibited for sale. Among the former was goldfields artist Samuel Thomas Gill's watercolour that captured the forbidding darkness and the raging sea as the *Dunbar* is swept onto the rocks. A fine line drawing by Évremond de Bérard depicted a despairing James Johnson on his ledge surrounded by *Dunbar* debris. Although it has never been confirmed as specifically representing the *Dunbar*, Conrad Martens' superb and evocative watercolour of a wrecked ship at precisely the point where the *Dunbar* foundered probably does. The former Royal Navy man and gold-seeker George Frederick Gregory painted the majestic *Dunbar* in the open sea, and also in its last moments as South Head menaces her under a leaden sky. Topographical artist Edmund Thomas was one of the many who rushed to South Head on the Saturday to witness what was left of the *Dunbar*. As well as his illustrations for James Fryer's booklet, he produced a striking panoramic watercolour. In its centre, the *Dunbar*'s topmast, protruding from the waves, is pounded by the swell. Other debris floats nearby. The skies are dirty brown and the sea a morbid grey. A reconnaissance steamer approaches the scene from around inner South Head. On the cliff-top in front of the signal station flag-staff stand two windswept figures, one pointing down to the wreck. In the left foreground, two uninterested goats occupy a ledge.

'The End of *Dunbar*' was a chapter in the 1864 novel, *Twenty Straws*, about convict transportation to Sydney. Its author was the Sydney actress Eliza Winstanley. *Twenty Straws* was dramatised and performed by a cast featuring Winstanley at the Britannia Theatre in London.

Poems about the *Dunbar* were published and recited in taverns and drawing rooms. Historian Samuel Bennett's 'The Wreck of the *Dunbar*' was likely modelled on Alfred, Lord Tennyson's galloping 1854 epic, 'Charge of the Light Brigade'. Bennett, like Tennyson, was guilty of a little poetic licence. For instance, Bennett has Captain Green deciding at first to stay out at sea, then changing his mind and making a run for Sydney Cove; and in the poem, the sun is shining on the Friday and Saturday after the wreck when the storm did not begin to abate until Monday.

Bennett's poem begins by chronicling the grandeur of the *Dunbar* and the optimism of its passengers as they sail from England, bound for Sydney:

Her broad wing spreading to the breeze, she sailed in all her pride
For the shores of far Australia—o'er the waste of waters wide;
France on her weather quarter—on her lee our fatherland,
A sturdy crew before the mast, a brave man in command
As rich a cargo in her hold, as good ship ever bore,
Her officers as staunch and bold as the old seadogs of yore.
Full-freighted, too, with English hearts her gilded cabins were—
The youthful and the talented, the beautiful, the fair,
The parent with his household, and the young and wealthy heir . . .

Music and dance on quarter deck, tough yarns before the mast,
With the merry souls in that good ship the time flew quickly past.
We see her with a channel breeze, spread every stitch of sail,

We see her topsails double-reefed before a Biscay gale;
Five thousand leagues of watery waste that gallant ship had crossed;
And still upon that watery waste her heaving hull was tossed.

And 'The Wreck of the *Dunbar*' ends with the clipper's demise:

The sudden shock of wind and tide
Brought down that proud ship on her side,
And made her topmasts reel,
And every timber groan and quake,
And every plank and stanchion shake,
From her bulwarks to her keel.

The passengers rushed crowding, half naked, from below—
The murky darkness shrouding their features pale with woe.
'Port! Hard your helm!' Those fatal words, alas! too soon were
given,
By the next sea that doomed ship was in the breakers driven.
The dark cliffs looming overhead—the mad waves driving past—
her rudder swaying helpless—torn hull and reeling mast.
With staggering shocks, the jagged rocks drove through her
quivering side,
And in their course, with crushing force, burst through the
whelming tide . . .

Ghostly gleamed those anxious faces,
Closely crowding in their flight—
Last adieus and wild embraces—
Spectres in that lurid light.
Scarce half awoke from slumber,
By voices loud and hurried,
Some of that fated number
Between the decks were buried.
Bewildered by the fearful crash,

Confusion, and dismay,
To the rushing waters' whelming dash
They fell an easy prey.

Through gaping seams the briny streams poured like a torrent in,
All cries for help and succour drowned in that horrid din.
Alas no power but heaven its aid could now afford;
Her hull is torn and riven, her masts gone by the board;
The wild winds hoarse pour all their force on that devoted wreck,
Huge seas break o'er her bulwarks and sweep her shattered deck;
Her loosened sails are thrashing, in a thousand ribbons torn,
Her keel and timbers crashing on great waves upborne . . .

In cavern dark the greedy shark
Feasted on morsels rare!
What food for him, the monster grim!
The brave, the young, the fair! . . .

The cargo of that gallant ship floats scattered o'er the main—
The choicest brands of distant lands—the ruddy wines of Spain,
And fruits from sunny Grecian isles, and spices from Cathay,
And gorgeous silks from Lyons looms, and furs from Hudson's Bay—
And prints from busy Manchester, and linens from Belfast,
And tweeds and drills from Glasgow mills were on the waters cast,
And diamonds from Golconda, and pearls from fair Ceylon
(Once rescued from the greedy sea) to that greedy sea have gone;
But valued more than ruby rare, or pearl, or diamond bright,
Were those loved ones who went down to death on that fatal
    August night . . .

Hot tears are dimming many an eye, and many a cheek is pale;
On every hand, as through the land, is told the dismal tale.
The widowed wife her husband mourns—the children mourn
    their sire,

And the loving eye of maiden sky has paled its wonted fire.
The sister for her brother weeps—the mother mourns her son;
Yet when they pray, shall each one say,
'Father, Thy will be done!'

In contrast to Bennett's rollicking ballad was Henry Kendall's restrained and mournful '*Dunbar, 1857*', which was written to be read rather than chanted in a tavern. The prolific bush poet's tribute to the clipper and those upon it was informed by his lifelong melancholia, his early years on a whaler and his ownership of a timber transport vessel on the south coast of New South Wales which sank in 1832 with the loss of all hands.

Gloomy cliffs so worn and wasted, with the washing of the waves,
Are ye not like giant tombstones round those lovely ocean graves?
Are ye not the sad memorials telling of a mighty grief
Dark with records ground and lettered into covered rock and reef?
Oh, ye show them, and I know them, and my thoughts in morning go
Down among your soulless caverns deep into the surf below.
Oh, ye bear them and declare them and o'er every cleft and scar,
I have wept for dear dead brothers, perished in the lost *Dunbar*.
Ye smitten—ye battered, and splintered and shattered, cliffs of
    the sea.
As we stooped and moaned in darkness, eyes might strain and
    hearts might plead
For our darlings crying widely, they would never rise nor heed!
Aye, we yearned into their faces, looking for life in vain,
Wailing like to children blinded in a mist of pain!
Dear hands clenched and dear eyes rigid, in a stern and stony stare,
Dear lips white from past afflictions, dead to all our mad despair.
Ah, the groanings and the moanings; ah! The thoughts rise in tears,
When we turn to all those loved ones, looking backwards through
    the years!
The fathers and mothers, and sisters and brothers, drowned at sea.

* * * *

217

Out in Port Jackson, pieces of the *Dunbar* still floated on the tide and lay on beaches. The police's campaign to arrest scavengers and unauthorised salvors plundering its cargo and wreckage was having only limited success, for as soon as night fell, scroungers descended on the *Dunbar*'s dismembered beams and planks and took its iron and copper. Mitchell & Co. Chandlers, the official salvor of the wreck with George Green, official receiver of the cargoes of the *Dunbar*, whose Lavender Bay shipyard was authorised to store and sell the timbers and other items from the clipper, and Muriel & Miller the auctioneer, published a notice:

> CAUTION, All persons who may have picked up or taken any portion of the wreck of the *Dunbar* are requested to deliver up the same to Mr George Green, or the undersigned, and all parties in whose possession any part of the property is found after Saturday next 29th August, will be prosecuted. This CAUTION is especially directed to several parties who are known to have been engaged removing the copper and bolts. (Signed) Mitchell & Co, Circular Quay.

Much of the clipper's timber collected from Outer South Head and the waters of Port Jackson was stored at George Green's boat yard in Lavender Bay. Green and his partner, whose name was Francis, purchased from the Dunbar line for £182 and 10 pence what was left of the uninsured *Dunbar*—which had cost £30,000 to build—that the scavengers had left behind—including teak and oak and copper fastenings and bolts. He sold the timber and iron to boat builders and furniture-makers at a profit. Attempts had been made to raise the *Dunbar*'s heavy anchors, which had wedged in rocks, but this had proved too difficult for hard-hat divers who were also thwarted by the undertow.

In George Green's possession were some of the *Dunbar* passengers' and crew's belongings. He posted an advertisement:

> To whom it may concern . . . I have collected a quantity of bale goods, wearing apparel, boots, shoes and other articles of merchandise,

upon which no marks are visible, and which can now be inspected upon application to me, and received by the owners on payment of expenses and my salvage. If not claimed within 20 days of this date, I will cause the same to be sold by public auction.

* * * *

As ubiquitous around Sydney as the *Dunbar* paintings, booklets, souvenirs and special edition newspapers were photographs of James Johnson. Another by-product of the tragedy was that he became the toast of Sydney, a genuine celebrity.

Having been the prime witness at the coronial inquest and the funeral and written about in newspapers and booklets, the 'miracle survivor' could not appear in public without attracting a crowd and being offered ale, food and clothing in return for telling his story.

Being the centre of attention must have discomfited this stolid, ingenuous man. Yet, for a while, Johnson had little choice but to play along. He was short of money—the agents of the *Dunbar* agreed to pay him his wages but, in a nineteenth-century Catch-22, he would have to collect them in London—and could not get on with his life because the maritime authorities and police kept summoning him for information about the wreck. Basil Lubbock wrote in *The Colonial Clippers*, 'Sympathy of a very practical nature poured in upon him and for some days he was the lion of Sydney, with pockets full of money, a girl on each arm, and a crowd of admirers in his train. He soon became a familiar figure in the streets and at theatres and music halls.'

There is no evidence to support Mark Twain's claim in *Following the Equator* that Johnson 'was a man with a practical turn of mind, and he hired a hall in Sydney and exhibited himself at sixpence a head till he exhausted the output of the goldfields that year'.

But James Johnson's 'pockets full of money' soon were empty again and for many months, while looking for employment, he survived on £51 donated by the citizens of Sydney in a charity drive organised by his admirers W.E. Lenthall, W. Whitbread and a photographer named J. Gow. Members of the public, rich and poor, as well as the politician, journalist, future long-serving premier of New South Wales and 'Father of Federation' Henry Parkes, gave money to Johnson. Parkes' contribution was £1 and 12 shillings. John Gough Waller, though grief-stricken himself, gave £1. Another prominent donor was John Fairfax, owner and publisher of the *Sydney Morning Herald* and founder of the media dynasty, who donated £1 and 1 shilling (a guinea) to the fund. Considering the record number of his newspapers that Johnson's name had sold, it seemed the least Fairfax could do.

To cash in on the colonists' obsession with the *Dunbar* and Johnson, a photographer, Thomas Glaister, photographed the survivor free of charge. He posted the large-format hand-coloured ambrotype photo prominently in the front window of his Excelsior Photographic Galleries in Pitt Street and sold prints to customers. We see Johnson from the waist up, half-turning to his left. It is just days after his rescue and his weather-beaten face and chapped lips and the haunted, dazed look in his dark eyes betray his nightmare on the ledge. Johnson's long hair is thick and black and his Captain Ahab–style chin beard is full. Johnson's powerful torso strains the seams of his heavy woollen coat with shoulder cloak and he wears a white shirt and scarf necktie. The clothing was likely a gift, or perhaps a photographer's prop.

Other photographers to profit from Johnson's time in the spotlight were J.W. Denslow who sold numerous prints of his photo of Johnson in a casual pose, and the Freeman brothers who photographed the Irishman and hawked 'worthy of a frame' prints of their collodiotype image on the streets 'so those who wish to possess a memorial of the shipwreck can procure copies'.

Johnson soon wearied of his celebrity; to avoid being recognised by well-meaning but intrusive strangers, he cut off his distinctive hair and shaved his beard. His makeover had an unfortunate outcome when Johnson and his supporters, Whitbread and Gow, arrived at the London Tavern in Paddington to solicit donations. A resident of the hotel, named Hatch, not recognising the clean-shaven Irishman, accused Whitbread of trying to extort money from him under false pretences. Hatch, Whitbread later told a magistrate, called him 'an impostor, a swindling scoundrel, and had applied other opprobrious designations which need not be repeated'. Because, averred Whitbread, the incident happened on a public street outside the London Tavern within earshot of passers-by, Whitbread sued Hatch for defamation. At the hearing, Hatch denied abusing Whitbread and claimed that their conversation occurred *inside* the hotel where nobody could hear what was said. Further, insisted Hatch, it was Whitbread who had vilified *him*. Whitbread's lawyer offered Hatch the chance to apologise to his client and pay court costs in return for Whitbread dropping his charges. Hatch refused. The judge somehow decided that, even if Hatch had called Whitbread an impostor and a swindling scoundrel, Whitbread's 'character had sustained no injury' and found for the defendant. There is no record of James Johnson being present at these proceedings, but, seeing that his newly cropped head and smooth cheeks were the catalyst for the unfortunate affair, and that he was grateful for Whitbread's kindness to him, he probably was.

Inevitably, the public's interest in Johnson waned and he lived quietly and anonymously in Sydney, working as a pilot boat crewman and then as a member of Captain Robert Pockley's boat crew. He went to Queensland to prospect for gold. Unsuccessful, he returned to Sydney and was employed as a customs officer. He married Mary Keenan in 1860, and they had four daughters, Mary, Jane, Catherine and Margaret. The family moved to Newcastle in 1870.

Johnson never returned to Great Britain, nor did he again voyage overseas, but he did watch over the sea, as assistant lighthouse keeper at Nobby's Head at Newcastle Harbour, and coxswain of the harbour master's boat. He was encouraged to take the assistant keeper's job by his brother, Henry, who was himself a lighthouse keeper. Johnson was on duty when an extraordinary irony dragged him back into the headlines, and rekindled memories of his glory days as the lone survivor of the wreck of the *Dunbar*.

22

Lightning strikes twice

On 7 September 1857, the teetering conservative Parker government resigned and, after a six-week election campaign, it was replaced by the progressive administration of Charles Cowper. Making Port Jackson safer for ships was high on the new administration's agenda, and, said Premier Cowper, as soon as the report of the Light, Pilot and Navigation Board was delivered, it would be acted upon.

But, even as the board's recommendations were being finalised, a second clipper came to grief in Port Jackson with loss of life and cargo.

Like the *Dunbar*, the *Catherine Adamson*, built in Aberdeen, Scotland, in 1855, was speedy and graceful. Known as 'The Queen Ship of the Anglo-Colonial Vessels' for its record-breaking passages, the 803-tonne, 54.5-metre *Catherine Adamson* was on its third voyage to Sydney.

On Friday, 23 October 1857, around 9.30 p.m., she was hove-to outside Sydney Heads after an 86-day voyage from Falmouth, England. Captain George Stewart, a master of 'zeal and perseverance', had ordered that a blue flare be fired to summon a pilot from Watsons Bay to guide his ship into Sydney Cove. The wind was fresh from the south-west, the seas rough and growing rougher. On board were eight passengers, 34 crew, four horses and two bulls. The cargo, valued at £75,000, included brass, copper and iron, perfume, jewellery, muslin, cotton and silk, and 10,000 gallons (45,000 litres) of rum, 4000 gallons (18,000 litres) of brandy, 1500 gallons (6800 litres) of other spirits, 4500 gallons (20,000 litres) of wine and 156 barrels of beer. With such liquid treasure on board, the vessel was eagerly awaited by a thirsty colony.

Although the pilot service had an aversion to piloting when it was needed—that is, in rough weather—the supervisor assigned experienced pilot Captain John Hawkes, who had been prominent in the search for the *Dunbar* victims and given evidence to the Light, Pilot and Navigation Board inquiry into maritime safety, to be rowed to the *Catherine Adamson*. Arriving at the clipper an hour after the blue flare was fired, Hawkes climbed a rope ladder onto the deck where he was welcomed by Captain Stewart. As was customary, Stewart gave Hawkes navigational control, while retaining overall command.

Once through the Heads, the *Catherine Adamson* encountered heavy rain and wind squalls. Captain Stewart feared the rising winds and waves would drive his ship onto North Head, and wanted to retreat back out through the Heads to weather the gathering storm at sea. He was countermanded by Hawkes who saw no reason not to continue to Sydney Cove. When Stewart protested, and ordered Hawkes to, 'Take her out to the open sea. With this ship you have to keep her clean full and haul the main yard around as soon as she is head to wind!', Hawkes snapped back, 'Don't tell me what to do. I've had so many of these ships that I know how to handle her well enough.' The men continued to squabble, but the pilot prevailed. He ordered that the foresail be set, the topsails, jib, courses and spanker double-reefed and that the helmsman press on into Sydney Cove.

Now the winds strengthened into a south-westerly gale—'blowing straight out of the Harbour', said Captain Stewart later—that tore away the *Catherine Adamson*'s foresheet and blasted the ship off course. Hawkes tried to make for the shelter of Watsons Bay, but then again changed his mind and ordered the crew to run for Spring Cove, just west of the quarantine station on inner North Head.

Their oilskins giving little protection from the rain and wind, the captain and the pilot continued to snarl and gesticulate at each other in front of alarmed passengers and crew. Stewart again cried that the clipper's only chance of survival was to run hard for the open sea. Hawkes, who was by now regretting his decision to reach Sydney Cove, responded, 'It's too late for that.'

The *Catherine Adamson* was at the mercy of the gale, swept helplessly leeward towards the reefs and rocky headlands of the southern-facing shore of North Head where rollers surged and broke. A 'highly agitated' Hawkes ordered both anchors dropped. The anchors bit, and the clipper, all its sails now clewed and furled, jolted to a halt 100 metres from a towering rock formation known as Old Man's Hat, after the flat tam-o'-shanter–shaped rock that seemed to teeter atop it. The vessel would be safe, for now.

Around midnight, the already powerful swell grew stronger and the *Catherine Adamson* began dragging its anchors and was heaved towards the rocks. Distress flares were lit and the paddle-steamer *Williams*, which had arrived in Port Jackson that night from the Hunter River, sped to the scene and pulled alongside the stricken clipper.

A *Catherine Adamson* passenger named Archibald Blair later testified at the coronial inquest:

> I called to the other passengers to come onto the poop, and requested the pilot to put us onboard the steamer, as we could be of no use to the ship, which I believed would soon go ashore, and I was apprehensive of danger. The pilot told us that there was no danger, that the ship was quite safe. I replied to the pilot that there *was* danger, that if the wind changed there was not room for the ship to play round.

Captain Creer on the *Williams* loud-hailed Hawkes to fling him a rope so the steamer could tow the *Catherine Adamson* to safety. Hawkes yelled back that the *Williams* did not have sufficient power and that Creer should hurry to Watsons Bay across the harbour and alert the signal station superintendent, James Graham, who would despatch a horseman to Sydney Cove to fetch the steam tug *Washington*. Bellowing above the wind, Creer replied that there was no time for that and, besides, 'We're 20 horsepower stronger than any tug! Send us a rope, you fool!' At that, Hawkes backed down and threw a rope to the *Williams*. It snapped.

Next, some crew members of the *Catherine Adamson* attached a tow cable to its bulwark and lowered a small boat, called a gig, to carry the rest of the cable to the *Williams*. In the wild seas, the gig collided with the *Williams'* paddle wheel and both were damaged. A pilot boat now appeared and tried to get a line across to the stricken clipper, to no avail.

Just before 3 a.m., a lifeboat with 21 occupants was lowered over the side of the *Catherine Adamson*. One of those occupants was Captain Stewart. Later, when called on to explain why he abandoned ship, he insisted that he simply wanted to instruct Captain Creer face to face on the best way to save his passengers, crew and cargo.

The lifeboat was still dangling above the water when the *Catherine Adamson*'s anchors finally slipped and it crunched stern-first onto the reef. The waves smashed the clipper repeatedly onto the rocks, and turned it broadside. The lifeboat dropped into the sea and was swamped. There were screams of 'Save us! Save us!' from those who'd climbed the masts and clung to the rigging. Said a survivor, 'I wept when I heard their cries.' The sea made a clean breach over the *Catherine Adamson*, its masts cracked and toppled and it came apart. Twenty-one perished.

Captain Creer and his paddle-steamer crew managed to haul on board some who clung to the lifeboat. Then, unable to do more and with the *Williams* in danger itself of being jammed onto the reef, Creer steamed to Watsons Bay to raise the alarm. The survivors huddled below decks dazed, injured and drenched.

When the *Williams*, a number of pilot boats and the steamer *Washington* returned to Old Man's Hat at dawn, the *Catherine Adamson*'s bowsprit and forecastle protruded forlornly from the water. Of the 21 who perished, only five bodies were found. Some had been attacked by sharks. One corpse was that of Captain John Hawkes.

A bull that had scrambled to shore stood under the overhang of Old Man's Hat, surrounded by flotsam and barrels of beer.

Human scavengers were as voracious as the sharks, with alcohol the most prized booty. Long before Captain Pockley, Captain McLerie and his water police, Lloyd's of London insurance agent Graham, and cargo receiver George Green arrived to claim the goods and wreckage scattered in the water and on the beaches and headlands of inner North Head, much had been taken by the swarming pilferers, no doubt including many who had also looted the *Dunbar*.

The five recovered bodies were formally identified at the Dead House, then interred in the same tomb as the *Dunbar*'s dead at Camperdown Cemetery.

When Captain Stewart appeared before the coronial inquest at the King's Arms pub in The Rocks he had much to explain. One juror said he should have shown 'greater intrepidity and decision [and] seized some of the many opportunities to put his passengers and crew in safety'. He had not attempted to help 'a crowd of passengers and seamen on the forecastle of his ship, stretching out their hands, uttering piercing cries for help, which never came'. Another criticism levelled at Stewart was that he had allowed himself to be bullied by Captain Hawkes. Coroner John Skottowe Parker said, 'We can believe Captain Stewart is both a humane and courageous man, but nothing can compensate for the loss of presence of mind in the hour of danger.' It was put to Stewart by a juror that his decision to leave his ship and clamber into the lifeboat was evidence of his 'selfish haste and unmanly despair'. Regardless, eight of the thirteen jurors exonerated Stewart of any blame for the loss of the *Catherine Adamson*.

But Captain John Hawkes, like James Green, was posthumously vilified. Despite Coroner Parker initially praising Hawkes, who was survived by a widow and four young children, as a 'sober, intelligent, and respectable man, of considerable experience as a sailor', he went on to say that 'the witnesses seem to have formed very contradictory opinions respecting his manner and sobriety: some say he was excited, confused'. This wording quickly led to nods and winks that Hawkes was drunk. One passenger testified that the ship had been 'ridiculously handled' by Hawkes. Another believed that if Hawkes, Stewart and Creer had not wasted time and energy arguing with each other, the disaster might have been averted. Survivor Blair did not believe that Hawkes was 'a careful and cautious man . . . I think blame was attachable, and that the pilot was in fault'.

The jury's final statement was that the deaths had been 'caused by an error in judgment by the late Mr Pilot Hawkes, in attempting to bring the ship *Catherine Adamson* into Harbour during the unfavourable state of the weather at the time, and that through that error the lives were lost'. Also, the crew of the *Catherine Adamson* should not have abandoned ship so quickly, 'thereby rendering themselves censurable'. And 'some effort should have been made with the lifeboat to save, if possible, more lives of the passengers and crew'.

The search for bodies continued into the following week. No more *Catherine Adamson* corpses were recovered, but the torso of a woman was found between the Heads. Because of its severely decomposed state, it was assumed she was yet another *Dunbar* victim.

It seemed the people of Sydney were still numbed by the *Dunbar* calamity and struggled to summon the same degree of shock and grief when the *Catherine Adamson* was lost. The funeral procession was low-key, and there were no commemorative books, paintings or poems. One who wrote a letter signing him- or herself 'A Friend of Humanity' wondered if the class system had reared its head in the colony.

I beg to draw your attention to the difference between the funeral obsequies of such bodies as were discovered from the wreck of the *Dunbar* and those of the *Catherine Adamson*. When the funeral took place of the sufferers in the *Dunbar* nearly every shop in the centre of the city was closed and most of what is called the Sydney nobility followed the bodies to their last resting place. Was that because most of them were very wealthy people? When the funeral of those recovered from the wreck of *Catherine Adamson* took place, not one person followed in its train. Why was this distinction made? Is not the body of one man the same in the eyes of the creator as that of any other?

23

Reforms

In the aftermath of the *Dunbar* tragedy, it was clear that if Sydney was to regain its reputation as Australia's safest and most accessible port for immigration and trade, urgent action was necessary. The group given the task of advising on those safety remedies was the Light, Pilot and Navigation Board. The eighteen members were selected by the government for their extensive seagoing experience and knowledge of Port Jackson and were mentored by former Royal Navy admiral Sir Henry Mangles Denham, the current master of the SMS *Herald*, who had spent the past five years surveying the flow and depth and potential hazards of the waterways of Australia, notably Port Jackson, and the south-west Pacific. The board's findings were tabled in parliament and publicly released on 28 October, five days after the *Catherine Adamson* was wrecked.

Echoing the seafarer 'DP' and the captains of the ships in the harbour, the board found that a second lighthouse, complementing Macquarie Light, on the low headland of South Head at the entrance to Port Jackson was a priority to assist vessels rounding the dangerous headland from the south.

The second major recommendation of the Light, Pilot and Navigation Board was the overhauling of the haphazard and inadequate pilot boat service, with its open whaling boats and crews who shied from rough weather and night work. It had to become a dependable aid to approaching ships.

Third, the government should replace the existing messenger riders and semaphore flags with an electric telegraph line from South Head Signal Station that beamed shipping news at all times and in all weather from the station to the Port Office in Sydney.

The new government rubber-stamped the findings of the board and commissioned the work.

* * * *

The location of Macquarie Light high on the cliff 2.2 kilometres south of the tip of South Head had long concerned sailors. Governor Macquarie's reasons for placing his cherished lighthouse there had been sound, to a point: it was high on the cliffs and could be seen from a distance by ships coming from all directions, telling seafarers that Port Jackson lay ahead. But Macquarie Light was a guide *to* the harbour, not *into* the harbour, and it could not be seen by a northbound vessel sailing close beneath the cliffs of South Head, let alone with obscuring low clouds and heavy rain, as beset the *Dunbar*. As one pundit of the day remarked, Macquarie Light 'is not unfrequently useless; it is even said that it is worse than useless, and calculated to produce some of those fatal errors which a lighthouse is especially intended to prevent'. The new lighthouse at the northern extremity of South Head would complement Macquarie Light, warning ships from the south that this was where the southern headland ended and the harbour fairway began. Whether due to the cost or projects they considered more pressing, successive governments had resisted building such a lighthouse. Had any of them done so, the *Dunbar* would almost certainly have arrived in Sydney safely.

Recommending the construction of the second lighthouse on South Head, the board quoted Captain Denham:

A light placed on the salient point of entering the Harbour, and which is, by being a comparatively low vanishing point of vital importance to be distinguished [by a vessel], I would ask for no other light than a light of 30ft [9.1 metres] high from the ground, which ground is 60ft [18.2 metres] above the high-water mark, upon the Inner South Head, directly over where the reef springs out . . . If a light were placed on the extremity of the inner South Head cliff it would be a rounding-to point for it under a northerly or easterly wind. With the present light-vessel [marking Sow and Pigs reef], the light I now propose, and the one of old standing on the South Head [Macquarie Light], I consider this port would be available to a ship under any circumstances . . . Under the circumstances I state, I consider that the approaches and entry of the port would be perfect.

Alexander Dawson, the architect responsible for Sydney Observatory and Sydney Registry Office, was to design and supervise the building of the new South Head lighthouse. Some £2732 was allocated to the project. The light would be named the Hornby Lighthouse, after Admiral Sir Phipps Hornby of the Royal Navy, father-in-law of Governor Denison. Its alternative name was the Lower Light, to distinguish it from Macquarie Light, or the Upper Light.

Just eight months later, in June 1858, Hornby Lighthouse, a 9.1 metre tall sandstone circular cylindrical tower with distinctive vertical red and white stripes and a balcony, stood on a jutting crag just short of the tip of Outer South Head. Its sixteen intense kerosene lamps each in front of a parabolic reflector shone from 27 metres above sea level. The light could be seen by mariners 14 nautical miles (26 kilometres) out to sea as well as by ships sailing close to the cliffs. It was ideally positioned to mark the entrance to Port Jackson as well as illuminate the jutting rocks and submerged reef extending 100 metres out to sea.

As extra safeguards for incoming ships, a stone marker and an obelisk were built on Inner South Head at, respectively, Laing's Point at Watsons Bay and at Parsley Bay.

Remarkably, the first Hornby Lighthouse keeper and occupant of the adjacent small sandstone keeper's cottage was Henry Johnson, brother of the *Dunbar* survivor James Johnson. Henry Johnson's children, Kate and Alfred, like their father and uncle, had salt water in their veins. Captain Alfred Johnson became the keeper of the lights at Twofold Bay on the south coast of New South Wales, and Smoky Cape and Seal Rocks on the state's north coast. He ended his career at Hornby Lighthouse where he'd been born. Kate married Captain Lambert, who was in charge of the lightship *Rose*, which warned vessels away from Sow and Pigs reef.

By no means was Hornby Light the last to be erected in Port Jackson. Fast forward to today and the night-time harbour and surrounding waterways are illuminated by Bradleys Head Light, Shark Island Light, Cremorne Light, Blues Point Light, the Eastern Channel Harbour Marker, the Western Channel Harbour Marker, the North Head Channel Marker, Vaucluse Bay Front Light, the Vaucluse Bay Rear Light, a light on Fort Denison, the Grotto Point Light and Rosherville Light.

* * * *

In January 1858, with appropriate fanfare, an electric telegraph line to relay emergency and routine shipping information from South Head Signal Station to the Royal Exchange Building in Bridge Street, Sydney, began operation. The 11.2 kilometre line cost £657, 6 shillings and 8 pence, higher than first thought because extra labour was required to drive 112 wooden telegraph poles into the rocky route. The days of semaphore flags and horseback messengers were over.

Like Hornby Lighthouse, the telegraph line had been a long time coming. Such a line could not have saved the *Dunbar*, but certainly a telegraph message to maritime headquarters warning of the *Catherine Adamson*'s predicament would have had the *Washington* speeding to the stricken clipper much sooner than had the message that was delivered on horseback.

* * * *

While the electric telegraph line was under construction, the pilot boat service was being revamped. The board's report had noted that 'the pilot service of Port Jackson, as at present constituted and conducted, is inefficient and requires to be remodelled'. To remedy such problems as assigned pilot boats taking too long to reach an incoming vessel (such as when it took pilot Hawkes more than an hour to draw alongside the *Catherine Adamson*), or not coming at all if the weather was threatening, it was recommended that, rather than being coordinated on a rotation basis by the Department of Lights, Pilots and Navigation, pilot crews compete among themselves to be first to assist a ship and receive payment from the ship's master, on top of their regular pay. Further, the board believed that for safety's sake, decked pilot boats ought at all times to be cruising off Port Jackson, ready for service, and that 'two cutters [a fast, single-masted sailing boat] of 70 tons, capable of keeping the sea in all weathers, be immediately built, purchased or hired' to speed pilots to a ship approaching the Heads. These, with the addition of a new whale boat, 'will be able to meet the present requirements of the trade'. Each boat would be manned by six licensed pilots paid between £300 and £400 per annum, less 2.5 per cent to provide a fund for the support of their widows or children should they die in service. But the board warned that the best pilot boat in the world would be of little use 'if she were not manned with more courage and alacrity' than the pilot boat had been on the night the *Catherine Adamson* went down.

George Bainbridge, a pilot of fourteen years' experience and now master of the steam tug *Washington*, was invited to address parliament. He felt strongly that pilots needed to be available in bad weather, whether day or night, and should be ready to lend assistance immediately once the incoming ship's blue light was seen. No vessel should be allowed to attempt to enter Port Jackson without a pilot on board. Bainbridge saw a need for a permanent pilot boat station at Camp Cove, rather than the loose encampment that had existed there since 1792, with a supervisor to ensure the pilots were licensed and fit for duty, and that the boats were shipshape. His recommendations were adopted.

Sydney's first permanent pilot station with pilots familiar with the local depths, tides and currents, and fast, reliable-in-all-weather closed-deck one-masted cutters and two- or more masted schooners were phased in throughout 1858 to replace the old open-deck whalers. Two years later, the government bought land at Watsons Bay and built a new pilot boat station. In 1862, cruising schooners and cutters with live-on-board crew were stationed off Sydney Heads and down to Botany Bay so they could swiftly assist all ships entering Port Jackson. The first boat to reach a vessel received a pilotage fee of £4 per ton, from which the pilot took £2 for himself, with the balance paying crew and for boat maintenance.

The Port Jackson Lifeboat Service, introduced in 1858 to save lives when a ship was in trouble, complemented the pilot boats. The lifeboat service operated two English-built 7 metre brown-painted timber clinker lifeboats with blue-and-white trim and benches for a crew of eight volunteers versed in heavy-weather rescues.

* * * *

Sailing ships, unforgiving cliffs, bad weather and a turbulent sea are always a risky combination and inevitably Sydney had not seen its last maritime calamity, but without Hornby Lighthouse, electric telegraph and effective pilot and lifeboat services, many more lives, ships and tonnes of cargo would have been lost. With the destruction of two magnificent clippers, more than 140 souls and £145,000 worth of cargo as the catalyst, within a year, Sydney's reputation as a safe port was restored. If any good at all came of the loss of the *Dunbar* and the *Catherine Adamson* it was this.

24

Three lives

Just like Thursday, 20 August 1857, Thursday, 12 July 1866 was a day when ferocious winds, hard rain and huge seas lashed the coast of New South Wales. Beaches were washed away and ships were sunk. Newcastle, 160 kilometres north of Sydney, bore the brunt of the storm. At around 1.30 p.m, the 471 tonne iron paddlewheel coastal steamer and sailing vessel *Cawarra* was plunging along the coast from Sydney, bound for Brisbane and Rockhampton. Off Newcastle, Captain Henry Chatfield feared that his ship might break up in the pounding seas, so decided to take refuge in Newcastle Harbour. On entering the channel, the *Cawarra* was smashed off course by large waves and swept towards the Oyster Bank, a notorious sandbank that had claimed vessels in the past. Chatfield ordered his helmsman to come about and, jib and mainsail set, retreat past Nobbys Head for the open sea. The *Cawarra* was pummelled by waves that extinguished the fires powering its steam engines. A plume of steam shot into the air. The wind shredded the ship's sails. Now helpless, the *Cawarra* was driven by the swell back onto the Oyster Bank. At 2.30 p.m., according to an eyewitness, the vessel, which, it was later learned, was overloaded, 'settled down head-first.

The funnel then went overboard', and at 3.20 p.m. the mainmast followed, taking with it 'a burden of human beings into the boiling, seething cauldron . . .'.

Sixty passengers and crew died when the *Cawarra* sank. Only one on board, a foredeck-hand named Frederick Hedges, was saved. His rescuer, of all people, was the *Dunbar* survivor, James Johnson.

The Irishman, now assistant lighthouse keeper at Nobbys Head, and Henry Hannell, the son of the keeper, Jesse Hannell, saw the *Cawarra* in distress from the lighthouse and rushed to it in a small lifeboat through the breakers, Hannell rowing and Johnson at the bow, eyes scanning the waves for survivors. There would be accusations that more lifeboats did not leave the lighthouse because crewmen were drunk. By the time Johnson and Hannell reached the Oyster Bank, only Hedges, who had tried to climb the *Cawarra*'s mast but been knocked overboard and clung to a piece of timber, as Johnson himself had, was left alive. Johnson saw Hedges on the timber and, as each roller threatened to swamp the lifeboat, pulled him on board. For their valour, Johnson and Hannell were hailed in Newcastle and, when word of Johnson's rescue of the *Cawarra*'s sole survivor Frederick Hedges reached Sydney Town, James Johnson was hailed there, too.

* * * *

While Johnson was being lauded, there was already another hero in the colony familiar to most who remembered the aftermath of the *Dunbar*'s demise. Sydney Mayor Alderman George Thornton's vivid eyewitness reports in newspapers and booklets on the wreck scene and the rescue of James Johnson, in which he played a part, earned him a level of fame that being a respected businessman and even mayor never had. And then Thornton's standing in the colony rose to an even higher level when, the year before Johnson's rescue of Hedges, he distinguished himself in another scarcely believable *Dunbar* coincidence.

Thornton was returning to Sydney from England on the *Dunbar*'s sister ship, the 1246 tonne luxury clipper *Duncan Dunbar*, which had arrived in Sydney on its maiden voyage just days after the *Dunbar* was wrecked. Now, eight years later, on 7 October 1865, the *Duncan Dunbar*, with Thornton and 116 others on board, ran aground and was swamped on Rocas Shoals off Cape São Roque, Brazil. Many panicked; not passenger Thornton. He helped Captain Swanson and his crew land every passenger, and stores of food and water, on a sandspit on the shoal. The captain and eight seamen set off in an open boat to find help. For the next ten days, Thornton held the fort. He maintained calm among the castaways, who included 35 women and children, and distributed rations. After a 200 kilometres passage, Captain Swanson and his crew were sighted by an American ship and delivered to the port of Recife on the coast of Pernambuco in north-east Brazil. The British consul there despatched the Royal Mail packet steamer *Oneida* to rescue the marooned voyagers and return them to Portsmouth. Thornton's fellow passengers on the *Duncan Dunbar* thanked him in a letter.

We, your fellow-sufferers at the wreck of the *Duncan Dunbar*, wish, before we separate, to express to you our very warm thanks for your untiring exertions on our behalf while on the reef Las Rocas. In our condition on the reef, without water or provisions, excepting such as could be recovered from the wrecked vessel, it was absolutely necessary that there should be adopted a regular system for the preservation and economical application of our limited resources. In this emergency you came forward, and, despite the many difficulties which beset the task, introduced system, and changed confusion into order. We bear in mind that this sacrifice of your time was not made without damage to your private interests, and that it prevented you from looking after the preservation of your own personal effects. It is impossible to over-estimate the value of such services. For what you undertook and did for us on the reef Las Rocas, accept, sir, our sincerest thanks, and believe that you will ever retain our lasting gratitude.

Insurance companies whose cargo he had helped save presented Thornton with a gold watch and chain. While grateful for the gesture, he later grumbled that the shipwreck had cost him £5845 when his own—uninsured—goods were lost.

After a full life in politics, banking and business, as a correspondent and author, a yachtsman, senior government official, rower—and *Duncan Dunbar* hero—Thornton, handsome and healthy until the end, died in 1901 of a sudden attack of dysentery at his home, Lang Syne, in Parramatta North. He'd attained the ripe age, for the time, of 82.

* * * *

Antonio Woolier, the boy who descended the terrifying Jacobs Ladder ravine then inched his way 190 metres along the wave-smashed rocks to reach and rescue James Johnson, lived a less auspicious life than George Thornton. In the years after his *Dunbar* heroics, Woolier had a modest gold strike and a few wins at the races, but he never again came close to attaining the lustre of the moments atop the cliff at Outer South Head when people thrust money and praise upon him.

The man who, for whatever reason, renamed himself Antonio Woolier was born on 28 November 1836, on the west coast of Iceland. Arni Olafsson's parents were Olafur, a farmer and chairman of the local council, and Helga Thorlacius. Olafur died when Arni was two months old, and Helga sent him to live with foster parents on the island of Ellidaey. When his foster parents passed away, ten-year-old Arni resided with his uncle and namesake, the merchant Arni Olafsson Thorlacius, at his grand home in Stykkisholmur. When the boy was confirmed at thirteen, in 1849, the priest described him as 'quite intelligent, well-learned and reasonably friendly'. The next that is known of him is that in August 1855 he was in Hong Kong, an able seaman on the freighter *Abeona*, sailing the Hong Kong–Sydney route. After Arni arrived in Sydney on 15 October 1855, he changed his name—sometimes his new surname would be spelled 'Woollier' or 'Wollier'. Possibly he wanted to conceal his whereabouts from his uncle; perhaps he had committed a crime. In Sydney, Woolier was employed as an apprentice watchmaker by the Elizabeth Street jeweller, Flower, who accompanied him to South Head that Saturday morning when word spread that the *Dunbar* had struck the cliff.

Woolier reportedly refused to accept payment for his bravery—'I did not go down for the money, but for the feeling in my heart'— but John Fairfax, the proprietor of the *Sydney Morning Herald* and prominent businessman who had chipped in for James Johnson, insisted he be compensated for his bravery. He opened a bank account in Woolier's name, into which public donations amounting to £88, 3 shillings and 6 pence were deposited. As the account's trustee, Fairfax invested £75 of the money in a twelve-month bank post bill bearing 5 per cent interest and the balance, was, said Fairfax, 'for Woolier's immediate wants'.

He had a few of those. By the end of 1858, Woolier was married, to Sarah Fitch, and digging for gold in Araluen, 311 kilometres south-west of Sydney. Three years later, the Wooliers were living in the nearby coastal town of Moruya. Antonio was a publican, and with his partner, John Roddy, sold mining supplies at the settlement of Gulf Diggings (today Nerragundah), but the pub and the store soon went broke, and an associate, Frederic Perry, was indicted for stealing £1105 from Woolier and Roddy. The money was not recovered.

Antonio and Sarah's firstborn, Rosetta, survived just weeks. One month later, Woolier and his friend Edward Smith struck gold at Gulf Diggings, and they sold their 250 ounces to a bank for £3 and 19 pence per ounce.

The Wooliers moved back to Sydney but stayed only months before relocating in Melbourne where a second daughter, Helga, was born in 1868 (Antonio's birth name, Arni Olafsson Thorlacius, is on Helga's birth certificate). Two years later, a third daughter, Alice, was born but she died at fifteen months. Woolier became a bookmaker taking bets in a tobacconist shop in Bourke Street and punted heavily at racecourses in Melbourne and Sydney. Woolier bought his own racehorse, named Royal Charlie, and rode it himself, with limited success. He had better fortune with his annual *Backer's Guide*, a booklet he compiled and sold for sixpence to bettors, offering 'pedigrees and performances of horses engaged in the Metropolitan Stakes and the Melbourne Cup' and other events on the racing calendar. He knew his subject, for it was reported that in 1873, Woolier won £4000 at the races. Sadly, he lost much of his winnings on mining shares.

Woolier was charged with illegal bookmaking at Flemington and Epsom racecourses after the new *Police Offences Statute Gambling Act*, which had been introduced in 1872. His bookmaker's licence was not renewed and he drank excessively. He was arrested and charged with assault after he attacked a baker. He barely scraped together the money to pay his fine. Had he not, he would have been gaoled.

There was nothing left to do but return to the goldfields. He prospected for gold and with a partner opened another mining supplies store in Lower Temora, 418 kilometres south-west of Sydney. Before the year was out, the store was insolvent and it was back to Melbourne for the Wooliers. Antonio's drinking worsened and Sarah left him and took Helga with her. Clinging to his religion, Woolier found a job as a gardener with the Congregational Church in Brighton, Victoria. Stomach cancer ended his diamonds-and-rocks life on 5 February 1889. He was 52. There were a few small obituaries in the Melbourne press, written by those who remembered his bookmaking days. There was even the occasional mention of his rescue of James Johnson all those years ago.

* * * *

The wrecks of the *Dunbar* and the *Cawarra* were not the last tribulations in James Johnson's life. A 74-year-old Sydney man named Leo Fitzpatrick announced in August 1983, that as a lad, he had been the elderly Johnson's friend and that Johnson confided to him that the greatest tragedy in his life was an accident in the Nobbys Head lighthouse where he had by now been appointed superintendent. 'With his wife expecting her first baby, Johnson slipped and accidentally pierced her eye with a pair of scissors. Before the baby was born, [Mary] became blind . . .' but, claimed Fitzpatrick, she 'could find her way around the lighthouse and do everything necessary for the children'. There is another story, although there is no known supporting evidence, that Mary was killed when she fell down the stairs at the lighthouse and accidentally stabbed herself with the scissors. Whatever scenario is true, and perhaps neither is, Mary Johnson died on 23 July 1889, and was buried in Sandgate Cemetery in Newcastle.

James Johnson was photographed towards the end of his 30-year term at the lighthouse. In one photo, the still-sturdy Irishman wears a natty derby, dark suit, white shirt and necktie, and sports a white goatee. In the other, he is hatless, revealing a fine head of thick dark hair.

In 1984, Johnson was remembered by an elderly woman named Ina O'Neill as a kind and friendly man who sat on the veranda of the hotel where he lived waiting for children to come out of school. 'We used to race to the hotel because the first one there would be able to sit on Mr Johnson's knee' and be entertained by his tales of shipwrecks and the sea.

When 'Loss of the *Dunbar*', yet another poem about his old ship, was published, Johnson congratulated the poet, Livingstone Clarke. 'Dear Sir,' he wrote:

I have received your poem on the loss of *Dunbar* and I am certain that it is the best account I have seen in print. You have made a slight error—instead of starboard it ought to be port; however, it is quite correct so far as the wreck is concerned. I am very grateful to you for your beautifully written poem, and I shall prize it as long as I live. I am going down to Newcastle to have it framed.

In the poem there are references to Jane Graham's dream in the signal station and to the barking of Macquarie Light keeper Joseph Siddins' dog as the clipper was breaking apart. Johnson told Clarke that he had never heard of Jane Graham's dream but that Siddins had mentioned to him in the days after the wreck 'that he had a dog that began barking about midnight, and that was shortly after we struck'.

Johnson was guest of honour at a lunch on 20 August 1887, the 30th anniversary of the wreck. The venue was the Royal Hotel at Watsons Bay, which was once the Marine Hotel where Johnson had recovered, and which, in 1950, would become Dunbar House. A guest wrote:

> Such was the terrific disaster which . . . is still vividly remembered, and advantage was taken of James Johnson's presence in Sydney to invite him to a commemorative lunch, which took place at a spot not many yards from the fatal place . . . The affair was conducted with excellent and memorable taste. A logical, sensible quietude, of course, prevailed. There was no roistering—there were none of the associations which dominate the typical dinner. There was a subdued, modified melancholy (of course not entirely untempered by the fact that 30 years had elapsed) about the affair, which was emotionally in keeping with the event recalled. Nothing of the kind (very naturally) had occurred since the event . . . It was a unique, semi-funereal gathering, sympathetic and reminiscent. Sixty gentlemen sat down to the repast, and after the genial Dan O'Connor had proposed the usual loyal toasts, the 'health of the survivor' was toasted. Johnson replied with evident feeling. The company afterwards adjourned to the edge of the cliffs and looked at the waves, which, dimpling in the sunshine, seemed as though they could never harbour, in their depths, the fierce elements of maritime disaster.

Johnson married again and with his new wife, Catherine Anne (or Annie), lived in Sydney's inner-west suburb of Dulwich Hill, at 85 The Boulevarde. Two of his daughters lived next door.

Although he moved on with his life, Johnson never completely severed the ties that bound him to the *Dunbar*. He rarely declined an invitation to a *Dunbar* commemoration. He was back at The Gap in 1910 when deep-sea diver Tom McNab recovered one of the *Dunbar*'s anchors at the wreck site. And two years later, nearing the end of his days, he was again the honoured guest at a 'Luncheon for Old Mariners' in Sydney. Photographed at this function, the 75-year-old's hair has at last turned white like his beard. His face, like that of any old man of the sea worth his salt, was deeply lined.

James Johnson died on 13 April 1915, aged 78. He was buried two days later in the Catholic section of Sandgate Cemetery, Newcastle, alongside his first wife, Mary.

A few obituarists remembered. They naturally recalled his rescue from the South Head cliff ledge and his pay-it-forward rescue in Newcastle Harbour nine years later. He had 'earned the respect of a wide circle of friends, having proved himself a most trustworthy and capable officer of the Navigation Department, and a worthy and intelligent citizen'. Only weeks before he died, noted another eulogist, Johnson had struck up a conversation on a Sydney tram with an elderly farrier named Mitchell. On Mitchell mentioning to Johnson that he immigrated to Australia in the year the *Dunbar* was wrecked and remembered the devastating effect the calamity had on the colony, Johnson was able to one-up him. If anyone had a more vivid memory of the *Dunbar* disaster, he declared, it was he. 'Oh, why?' had wondered Mitchell. 'Because,' Johnson had replied, 'I am the sole survivor of the wreck.' The obituary continued, 'After further conversation, the two old gentlemen arranged to visit each other, but before this arrangement could be consummated, Mr Johnson passed over to the great majority.'

Another tribute ran in *Freeman's Journal* on 29 April 1915:

A brave, true Irishman, James Johnson, hero of the *Dunbar*, 'put out to sea' on Tuesday, 13th April, aged 78 years, leaving his four daughters to mourn his loss . . . His familiar figure, no matter the weather, was always to be seen in St Mary's Church. One of the first to join the Hibernian Society in the Coal City, he remained till his death an ardent friend and supporter, until 15 years ago he retired on a well-earned pension, and resided at The Boulevarde, Lewisham. A model of piety and devotion to his Church, he was a friend to all the children, who would stop to have a chat with the historic one 'cast up by the sea'. He was first seriously ill on the 4th January, but recovering, was able to spend some four or five weeks at the Mountains. He was present at Mass on the Sunday prior to his collapse suddenly on Tuesday, 13th April. The body was taken to Newcastle for interment at Sandgate . . . It was met by a great concourse, including Mr James (Anglican), an old friend of Mr Johnson. Father Kelly read the last prayers at the grave of the sailor who through life had always hoped 'to meet his Pilot face to face'.—RIP.

Richard Blair of Marrickville Heritage Society delved into the life of James Johnson in 2005 for an article in the society's newsletter. He learned that Johnson named his Dulwich Hill house Beaulieu. Then he read that, 'About 5km from Drogheda [where Johnson was born], on the banks of the River Boyne, is a 1660s mansion which was one of the first unfortified houses in Ireland. Its name is "Beaulieu".'

The English translation of Beaulieu is 'lovely place', which, it is nice to think, is a clue that James Johnson's last years, at the end of a turbulent life, were happy ones.

25

Unreliable memories

The wreck of the *Dunbar* continued to obsess Sydneysiders long after the events of 20 August 1857, and especially on anniversaries of the disaster. In August 1887, 30 years after the *Dunbar* ran aground, Alderman George Thornton's published account of the rescue of James Johnson, considered the official version—and the versions of others who concurred with him—was questioned by some who stepped from the shadows of anonymity to proclaim that it had been them, and not Antonio Woolier, who had saved Johnson.

Thomas Williams of Wynyard Square insisted that he had attached a rope to an oar, and lowered it down to Johnson on his ledge. Johnson had straddled Williams' oar and 'was carefully drawn up, sustaining some bruises in the course' of his ride to the top of the cliff. There was no mention of Woolier in Williams' account.

George James of Woollahra, at a *Dunbar* commemorative banquet at Watsons Bay's Signal Hotel, boasted that *he* had been the hero of the day. James said that after he had grown impatient with police and others' timidity and indecisiveness at the cliff-top, he had boldly taken the rescue into his own hands. James claimed that 'without any ceremony' he had taken a rope from a pilot named Gibson and, ordering two men to hang on to his coat-tails to save him from falling to his death, leaned over the precipice and lowered the rope to Johnson below. When the wind blew the rope away from Johnson's outstretched arms, James had regathered the rope, tied a bag of stones to its end and this time it had fallen straight down to the survivor. Johnson, according to James, had then tied the rope to his waist and been hauled to safety. Halfway up the cliff, Johnson began to twist in the wind. James had yelled manfully, 'Hold on, lad!' and, although Johnson's sou'-wester was blown from his head, the rescue was completed. A grateful Johnson had given his name, rank and ship to none but his saviour, George James. James allowed that Antonio Woolier *was* on the scene, somewhere, but insisted that James Johnson had been rescued for an hour before the Icelander descended to the water's edge to search for more survivors. James claimed that he had been the first to volunteer to descend to the bottom of the cliff but was deemed too heavy and the task was given to Woolier by default.

The guest of honour at the Signal Hotel banquet was James Johnson himself, who fell in with George James. According to James' later account, Johnson had told the room, 'Gentlemen, every word Mr James has said, as far as to how I was hauled up, is true, even to the losing of my sou'-wester. I watched it go down but I didn't want to go after it.'

Some diners, and others who learned of George James' claim later, suggested that James' version of events may have been distorted by wishful thinking and too much ale, and wondered if Johnson had been matching James tankard for tankard. Either that or Johnson, in his 'insensible' state after his ordeal, had scrambled memories of his rescue. In response to George James' elbowing his way into the limelight, eyewitnesses reiterated that Woolier, not George James or Thomas Williams, had rescued Johnson and that, when seen down on the ledge, Johnson was bare-headed and wore only a drenched and ragged blue shirt and cotton trousers. Until the banquet there had never been mention of a sou'-wester. Or of George James.

Alderman Thornton himself indignantly confirmed his account of three decades before. And Philip Cohen, who had famously (but probably apocryphally) tried to prise a *Dunbar* victim from the jaws of a shark at Manly Cove, angrily rebutted James in a public announcement.

> To my utter astonishment, a Mr James appeared at the banquet as the rescuer and deliverer of James Johnson . . . Permit me to say that this is the first time that I have ever heard of anyone named James being in any way concerned with the rescue of Johnson. The real hero to whom the latter owes his life was a Norwegian [sic] lad named Antonio Woolier . . . This intrepid boy stepped forth in response to a call for a volunteer [to go down Jacobs Ladder] . . . I well remember how men shuddered and women wept when that fragile boy clambered over and disappeared down the jagged and perpendicular rocks. Scarcely a sound was heard from the assembled thousands, and a mighty roar announced the rescue of Johnson and the subsequent recovery of his brave deliverer, Antonio Woolier . . . The story about the bag filled with stones is a pure fabrication; but the most amazing result obtained at the banquet was the recognition of James by Johnson and the verification of the former's statement as to how he rescued the latter. When Johnson was hauled over the brow of the cliff he was in a perfectly dazed condition, if not quite unconscious. Surely there must be numbers of people living in the present day who will bear me out in this statement.

There were. A district court judge named Forbes, who was present at the rescue, called George James' story 'quite incorrect' and confirmed the truth of the Thornton version. One Watsons Bay local who was on the scene had no recollection of James but pointedly suggested that perhaps he 'was amongst the crowd which partook of congratulatory refreshments at the hotel'. Henry Packer, who was James Graham's assistant at the signal station in 1857, attested to Woolier's descent. Another veteran seaman scoffed at James' claims.

> Mr James might have been there with his bag of stones. I do not remember that circumstance, and yet I took part in helping to rig up

the boom. I suppose it is meritorious to wish to be connected with anything of an especially heroic character. The heroes of the celebrated charge at Balaclava must have another cypher added to the 600, to supply all the claimants who desire to share in that military blunder, and so with Waterloo and other events of a kindred character.

Finally, there was no reason for Alderman George Thornton to invent his narrative of Woolier's involvement in the rescue of Johnson. Thornton had nothing to gain. He did not claim to have done anything heroic himself. Thornton was a well-known and well-respected public figure, so surely, if he had fabricated the story of Woolier's descent and it was printed in every newspaper and in the booklets that were read by tens of thousands in the days after the wreck, he would have been quickly taken to task. That it took 30 years for anyone to contradict Thornton's version suggests that the way the mayor had told it was the way it had been.

* * * *

The *Dunbar* wreck site was officially confirmed as being around 260 metres north of the signal station on 24 June 1861, two months shy of the fourth anniversary of the ship's foundering. A member of the Sydney pilot service, E.W. Blakeney, and signal station telegraph operator Harry Gibson were standing atop the cliff watching for incoming ships on one of those rare days when the surface of the sea off Outer South Head was smooth and underwater visibility good. Down below, they saw under the water a ship's cables and two bow anchors. The men realised that these were the remnants of the *Dunbar*. Gibson alerted John Crook, Captain Robert Pockley's successor as Sydney harbour master, who ordered that a search and salvage operation immediately be conducted to 'ascertain the state of the wreck', and, if possible, salvage the anchors, chains and any other relics.

The following day was also bright and still with placid seas. The steam tug *Washington*, commanded by Captain Williamson, chugged out of the Heads, turned right and saw shapes on the ocean floor, 20 metres out from the base of the cliffs and 4 metres under the unruffled surface. He dropped anchor. A commercial diver, one of the few in the colony, named Tom McNab, trussed up in his metal-and-rubber diving suit, boots and helmet with air hose attached, went down. McNab (who would drown in a diving mishap in Torres Strait ten years later) located two large anchors embedded in the rocks, and scattered around them was corroded copper, pig-iron ballast, and 'iron, both round and square, lying in a heap'. Piled on the iron were chain cables and one small kedge anchor, 'just as it had fallen through the decks' on impact. But 'the only things that could be readily got at', reported McNab, were metal sheathing, copper bars, a bell, a handful of the 1.5 tonnes of Hanks & Lloyd and Lasseter penny tokens that the *Dunbar* had carried, gudgeons and pintles (which formed hinges on the ship) and an unopened bottle of champagne. Hampered by his unwieldy diving apparatus, McNab's search was restricted to the area directly below the steam tug. Had he been able to look just a little further afield he would have located more than nuts, bolts and a bottle of bubbly.

Divers with more modern equipment who came after McNab would have better luck, unearthing relics to satisfy the most avaricious plunderer of pirate days.

It was another 49 years before another serious attempt, ordered by Superintendent of Navigation Captain Henry Newton, was made to salvage *Dunbar* relics. On a July day in 1910 when the conditions were right, a reconnaissance team of 'gentlemen residents of Watson's Bay' and local pilots and salvors George Jenkinson, Harry Dunn, Harold Dunn, H. Robinson and Samuel Toye aboard the salvage steamer *Federal* sighted what Williamson and McNab had seen on the ocean floor: two large rusted and corroded anchors and other wreckage 20 metres offshore.

An operation to raise the largest anchor, which was 3.9 metres long, weighed 3.6 tonnes and was wedged between large boulders and coated in sea vegetation and rock coral, got underway. When hauling gear powered by a donkey engine failed to dislodge it, Plan B—dynamite—was put into action. As well as freeing the anchor, the blast killed scores of fish that floated belly-up to the surface. A crowd on the cliff-top, which included 73-year-old James Johnson who'd come for the occasion, applauded as the anchor was chained to a tug. After lunch, a diver named Anderson and his team raised a smaller anchor, three breast hooks, a davit (a crane-like device), two iron knees, bolts, a candlestick, a silver spoon inscribed with the ship's name, and a fragment of a china saucer decorated with green flowers on a yellow background. All were displayed on a wooden platform in a tin and timber shed grandly called the *Dunbar* Relics Museum behind Vaucluse Council Chambers in Gap Road, Watsons Bay.

Then, just as the salvors were congratulating themselves on a job well done, materialised the now-elderly, and ubiquitous at any *Dunbar* gathering, former signal station assistant, Henry Packer, with an axe to grind. He distinctly remembered that the wreck site was not north of the signal station but further south between the signal station and Macquarie Light, and therefore the anchors could not possibly be the *Dunbar*'s.

The emotional grip that the wreck still had on the community was evinced by a furious barrage of rebuttals. A witness to the aftermath of the wreck, Vaucluse Council employee Frederick Dunn, retorted: 'Our friend Packer is all astray. I am positive that Mr Packer's memory is failing him when he talks about the wreck taking place between [Macquarie] lighthouse and the Signal Station.' Besides, continued Dunn, the anchors *had* to be the *Dunbar*'s because no other ship with anchors that size had foundered or lost their anchors anywhere near this location. Local man George Newton joined the fray.

> Mr Packer is talking nonsense. I was one of the first to discover the wreck. I have lived in Watsons Bay all my life, and my father before me. I know those cliffs as well as I know my backyard, and I tell you that *Dunbar* was wrecked to the south of Jacob's Ladder, abreast of

where Johnson was washed up, and I can show you the rock he was behind when in my presence they hauled him up the cliffs. There are not many who know that rock but I have fished from it and around it thousands of times. As Johnson himself says, when he left the ship he was washed straight up.

On the morning after the wreck, George Newton continued, he had walked up to The Gap and seen men looking over.

Captain Hawkes, one of the pilots, was one of them. Poor Captain Hawkes, he was drowned while bringing the *Catherine Adamson* in a month later. Well, these men were watching something. I strolled up to them and there I saw all the bodies of the victims being tossed about in the waves as they beat up against The Gap. We walked along a bit towards the [signal station] flagstaff and there we saw the wreck, just where I told you, a little south of Jacob's Ladder . . . It was close to what we fishermen know as the Bombora, which is a big flat rock and I am told that this was where the anchors were found the other day. At any rate, anyone who says *Dunbar* was not wrecked where I told you is a madman!

Mark Twain added to the confusion in his memoir *Following the Equator*. Twain got wrong not only the site of the wreck, but also the name of the ship when he wrote that the *Duncan Dunbar* struck at The Gap. He also had Captain Green, who, he wrote, had entered Sydney Heads seventeen times in the past, being browbeaten by passengers anxious to arrive home into running for Sydney Cove, and that 200 perished. According to Twain, Johnson was flung 15 metres into the air onto his ledge, and he was rescued next day.

Further evidence that the *Dunbar* foundered 190 metres south of Jacobs Ladder is a makeshift memorial on the very edge of the cliff-top at the point where Johnson was pulled to safety. Five days after the wreck, somebody, whom we can only know as 'CP', scratched into a flat piece of sandstone the words: '*Dunbar*, CP, 25th Aug 1857.'

26

All that remains

The Australian National Maritime Museum in Sydney's Darling Harbour has preserved and catalogued a vast trove of *Dunbar* artefacts. Museum assistant curator Myffanwy Bryant invited this author to view the jewellery, bells, buckles, picture frames, utensils . . . and gold dentures that had been taken from the wreck site by scuba divers last century. It was moving to realise that every item once belonged to a *Dunbar* victim, an everyday talisman of a life lived and lost. A small silver ring caught our eye. Words had been engraved around its circumference but were too small to be read by the naked eye. Myf Bryant, as irrepressible as she is knowledgeable, set off to find a magnifying glass. That afternoon an email arrived. The mystery inscription, said Myf, was in Latin: '*Si fuerit deus mecum*' which translates as 'God is with me'. And she added, 'In light of the fate of whoever wore the ring, quite poignant, I think.'

* * * *

More than a century and a half after it shattered on Outer South Head, the *Dunbar* remains an intrinsic part of the history of the city she almost reached. There are vestiges of it everywhere.

People can see *Dunbar* graves and monuments at Sydney's cemeteries. Buildings and streets are named for the clipper. Artefacts and relics from it are in museums and libraries and churches, and moulder in the wardrobes and garages of private homes.

Every year, on the anniversary of the disaster, services are held at St Stephen's Church in the grounds of Camperdown Cemetery, St John's Anglican Church at Darlinghurst and at the *Dunbar* memorial atop The Gap.

Hornby Lighthouse, its jolly red candy-striping belying its deadly serious function, was built to prevent ships sharing the *Dunbar*'s fate. Some of the buildings of South Head Signal Station still stand and there are tours of Macquarie Light, whose beam broke the clouds all too late for the *Dunbar*. The latter lighthouse is not Governor Macquarie and Francis Greenway's original tower but one constructed in 1883 that, its modern lantern technology excepted, replicates the original lighthouse.

Art galleries exhibit *Dunbar*-related paintings and lithographs by Conrad Martens, Évremond de Bérard, G.F. Gregory, Samuel Thomas Gill, Edmund Thomas and George French Angas. The portrait of victims Marian Egan and her children Gertrude and Henry is at the National Portrait Gallery in Canberra. Photographs exist of survivor James Johnson and third officer John Pascoe, and there is the remarkable photo by Robert Hunt of the ship's salvaged timbers.

In its way, Hunt's photograph is as poignant as the best of the *Dunbar* paintings and illustrations. It is a strikingly clear image of *Dunbar* debris, taken on 13 December 1857, by Hunt, the brother of Sarah and Emily Hunt, the eighteen- and twenty-year-old sisters who were returning on the *Dunbar* after school in Bordeaux. Hunt's image may well be Australia's first news photograph and can be seen in books, museums and libraries. Heartbroken by his sisters' deaths, Hunt, deputy master of the Sydney Mint and a keen photographer who specialised in harbourside scenes taken from his skiff the *Terror*, searched the harbour bays and beaches for weeks for some trace of Sarah and Emily. He found a pillow embroidered with the letters 'SH' and, because the *Dunbar*'s passenger and crew lists showed nobody else with those initials, Hunt was convinced it was his sister Sarah's. At Lavender Bay on the north shore of the harbour, Hunt came upon the Official Receiver of Cargoes George Green's boatshed where salvaged timbers from the *Dunbar* were stacked and he photographed the wreckage. It is hard to believe that the forlorn pile of wood lying in the yard by the water was once the *Dunbar*, the finest clipper afloat.

* * * *

On 23 August 1930, a team of men hauling on a pulley-and-hoist contraption lifted onto the bed of a truck the rusted 3.6 tonne, 3.9 metre long *Dunbar* bow anchor that had been on display for the past twenty years at the *Dunbar* Relics Museum at Watsons Bay. Its load secured, the truck rumbled along Gap Road to the cliff-top above the south end of The Gap, where the anchor was unloaded and positioned on a stone plinth that had been bonded into the vertical sandstone face. Metal bands were attached to hold the anchor fast.

Later, a commemorative plaque completed the *Dunbar* memorial. It was inscribed: 'The *Dunbar* was wrecked about 500 yards south of this spot in a heavy north east gale at night Aug. 20th 1857. From a total of 122 there was only one survivor. This her anchor was recovered by local residents 50 years later and is now set up in memory of the tragic event.'

Before the flag that covered the plaque was drawn aside with appropriate ceremony by local alderman C.B. Combes, Captain J.H. Watson regaled walrus-moustached derby-hatted members of the Royal Australian Historical Society and Vaucluse Council with tales of the great clipper ships of the 1850s, and Royal Navy man Francis J. Bayldon spoke on the *Dunbar* disaster. Dr Harold Norrie, president of the Historical Society, concluded, 'This ceremony marks a pathetic event which has lingered in the minds of Sydney people and will do as long as the cliffs, against which so many persons, almost within sight of their homes, were dashed to pieces, remain to mark the spot.'

Three errors in the plaque inscription at the *Dunbar* memorial at The Gap remain uncorrected to this day. The gale blew from the south-east and the east-south-east, not the north-east. The *Dunbar* was destroyed around 850 metres south of The Gap, not 500 yards, or 460 metres. And the anchor was raised from the depths in 1910, 53 years, not 50 years, after the *Dunbar* went down.

Another common misconception was, and is, that the *Dunbar* foundered at The Gap. The location of the *Dunbar*'s anchor memorial at The Gap has compounded the error. Blame also the vivid memories, passed down through generations, of the debris and bodies, swept onto the rock shelf. And at the coronial inquest, one witness stated that the clipper had smashed into The Gap, and his testimony was widely published in newspapers.

To set the record straight, on Saturday, 12 September 1993, a plaque was set in the footpath on the cliff-top directly above where the *Dunbar* was wrecked. (The plaque is across the road from 248 Old South Head Road.) A brochure to attract people to the unveiling by the Mayor of Woollahra, Alderman Cathy Lemech, read, 'The plaque has been positioned to indicate the site of the disaster and help to dispel the oft-repeated premise that the *Dunbar* was wrecked at The Gap . . . This mistaken belief is deep-seated in the community and surfaces almost every time the disaster is recalled to memory—it has helped in no small way to engender the awe and morbidity in which The Gap is held.'

Near the plaque but inaccessible today behind a safety fence because it edges the precipice, is the simple *Dunbar* tribute that was chiselled into the sandstone five days after the wreck by 'CP' marking the exact spot where James Johnson was pulled up over the cliff-top to safety. In 1906, 49 years to the day since the *Dunbar* was lost, Vaucluse Council town clerk Edwin Stanhope Sautelle happened upon the rock but by then all that was legible was '—*bar*, CP'. Sautelle re-inscribed CP's original wording, and then to reward himself for his enterprise, added 'recut by ESS 20 Aug 1906'.

* * * *

255

Considering its dramatic history, the *Dunbar* wreck site can disappoint divers who descend on calm water days to explore what is left of the grand clipper and try to imagine how it looked in its heyday. Scuba-diving salvors and scavengers since the '50s and the relentless ocean swells since 1857 have left little to see. A Porter's anchor lies beneath a submerged rock overhang. Some 4 metres south of that is an Admiralty anchor. Its broken arm rests between the two anchors. Nearby, a chain cable and a brass fastener are covered in black concretion formed by the decomposing iron. To the south of the anchors is more chain cable, iron knees and copper sheathing, some of it concreted between sandstone boulders. There are pig-iron ballast blocks. A few trinkets and ceramic and glass fragments are sometimes seen tumbling among the rocks, kelp and shifting sands.

Kieran Hosty, head of curatorial and research and maritime archaeologist at the Australian National Maritime Museum, who has dived the wreck site many times, describes it this way:

> The site is around 125 metres long, and 15 metres wide at its widest point. It runs north–south, with the bow facing to north. It's hard to locate because of the kelp and can only be dived in June, July and August when the westerlies come. Even then it can be rough offshore, but against the cliffs there is no swell. If you're expecting to see lots of stuff down there, the site can be underwhelming, but to me it's beautiful. There are still anchors there, iron framing and scattered ceramic and glass artefacts. We found a ceramic teapot two years ago, concreted to the stone under boulders.

Like Kieran Hosty, Stirling Smith, formerly maritime archaeologist at the National Maritime Museum and now senior maritime archaeological officer at Heritage New South Wales, Department of Premier and Cabinet, has dived the *Dunbar* often. 'Even on calm days, the wash that comes back off the cliff makes you feel like you're in a washing machine. It's really evocative because when you surface you are right underneath those cliffs and you wonder how James Johnson survived. It's a scary place. Those cliffs are intimidating. Every time I dive there or sail past I think of those poor souls on the *Dunbar*.'

Stirling Smith is another who is captured by the mystique of the *Dunbar*. 'We'll never know with *absolute* certainty what happened, but the most probable explanation is that in that terrible storm with poor visibility and the north-west current slowing his progress, Captain Green mistook the waves breaking on The Gap for North Head and turned *Dunbar* into the cliffs. That's the best theory based on available information but people will be debating why *Dunbar* foundered for another 100 years.'

The wreck was left largely alone until the 1950s when old-style diving outfits—full rubber suit and weighted boots and a metal helmet attached to an air hose connected to a pump in a crewed boat—were superseded by relatively cheap, lighter, self-contained scuba diving equipment: wetsuit, single hose regulator, weight belt, compressed air tanks, mask, fins. Helped along by television series *Sea Hunt* and *The Aquanauts*, wreck diving now became a popular recreation. The *Dunbar* site, largely untouched since 1910, was rediscovered by members of the Underwater Explorers Club, the Underwater Skin-divers and Fishermen's Association and other divers.

'When scuba diving was introduced in the 1950s,' says Stirling Smith, 'people were looking for wrecks to dive on, so you have Australia's biggest city with reasonably wealthy people getting into this new sport called scuba diving. The *Dunbar* was the obvious wreck to dive, and, for some, to loot.'

Whenever the waters off South Head were accessible to boats and divers, the *Dunbar* site was swarmed. Some divers were not content to simply look, but wanted to make money from the wreck by taking and keeping or selling its artefacts. Runabouts and dinghies and boats towing pontoons packed with people jockeyed for position above the site and divers descended to remove anchors, cannon, coins, candlesticks, jewellery, dentures, buttons, compasses, cutlery, specta-cles, telescopes, glass objects, pewter tankards, watches, rifles, brass buckles (some from the Crimean War), shoes, rings, lamps, pottery and ceramic plates and cups, copper and brass pieces, pocket watches, a gold brooch in which was lodged a shark's tooth. There is a photograph of a diver named Denis Robertson holding a human bone recovered from the *Dunbar* in author Tom Byron's book, *History of Spearfishing and Scuba Diving in Australia*.

In the 1950s, '60s and well into the '70s, there was no law against scavenging on wrecks, and virtually any relic that could be snatched up by gloved hands or forced free with a crowbar, wrench, hacksaw, knife, suction pump or explosives was removed. Large rubber tyres and 44-gallon drums inflated underwater with compressed air from a cylinder were used to raise anchors and cannon. A rumour that a chest containing 5000 gold sovereigns had gone down with the ship fuelled the frenzy. Loose gold sovereigns *were* unearthed but no treasure chest has been found. In his autobiography, *Blood in the Water*, spearfisher, filmmaker and shark hunter Ben Cropp wrote:

> Our technique was effective, but uncomplicated. We would buy gelignite and head out to a wreck in my tinnie. I'd dive down and place the charges, swim back to the boat and set them off. I'd bring up the pieces of metal and at the end of the day we'd take a trailer load to the wreckers ... Lost in the wreck of the *Dunbar* were thousands of coins, mostly copper penny tokens but also some gold sovereigns [and personal belongings of the passengers and crew]. Over the years these had fused together in a conglomerate of rock, and [we] had to use gelignite to separate them. It was well worth it. I could sell one gold sovereign for the equivalent of one week's wages.

Some divers descended in dangerous conditions to get their share of the booty. Professional diver Stephen Wagstaffe told in the 1970s how there were 'turbulence and other grave dangers for the diver who is not constantly aware of the treacherous swell. Several times I have sustained injuries and once I split my head open and was washed up in the same spot where they found James Johnson. That was while I was recovering a cannon.'

Removing relics from the *Dunbar* was banned when the site was granted provisional protection as a historic shipwreck site under the Commonwealth *Historic Shipwrecks Act 1976* until further archaeological and historical research was conducted. That research completed, in October 1991 the remains of the *Dunbar* were officially designated as having 'historical, archaeological and symbolic significance'. The following year, the government's Maritime Heritage Program's David Nutley and Tim Smith conceived the *Dunbar* Conservation Management Plan.

In 1998–99, the Commonwealth Department of the Arts and Administrative Services declared a twelve-month amnesty from prosecution for those who handed over undeclared souvenirs taken from shipwreck sites. Anyone still with artefacts after the amnesty expired faced a $5000 fine or ten years in prison. The department hoped this would encourage hoarders to relinquish their pieces for recording, preservation and public display in museums and libraries, such as the Australian National Maritime Museum, the Museum of Applied Arts and Sciences/Powerhouse Museum, Sydney Living Museums, the Historic Houses Trust and the State Library of New South Wales.

On 17 October 2003, the *Dunbar* wreck site was added to the New South Wales State Heritage Register. The Statement of Significance says, among other things:

> The . . . site and its associated relics are a significant component of Australia's maritime heritage by virtue of the shipwreck's impact on the developing colony of Sydney, its influence on the improvement of navigational aids and its potential for interpretation through public education programs. The wreck site maintains an important and continuing association with descendants of the victims and as one of the most well-known Australian maritime tragedies.

The New South Wales Heritage Office manages the site; its brief is to 'ensure the survival of the site and all associated materials that have been established to be irreplaceable items of cultural heritage'.

Dr Brad Duncan, senior maritime archaeologist, Heritage New South Wales, Department of Premier and Cabinet, is another who has continued the management of the wreck and relics. Duncan has carried on the work of the Maritime Heritage Program's Nutley and Smith. To Duncan, the *Dunbar* is much, much more than a few pieces of iron strewn on the ocean floor.

> I started off regarding the site strictly as another archaeological location with artefacts, but I came to understand what the wreck of the *Dunbar* meant to the colony, and still means to the community. So many lives ended when the ship went down, and not only the victims' loved ones but all of Sydney mourned. People coming to South Head today still consider it a gravesite and become moved and even upset. Sydneysiders appreciate what a moment it was in our story. People stood on the cliffs and looked down at the bodies, some of whom they would have recognised, and the sharks. To me the site is not a time capsule, as there are ongoing events that went on after the wreck (including the rescue of James Johnson and divers salvaging of the site, and later historic site management and recording), which add multiple ongoing chapters to the story. Objects at the site are not just *things*, they were someone's personal property. The buckles belonged to someone's belt, the dentures were once in somebody's mouth. Then there were all the safety changes—Hornby Lighthouse, telecommunications, the improved pilot service—that were made to ensure that such a tragedy never happened again. That all makes it a very special place for me.

Dr Duncan finds diving the *Dunbar* an unnerving experience. 'There's a 60-metre cliff above you so it's dark down there, and visibility is poor. There are shadows, a sense of danger.' Other divers have told him that they get chills that have nothing to do with the cold water. He acknowledges that in Sydney there was a 'finders keepers' tradition among early divers. Whatever somebody found washed off a wreck became their property. 'Locals felt entitled to scavenge. When wrecks occurred along the coast and all this stuff washed ashore it was like a field day, a gift from God for communities with not a lot of wealth. Everyone would flock to help themselves, make tables, or build houses from the timber wreckage, take chairs, clothing, anything they could lay their hands on.'

One who took advantage of the *Dunbar* artefacts amnesty was Sydney diver and spearfisher John Gillies. From the mid-1950s to 1974, Gillies reportedly retrieved more than 5000 objects from the wreck site. Conscience may have played a role in Gillies' disclosure of his trove, which maritime archaeologist David Nutley described as 'mind-boggling'. Gillies told journalist Frank Robson of the *Sydney Morning Herald*'s *Good Weekend* magazine in 1994 that he had nightmares about the way he, and other divers, had treated the *Dunbar*. 'I'm still ashamed of some of the things I've done with [explosives], but not as ashamed as a lot of others should be . . . Divers in the 1950s and '60s were looking for a bit of money on the side and nobody cared about wreck preservation.'

Also, John Gillies was ill and was facing medical bills. After he notified the Department of Planning of his hoard, Gillies was allowed to auction his artefacts at Sotheby's Australia, but only after they had been photographed and catalogued. There was also a stipulation that the relics, which included a valuable 1855 Sydney sovereign, had to be sold in one lot and remain in Australia. David Nutley confirmed the collection's significance. The objects, he said, 'bring the *Dunbar* and all it stood for into much clearer perspective. These were the materials that the people on *Dunbar* were familiar with. This was their life—it's a very poignant collection.'

Private collectors were keen to get their hands on the *Dunbar*'s artefacts, but the Australian National Maritime Museum was alarmed at the prospect of the relics being resold and dispersed, never preserved or seen by the public. So in 1994, with the backing of the Office of the Environment and Heritage and the Andrew Thyne Reid Charitable Trust, the museum negotiated an out-of-auction settlement with John Gillies.

'Ethically, we are not allowed to buy relics from wrecks because that may encourage an illegal market,' explains the National Maritime Museum's Kieran Hosty.

We wanted to save the Gillies Collection, so the Trust bought the 5000 pieces on our behalf. John Gillies received $55,000 for his medical expenses but with the auction house's buyer's premium, the total cost of the collection was about $67,000. John knew he was very sick. I met him a couple of times: when we acquired his relics and later when he talked me through the pieces. He died within two years.

'Since then,' says Hosty, 'thousands of *Dunbar* artefacts have undergone conservation, photography, registration and curatorial research, and been seen by visitors to the Museum.' The relics are detailed in Hosty's book, Dunbar *1857: Disaster on Our Doorstep*, published to mark the 150th anniversary of the *Dunbar*'s foundering. Hosty wrote in *Disaster on Our Doorstep* that, because the museum acquired the relics from divers:

It is unfortunate that this collection lacks the rigorous scientific documentation that is provided by professional archaeological excavations, including context—the positional relationships between artefacts and the site they come from. Nonetheless, the collection still has the potential to provide a snapshot of what life was like in colonies during the gold rushes of the 1850s. It also stands as a record of early shipwreck salvage activities and the impact that uncontrolled access had on these fragile sites.

The relics continue to turn up. Stirling Smith and Dr Brad Duncan at Heritage New South Wales were contacted by a man in his eighties wanting to donate his *Dunbar* relics. 'He said he used to dive with John Gillies,' said Smith.

He realised he may not be around much longer to enjoy his artefacts and his family didn't want them cluttering up the house—'Get these rusty old things out of here!'—and he was happy for us to take them off his hands. I had a look and because they'd been in the open air for 50 years they'd deteriorated a lot, but I organised for the Observatory Hill Archaeology Program to use the artefacts as teaching aids. That man's relics were authentic, but a number we're asked to look at or which turn up on eBay are not. You have to be circumspect.

Among the Australian National Maritime Museum's splendid collection of *Dunbar* artefacts is a metal ornament depicting two soldiers shaking hands, possibly commemorating the end of the Crimean War in 1856. There are more than a hundred silver and copper-alloy coins, one of the oldest being an 1816 King George III sixpence, and more than a thousand coin-shaped Hanks & Lloyd–minted metal tokens planned to be used in the colony as legal tender. Among the most affecting relics are wedding and signet rings, many, like the tiny ring with *Si fuerit deus mecum* etched upon it, with a personal inscription, and there are earrings, pendants, brooches and watches. The collection includes clay pipes, keys, metal and mother-of-pearl buttons, a copper-alloy sailor's belt buckle featuring a rope entwined around an anchor, a silver nib and bone shaft pen, iron bedframes, furniture fittings and firearms.

Not all of the Australian National Maritime Museum's *Dunbar* items were acquired from John Gillies. One of its most notable items is the captain's chair. Not Captain James Green's personal seat, but a solid polished wood chair most likely fashioned by a carpenter from *Dunbar* timbers found floating in Port Jackson or washed up on a beach.

The Maritime Museum's Myffanwy Bryant has written on the Museum's website about the collection's 'hundreds of everyday objects that do not often survive the rigours of domesticity but tell the story of life in a growing colony. In effect the wreck [preserves] together the materials of many different industries and areas of life.'

Myf Bryant is intrigued by the denture plates Gillies took from the wreck and that are now with the museum.

These are made of gold and . . . are surprisingly delicate and one of the many wonders of what could survive a devastating shipwreck such as the *Dunbar*. It did get me wondering what the state of dentistry was in the colony of Sydney in 1857 . . . By the 1850s, denture plates could be made of platinum, silver or gold, such as those from *Dunbar* . . . The artificial teeth used in the dentures were made either from porcelain, which was prone to chipping and grating, or [they were] human . . . [which were] more natural looking than their porcelain counterparts, kept their colour longer and were tougher . . . Dentists had two options, obtaining them from the poor who sold them or to purchase those taken from cadavers . . . Wars were a reliable source of teeth and during the Crimean War of 1853 . . . the supply was steady.

Sydney's Powerhouse Museum, a branch of the Museum of Applied Arts and Sciences, has a number of *Dunbar* artefacts. One of the items preserved at the Powerhouse is a colourised ambrotype portrait of the *Dunbar*'s third mate, John Pascoe. The image's hinged glass, metal, wood, leather and textile case protected it from water damage. The doomed Pascoe, from Cornwall, looks proudly at the photographer. His long dark hair is tucked into a fine sailor's cap with gold braiding and his uniform is decorated with gold buttons and chain. His left hand rests easily on his hip. At his death, Pascoe was just eighteen.

After a piece of ribbon, described as 'fragile and rather lovely' and perhaps used to tie back the hair of a *Dunbar* passenger, was recovered from the harbour, it somehow turned up in a London antique market in 1965. When a Mrs Rita Spector read the attached note revealing that the ribbon was from the *Dunbar*, she presented it to the National Library of Australia in Canberra. Today it is stored in the Library's vault. The National Library also keeps *Dunbar* shirts, dresses, hats, silk and linen drapery, carpets, candles and children's toys.

27

Last respects

Captain James Green's body was never recovered, but those wishing to can stand before a memorial plaque dedicated to him by his friends and supporters at the colonial St James' Church, off King Street in the city. And at South Head Cemetery on Old South Head Road, not too far from where he met his death, there is a marble monument to Green and his seafaring brother, Malcolm. The monument was installed after Malcolm's death in 1904. Its inscription ends: 'Their anchors are cast in the haven of rest. They sail the wild seas no more.'

* * * *

Camperdown Cemetery, serene and beautiful by day, can ice the blood on a winter's night. Then, with its skeletal trees, sunken graves and tilted, crumbling headstones, the 173-year-old cemetery could be the setting for a dark fable by Poe or the Brothers Grimm.

Sadness seems to float like fog among the cemetery's decaying graves, and nowhere is the sense of despondency more pronounced than the south-east corner of the graveyard where the unidentified bodies or body parts of 24 *Dunbar* victims were interred together in a rectangular sandstone tomb after the funeral procession that brought Sydney to a halt on 24 August 1857. Captain John Steane is buried nearby, and the bodies of Maria and Mary (or Polly) Waller and their servant lie beneath a formidable monument that also commemorates the six Waller family members whose bodies were never found. William Butler Williams and John Jerram rest in their own plots elsewhere in the cemetery.

The first official *Dunbar* remembrance service was conducted at the tomb on 21 August 1926. Four hundred attended. Prayers were read and the church bell tolled 121 times, once for each victim. Organised annual commemorations ceased when the Great Depression and then World War II preoccupied Sydneysiders. The services began again in 1992, and since then have been held at Camperdown Cemetery and St Stephen's Church in the cemetery grounds on the closest Sunday to 20 August every year.

Flowers often decorate the *Dunbar* tomb, and not just on 20 August. The gravesite, which even more than the graves of colonial surveyor and explorer Sir Thomas Mitchell and Eliza Donnithorne, reputedly the inspiration for Charles Dickens' Miss Havisham in *Great Expectations*, draws visitors to the cemetery. It is a Sydney thing to do to stand at the *Dunbar* tomb and the recovered *Dunbar* anchor and chain, which were incorporated in the monument in 1933.

Naturally, there is a *Dunbar* ghost story. It involves the dashing retired Royal Navy captain, John Steane. Perhaps it was a nocturnal visitor who, eyes wide and knees knocking, conjured up the tale that has been recycled in books and magazines and by word of mouth since the 1990s. Whoever is responsible for propagating it, the legend lives on. The story goes that Hannah Watson, the—if colonial artist Joseph Backler's 1849 portrait of her is accurate—heavy-set, stern-faced and, by her velvet dress and gold jewellery, wealthy wife of Port Jackson harbour master and inaugural keeper of Macquarie Light Captain Thomas Watson, was having an affair with Captain Steane. Thomas found out and put a curse on the lovers. Hannah Watson wrote to Steane, who was visiting England, suggesting that, considering her cuckolded husband's fury, he'd be wise to lie low there for a while. Hannah promptly, whether due to Thomas's curse or a more mundane cause, died and was buried in Camperdown Cemetery. Captain Steane never received her warning letter. When it arrived in England, he was already bound for Sydney on the *Dunbar*. So, it's said, on nights when the wind blows and the rain pelts down, like it did on 20 August 1857, Hannah's wispy grey phantom wafts from her grave and keeps Captain Steane company in his. A good yarn, certainly, although there is no proof that Hannah Watson and John Steane were lovers, either pre- or post-mortem.

Nowadays, Camperdown Cemetery, where 18,000 souls were buried, is officially deemed to be in a state of 'graceful decay'. Its last burial (save for a few who had pre-booked their plot) was in 1948, two years after the brutal rape and murder of an eleven-year-old local girl, Joan Norma Ginn, saw the place declared 'dangerous and decadent'. Two-thirds of the cemetery was closed and designated open parkland, leaving the graves around St Stephen's and its stately Moreton Bay fig as a memorial to the dead.

Camperdown Cemetery is an atmospheric and tangible link to colonial days, and to the *Dunbar*.

On the Sunday this author strolled through Camperdown Cemetery to view the *Dunbar* mass tomb and find the other victims' graves, around 60 visitors were doing the same, quietly and reverently trying to read the weather-blasted wording on the sandstone headstones and admiring the beauty of the stone monuments—urns, crosses, angels and ships (the latter because so many died on the water then). Not so reverent was a group of around 40 young people, self-styled 'Goths', affecting a uniform of black clothing, black-dyed hair and black eye and lip make-up, straining to be macabre and exotic as they draped themselves over the vaults and headstones and gambolled like sprites among the palms and gums. A few people grumbled that the Goths were being sacrilegious, but not many others seemed to mind, least of all the occupants of the graves.

* * * *

The so-called 'Dunbar Bible' is kept in the safe at St Stephen's Church at Camperdown Cemetery. The day after the clipper foundered, Daniel and William Whealey were on Forty Baskets Beach, near their home. They were fossicking through debris, obviously from a shipwreck, that had washed ashore overnight. They came upon a Bible in a box. The Bible, the lads would learn, had been the property of a *Dunbar* victim. Remarkably, it was only slightly water-stained. In 1955, the boys' descendants presented the Bible to St Stephen's Church, and it was read from at the church's *Dunbar* centenary service in 1957.

* * * *

On Sunday morning, 19 August 2007—on what John Lanser of the Australasian Pioneers' Club, who was there, called 'a rotten day . . . foul weather, a *Dunbar* day'—there was a sesquicentenary of the loss of the *Dunbar* service at Camperdown Cemetery. The Reverend Peter Rodgers led prayers at the *Dunbar* tomb. With him were New South Wales Governor Professor Marie Bashir; her husband, the former Lord Mayor of Sydney, Sir Nicholas Shehadie; and the Mayor of Marrickville, Alderman Morris Hanna. Descendants of survivor James Johnson and victims Marian Egan and John Ridley Jerram attended. Former State Coroner Kevin Waller, a descendant of John Gough Waller, the brother of Kilner Waller, brother-in-law of Maria Waller, and uncle of the six Waller children, all of whom died on the *Dunbar*, was there that day. With him were members of his family, including his son Steven. Kevin Waller, a late twentieth-century counterpart of *Dunbar*-era Coroner John Skottowe Parker, between 1988 and 1992 conducted inquests into some of New South Wales' worst disasters. Dr Christian Garland, a descendant of Marian Egan, who died with her children, Gertrude and Henry Cahuac, was there. Kieran Hosty needed no guide to the cemetery, having lived in St Stephen's sexton's cottage, as old as the cemetery itself, for ten years from 1998. 'That's where my *Dunbar* passion began' he said.

In his eulogy, Reverend Rodgers said that the loss of the *Dunbar* and her passengers and crew should remind us of the fragility of life. He then read from James Johnson's testimony to the coronial inquest 150 years before. 'And then we struck and the screaming began, the passengers running about the decks in nightdresses, screaming for mercy. Almost immediately the decks burst up from the pressure of the water, the ship was rammed into a thousand pieces and all on board were hurried into the foaming, terrific sea.'

Wreaths of wildflowers were laid on the tomb, which glistened in the rain. At the end, St Stephen's bells chimed, and the congregation recited the names of the 121 *Dunbar* victims.

Dr Christian Garland recalled that rainy morning. 'It was a very sombre occasion, then Governor Marie Bashir climbed up onto a plinth supporting the mass grave, and she slipped on the wet surface and was almost impaled on the sharp points of the fence around the grave. We almost had another *Dunbar* tragedy! The near-accident broke our gloomy mood and everyone, including the governor, had a good giggle.'

And Steven Waller had a disconcerting encounter with someone more interested in making a dollar than paying his respects.

This bloke sidled up to me, salt of the earth, rough and tumble, someone who'd obviously spent a lot of time in the sun. He said, 'So you're one of the Wallers?' When I told him that I was, he said, 'You're clearly not descended from Kilner Waller because all of his family perished.' I told him I was descended from Kilner's brother, John Gough Waller. 'Well,' he went on, 'I've got a lot of your family jewellery.' Which was a not-so-subtle suggestion that I purchase it from him. I said, 'So you're one of those who pillaged the wreck?' And he said, 'Yep, but it wasn't illegal when I did it.' He was quite brazen, but when it was clear he was not going to get a sale, he left me alone. How did he know the jewellery he had was our family's? Maybe it was a monogrammed jewel case . . . Maybe he had no evidence and was trying to con me.

Later, in the church, the Shipshape Theatre Company performed *Dunbar: A Folk Opera* in thirteen scenes, and folklorist Warren Fahey sang, accompanied by appropriately mournful violin, his ballad 'Dreadful Wreck 1857': 'Upon their lee the breakers roar and dark cliffs frowning loom/the thunders crash, the lightnings flash, break through the awful gloom . . .'

* * * *

While its former owner, Dr Christian Garland, is unconvinced that it is a great example of portraiture, there is a painting at the National Portrait Gallery in Canberra whose poignancy transcends any notions of artistic merit: *Dunbar* victims Marian Egan, wife of the Sydney politician and businessman Daniel Egan, and her children, Gertrude and Henry Cahuac, who had sat for the now-unknown artist shortly before boarding the *Dunbar* on its final journey. Attractive and well dressed, in the portrait they seem serenely content with life, looking forward to returning to Australia after an English and Continental holiday. Surely, ahead can lie only happiness. It was unfinished when the three sailed from England. The artist kept his promise to despatch the completed work on the next ship to Sydney, the *Dunbar*'s sister ship, the *La Hogue*, addressed to Daniel Egan. According to historian Annette Lemercier, Egan presumably gave the painting to Marian's sister Elizabeth Evans, who bequeathed it to her son, Alfred. On Alfred's death, his widow, Fanny, hung it at her home in Lauderdale Avenue, Manly. 'Her eldest daughter, Grace Elizabeth O'Rourke, inherited it and Grace in turn passed it to her great-grandson Dr Christian Garland.'

Dr Garland, a microbiologist who now lives in Adelaide, elaborated. 'I was four years old and visiting the Manly home of my great-grandmother, Grace, and I was entranced by the portrait of Marian, Gertrude and Henry. Later, I learned about them and immersed myself in the romance and tragedy of the *Dunbar* story. I inherited the painting when Grace died in 1966.' On having it cleaned in the 1980s, Dr Garland said:

My eyes popped out and I nearly fell over . . . It burst to life, especially the fresh skin tones, and a necklace appeared on Gertrude's neck! When I hung the painting in my house, Marian, Gertrude and Henry truly came back to life, their eyes followed me around the room and it spooked me to the point I had to turn away. There is something haunting about the faces of those people, perhaps because they do not know their fate, and we do.

Dr Garland tried to discover the identity of the artist. 'I took it to the Art Gallery of New South Wales and the painting was x-rayed. We found bits and pieces underneath, sketches of some slightly different poses, but there was no signature. The style is similar to that of Robert Hawker Dowling, but it's impossible to say if it is his work.'

When he went to work in the Philippines in 2011, Dr Garland lent the painting to the Pioneers' Club, and on his return he sold it to the National Portrait Gallery. 'I thought, "Why not? I've had it for 50 years."'

And there today at the gallery are Marian, Gertrude and Henry, their portrait yet another link to the *Dunbar*, frozen in time, dreamy-eyed, happy, privileged, contemplating a sunny future in Sydney town that they would never have.

On Marian's death, a grieving Daniel Egan commissioned for £70 from the renowned stained-glass artist John Hardman of Birmingham, England, a window comprising three panels memorialising his wife and her children. The window was installed in Sydney's St Mary's Cathedral in 1860. There was an inscription: 'Pray for the souls of Marian Egan and her children Henry and Gertrude drowned in the wreck of the *Dunbar* on the South Head of Port Jackson on March [sic] 20th, 1857'. The central panel depicts Mary Immaculate above the storm-tossed *Dunbar*, with Marian Egan on board. The side panels feature Henry and Gertrude Cahuac kneeling at the feet of their patron saints St Henry, the tenth-century Bavarian Holy Roman emperor, and St Gertrude of Helfta, a thirteenth-century

German nun. The siblings are pleading with Mary to save them from the tempest.

When fire destroyed St Mary's on 29 June 1865, the central panel featuring Marian was destroyed. The side panels survived and were relocated at the Benedictine nuns' convent Subiaco, in Rydalmere, western Sydney. Since 1980, they have graced the chapel of the Benedictine monastery at Arcadia, north-west of Sydney.

* * * *

A number of the *Dunbar* victims' loved ones and friends were parishioners at St John's Anglican Church, Darlinghurst, which held its first service in 1858, the year following the clipper's destruction. In homage to the *Dunbar*, the nave of the church was designed to evoke the interior of a ship. Says St John's caretaker and historian, Laurie Alexander, 'It's possible that a number of the voyagers who died had subscribed to help build the church, so it's fitting that today there are *Dunbar* artefacts at St John's that the public can see.'

The ship's bell is at the church. Perhaps it is the one that summoned the *Dunbar* passengers to breakfast at 8 a.m., lunch at 1 p.m. and dinner at 6 p.m. It was one of the items salvaged by diver Tom McNab on 25 June 1861, when he first dived the wreck in his heavy helmet, suit and boots. The bell was bought by St John's at an auction of *Dunbar* relics in the late 1800s. It hung in a turret at the western end of the church and was tolled to call parishioners to Sunday service. There it remained until 1903 when it was taken to the bell tower of St John's parish hall and primary school and for 63 years was rung to summon children to classes. When the school was demolished in 1966, the bell was given a new home in the vestibule of St John's.

On a wall of the church, alongside a painting of the *Dunbar* under full sail, is a marble memorial dedicated by their parents to the memory of the doomed Logan children—Ida, Arthur and Charles. Beneath a cross is a plaque: 'Sacred to the memory of Ida, aged 18, Charles Alfred, aged 11, Arthur P, aged 9, the beloved children of Charles and Mary Logan . . .' Then, from 2 Samuel 1:23, 'They were lovely and pleasant in their lives, and in their death they were not divided.'

A chair made from *Dunbar* timber is at St John's, and a small wooden chest belonging to Captain John Steane. The chest was not unduly damaged in the wreck or by salt water. On its front it reads 'J Stean'. The final 'e' is long lost.

* * * *

The Australasian Pioneers' Club in Macquarie Street, Sydney, hosts a *Dunbar* lunch each year on the nearest Tuesday to 20 August. One of the club's treasures is a heavy round table. Former Pioneers' Club president, John Lanser, believes a salvor would have sold the floating timber to George Green's boat yard in Lavender Bay, and it was then on-sold by Green to a carpenter who built the table. Lanser said, 'I'm the great-great-great grandson of George Green, who handled a lot of *Dunbar* wreckage, and whose boat yard features in the wonderful photo by Robert Hunt, who was the brother of the Misses Hunt . . . So many coincidences.'

* * * *

What does *not* exist is a film, *The Wreck of the* Dunbar, *Or the Yeoman's Wedding.* The lost 39-minute silent movie was directed in 1912 by Gaston Mervale. It starred Louise Carbasse who, in one more *Dunbar* irony, had attended St John's Anglican Church primary school in Darlinghurst and would have hurried to class on hearing the *Dunbar*'s recovered bell rung. The film was based on an 1887 play, *The Wreck of the* Dunbar, that was performed at Sydney's Royal Standard Theatre on Castlereagh Street and that, going by the reviews, seems to have been more notable for the rowdy behaviour of the audience than the acting talent of the players. The film, like the play, was a ripe melodrama that piled a steamy love triangle between orphan Hettie Parker, pilot Joe Trueheart and the *Dunbar* survivor, who was given the name Ralph Johnson, pathos, pratfalls, belief-defying coincidences and suicide on to a loose retelling of the *Dunbar*'s demise. The film had a three-week run. It is not known whether the trinkets purportedly beaten from *Dunbar* copper that were handed out to cinema patrons helped extend the season.

Epilogue

The bay

Though much has changed about Watsons Bay, its harbourside village heart still beats, if fainter than in the old days.

On the 161st anniversary of the *Dunbar* wreck, in 2018, a group came together in swirling mid-winter winds on the cliff atop the wreck site to see members of New South Wales Police Rescue re-enact the rescue of James Johnson. New South Wales Minister for the Environment Gabrielle Upton called the loss of the *Dunbar* one of the saddest stories in Australian history. 'Instead of welcoming their loved ones in Sydney Cove,' she told the gathering, 'Sydneysiders watched from these cliffs in horror as bodies were pounded on the rocks below [by waves] as high as mountains.' Maritime archaeologists Kieran Hosty, Stirling Smith and Dr Brad Duncan attended. So too, did members of groups and individuals determined to preserve the traditional character of South Head, including film director George Miller (the *Mad Max* franchise, *Babe*, *Happy Feet*), local historians Bruce Crosson, Roger Bayliss and Peter Poland, and Dr James Hanson, great-great-great-grandson of lone survivor James Johnson's brother Henry, the first keeper of Hornby Lighthouse.

South Head, because of its extraordinary beauty and location, is constantly besieged by developers tone-deaf to heritage and history. Their sprawling concrete-and-glass boxes, which have replaced many of the old weatherboard fishermen's cottages, monster the landscape and their planned massive wedding and convention palaces, thankfully thwarted (so far), would have turned South Head into a party peninsula. House prices at Watsons Bay have risen beyond the reach of the fishermen and sailors and boat builders, the artists, the writers, the historians, the young families who gave it its laidback, egalitarian character. All this is radically changing the demographic of Watsons Bay.

George Miller, Dr James Hanson and their colleagues are fiercely protective of their patch of paradise, and there is much worth protecting. In Watsons Bay, the past comes alive. The remaining century-old weatherboard fishermen's cottages on narrow, winding streets. Camp Cove, where Arthur Phillip first set foot on the shores of Port Jackson and the pilot boat service was founded. The Gadigal rock carvings, hard to find, but there. Hornby and Macquarie lighthouses, the signal station (though it beamed its final message in 1992). The Gap. The stone obelisk on the rocks at Green Point Reserve (formerly Laing's Point). The colossal fig trees in Robertson Park by the beach, gently sloping Robertson Park itself, where people picnic today as Lady Macquarie did two centuries ago. Don Ritchie Grove near Jacobs Ladder, honouring local Samaritan Ritchie who, over five decades, is said to have dissuaded more than 160 people from suiciding at The Gap. A German shepherd named Rexie is also remembered with a plaque; the local dog could apparently sense a potential suicide and draw attention to the person by barking, and is credited with saving more than 30 lives. Con's Milk Bar (though long-time proprietor Con Georgiou sold up in 2021) where long-time Watsons Bay denizens such as Roger Bayliss, Terry Wolfe, Costa Akon, Michael Rigg and others sip coffee, solve the problems of the world and celebrate their village. The wharf where ferries dock and disgorge day-trippers and take commuters to work in the city, and where once shark fishermen weighed their catch. The sharks were concealed behind a screen and the public was charged a penny entrance fee for a close look. The houses in Pacific Street, nos. 14 and 22 respectively, where novelist Christina Stead and impressionist artist John Peter Russell lived, and artist John Olsen's home at 12 Cliff Street.

There are many worse ways to spend a day in Sydney than to look down into the roaring maw of The Gap, then enjoy the views from Gap Bluff. Gaze far out to sea, up the coast, or back to Sydney Harbour and further west towards Parramatta, just as people did 200 years ago. Ships from Britain and elsewhere still round South Head and enter Port Jackson, even if the majestic clippers like the *Dunbar* have been replaced by multi-storeyed tourist-laden ocean liners that negotiate the Heads without a hitch.

Then, perhaps, wander up the pathway to the *Dunbar* Memorial, touch the gnarly old anchor and read the inscription before swimming at Watsons Bay Baths by Marine Parade, eating fish and chips at Doyle's kiosk and restaurant (although the restaurant is not the family-priced, simple seaside eatery it once was) or quenching a thirst at the Watsons Bay pub, both on the beach with sweeping Port Jackson views. The Marine Hotel, where James Johnson recuperated after his rescue, not too much changed since 1857, is today Dunbar House cafe and restaurant. Watsons Bay has a Dunbar Street, and the cliffs of Outer South Head between the signal station and Macquarie Light are now officially known as Dunbar Head.

There is no better time than at the end of the day when the sun slips behind the glittering metropolis that grew from Phillip's 'wretched hovels' and its dying rays briefly turn the waters of Sydney Harbour to liquid gold, to sit by a particular smallish fig tree near the beach front. It was planted in 1991 to replace, and commemorate, a giant fig known as the Tree of Knowledge, where fishermen and seafarers gathered in days gone by.

* * * *

Some Watsons Bay locals speak of the melancholy aura that can pervade Watsons Bay and cling to the monolithic sandstone cliffs of Outer South Head, the same cliffs upon which the *Dunbar* was destroyed. The Gap, to the north of the wreck site where the *Dunbar* bodies and wreckage were trapped, is Australia's most notorious suicide spot, and considering its tragic legacy, that is no real surprise.

Dr James Hanson, descendant of James Johnson's brother Henry, is an academic in the School of Business at UNSW Canberra. He works in the national capital, but his home, like that of his ancestors, is Watsons Bay. Whatever the weather, Hanson, a big, handsome man with a rakish ponytail, and a sailor himself, walks from his home in the village to Hornby Lighthouse, where Henry Johnson was the keeper 160 years ago. Hanson tells how when Henry died in 1884 his wife, Mary-Anne, left their cottage at the lighthouse and lived in Watsons Bay village, 'a stone's throw from where I live today'.

Watsons Bay is James Hanson's place of the heart. 'I love its history, the streets, the cottages and the people. I like to be surrounded by the sea, to get as much salt water around me as I can get. When people learn that I'm distantly related to the sole survivor of the *Dunbar*, they want to touch me on the shoulder for good luck.'

On his strolls along the cliff-tops, James Hanson returns again and again in his mind—like Kieran Hosty and Stirling Smith and Steven Waller and all those who've been entranced by the sad saga of the *Dunbar*—to the events of 20 August 1857. 'It's important to remember those who died that night, and the families who mourned them. Our family was lucky.'

James Hanson attests to Watsons Bay's forbidding ambience. Not, he insists, on sunny days when hordes of happy day-trippers in their bright cossies converge from all over Sydney and overseas to swim and picnic and queue for crisp hot fish and chips at Doyle's kiosk. But on historian John Lanser's *Dunbar* nights, when mighty waves pound the cliffs and the rain falls in sheets and the wind howls and seagulls wheel and scream and a sliver of yellow moon shows itself through helter-skelter clouds, then, says Hanson, you can sense that something terrible happened here.

My academic mind says don't be silly, but still . . . *Dunbar* has left her mark on Watsons Bay. There's definitely a spookiness. I know some who refuse to go up to The Gap at night. I've seen them turn white and freeze at the bottom of the steps leading up to the lookout. On dark winter days I find The Gap and the cliffs and the heaving mass of water below unsettling, yet I never turn back. I feel safe on the cliff-top. I look down into The Gap and I walk to the *Dunbar* anchor memorial and I'm at peace. If there *are* ghosts there, I know they're my friends.

Acknowledgements

Many people helped me during the process of researching and writing *The Shipwreck*.

Sandy Peacock and Damien Parkes, men of the sea and veteran sailors both, who have a wealth of knowledge, practical and theoretical, about ships and sailing, fact-checked my manuscript and rescued me from making any embarrassing blunders. It's easy to run aground when writing about the technicalities of sailing, its lore and arcane vernacular. That said, any errors in this book are mine.

Jennie Fairs, president of Botany Bay Family History Society, unearthed birth, death and marriage certificates, family trees and long-lost newspaper clippings about the *Dunbar* victims and other key protagonists. If these long-dead people breathe again in this book, which was my aim, much of the credit belongs to Jennie's diligent sleuthing.

Steve Waller is a descendant of John Gough Waller, brother of Kilner Waller who, with his wife and six children, perished on the *Dunbar*. Steve is steeped in both his family and *Dunbar* lore, and the information about both that he graciously imparted to me when I visited him at his home in great part enabled me to portray the remarkable Wallers as real people and not simply as sad statistics. On Steve's dining table is a replica of the *Dunbar*.

Jill Rowbotham, journalist at *The Australian*, who wrote a lovely piece on the Waller family's connection to the *Dunbar* tragedy, put me in contact with Steve Waller.

Dr James Hanson of the School of Business, UNSW Canberra, was, like Steve Waller, a godsend to this book. James is the great-great-great-grandson of the *Dunbar*'s sole survivor James Johnson's brother Henry, who was the first keeper of Hornby Lighthouse. A sailor himself, James regaled me with stories of his ancestors and his insights into the life of the enigmatic James Johnson after his miraculous rescue. James and I walked together in Watsons Bay and he gave me a deeper appreciation than I previously had of the mystique of South Head and the ways in which the *Dunbar* calamity continues to haunt the village.

Kieran Hosty's contribution to this book was considerable. Kieran is head of curatorial and research and maritime archaeologist at the Australian National Maritime Museum, and a *Dunbar* authority. Kieran has done much to preserve relics from the wreck. He has written a fine book, Dunbar *1857: Disaster on our doorstep*, for the Maritime Museum, and his description of the acquisition and preservation of the clipper's relics is as exciting as any passage in an adventure novel. Kieran allowed me access to rare research materials. I thank him for his generosity.

I'm indebted to two offspring of renowned authors who have become important authors in their own right. Adam Courtenay, son of Bryce and author of *The Ghost and the Bounty Hunter* and *The Ship that Never Was*, suggested I call Meg Keneally, daughter of Thomas, whose recent novels, *Fled* and *The Wreck*, vividly evoke life in the colony in the first half of the nineteenth century. Meg, as generous as she is talented, in turn introduced me to Stirling Smith, formerly maritime archaeologist at the National Maritime Museum and now senior maritime archaeological officer at Heritage New South Wales, Department of Premier and Cabinet. Like Kieran Hosty, Stirling has dived what is left of the *Dunbar* often and has a wealth of knowledge of the ship, its place in our history, and its relics. Our interview was enlightening and a pleasure.

Stirling's colleague, Dr Brad Duncan, senior maritime archaeologist, Heritage New South Wales, Department of Premier and

Cabinet, was one of those who helped manage the *Dunbar* wreck and preserve its relics. Brad gave me goosebumps when he described the challenges of diving on the *Dunbar* in the shadow of the South Head cliffs on a rough-water day. Brad has continued the work of the Maritime Heritage Program's David Nutley and Tim Smith who conceived the *Dunbar* Conservation Management Plan and were instrumental in having the wreck declared a Heritage site.

One of the most fascinating interviews I conducted was with Laurie Alexander, caretaker at St John's Church, Darlinghurst. Laurie imparted his knowledge of this enduring shrine to the *Dunbar* and its passengers, and showed me paintings and artefacts related to the ship and—a great thrill—allowed me to ring the bell that was recovered from the *Dunbar* and that now graces the vestibule of the church.

Xanthe Reid, office manager of NEAC (Newtown Erskineville Anglican Church), organised a guided visit to Camperdown Cemetery. There I stood at the *Dunbar* memorial and the victims' graves and absorbed the melancholy, yet sublime, atmosphere of the crumbling burial ground. The experience informed my chapter on the mass burial of the *Dunbar* victims and the cemetery today.

After I told him of my project, nothing was too much trouble for Roger Bayliss, president of the Watsons Bay Association, a group dedicated to protesting the commercial development of South Head. Roger introduced me to authorities on the *Dunbar* and Watsons Bay. Speaking with and reading the writings of this notable group of historians and chroniclers helped me to understand the tragedy and its ongoing significance. Thank you, Kosta Akon, former proprietor and editor of *Bay Lief*, the bulletin of the Watsons Bay Society. Retired naval officer and author Peter Poland of the Woollahra History and Heritage Society, and John Lanser, former president of the Australasian Pioneers' Club, who invited me to his club for an interview and to sit at a handsome table made from *Dunbar* timbers. My knowledge was increased by the writings of historians Robin Derricourt, Bruce Crosson, Vincent Marinato and Jack Woodward.

Another valuable contributor to this book was Captain Mike Plant who, like his father, went to sea as an apprentice at the age of sixteen, and, after captaining container ships, became a Torres Strait pilot, the pinnacle of pilotage in Australia. Captain Mike helped me understand the hazards of entering Sydney Heads and the conditions that would have been faced by Captain James Green on 20 August 1857.

I felt that it was important to give readers a vicarious sense of what it is to be at the mercy of huge seas and a roaring gale. To that end, I sat with John 'Steamer' Stanley who was one of eight crewing the *Winston Churchill*, which was smashed and sunk by mountainous seas, and notably one 20 metre monster, in the infamous Sydney–Hobart Yacht Race of 1998. After the *Winston Churchill* sank, the crew took to two separate life rafts. Skipper Richard Winning, Bruce Gould, Michael Rynan, Paul Lumtin and Stanley, with his leg badly broken, were rescued. Tragically, fellow crewmen John Dean, Jim Lawler and Michael Bannister died. John Stanley's recounting of his ordeal, during which he experienced the horror of imminent death in raging seas, as did many of those on the *Dunbar*, and, like the *Dunbar*'s lone survivor, James Johnson, the enormous relief of being saved at the last, informed this book.

Spending a morning with Myffanwy Bryant at the Australian National Maritime Museum where she is assistant curator was a delight. A highlight of my research was when Myf spread on a table in front of me the museum's *Dunbar* relics that had been taken from the wreck site by scuba divers last century: jewellery, bells, buckles, picture frames, utensils—and gold dentures. Myf's eyes shone as she described the items, especially the tiny ring with the poignant inscription described in the text.

I'm grateful to my friend Tony Baine, who connected me to a group of long-time Watsons Bay denizens who meet at Con's Milk Bar, a retro cafe on Military Road just down from The Gap. On hearing that I was writing a book on the *Dunbar*, a talisman in all their lives, they invited me to join them for coffee and yarns. Just sitting and chatting, I learned so much, those little details that bring a book to life and lend it authenticity. Thank you, John Blondin, Michael Rigg, Grant Walter, Tony O'Neill and especially Terry Wolfe with his voluminous Watsons Bay history tomes and scrapbooks comprised of pages from the long-defunct *Bay Lief*.

Another to share her knowledge with me in my search for information on the *Dunbar* victims was historian, genealogist and *Australian Dictionary of Biography* contributor Annette Lemercier. Annette is a fifth-generation descendant of James Cheers, brother of Marian Egan. Annette is an authority on Marian, her husband, Daniel, and life in Sydney in the 1850s.

Through Annette Lemercier and John Lanser, I tracked down in Adelaide Dr Christian Garland, a one-time owner of a poignant portrait of *Dunbar* victim Marian Egan and her children. Christian told me the exciting history of the painting, which deserves a book of its own. Maria Ramsden, collection manager at the National Portrait Gallery in Canberra accompanied me into the gallery's archives to view the painting, which Christian presented to the gallery. Maria made history come alive.

Mori Flapan has an extraordinary knowledge of ships and the sea, and it was my great fortune that he was delighted to share his knowledge with me. Mori joined the Australian National Maritime Museum in 1971 where he worked tirelessly on the museum's fleet and for 30 years wrote articles for the museum's *Australian Sea Heritage* magazine. As well as bombarding me with facts, figures and stories about the great ships of the *Dunbar* era and their vital role in forging the colony of New South Wales, Mori unearthed some of the photographs in this book. Thanks to my friend and historian Jim Boyce for putting me in touch with Mori.

On a day when the wind was a gentle westerly and it was safe to do so, yet another experienced seaman and friend, Mike Rose, took me in a powerboat out through the Heads and down past The Gap to the exact spot where the *Dunbar* was wrecked. We ventured in as close to the cliffs as we could go without being dashed on the rocks ourselves and gazed up in awe at the implacable golden cliff face that rose above us and at the ledge at its base where James Johnson clambered and to which he clung for dear life after he was thrown into the sea. Even on this gentle day, the strength of the swell and the roar of the waves as they thundered onto the cliff where the poor *Dunbar* lay prostrate and then broke apart, left us in no doubt that Nature was boss.

Sydney's Powerhouse Museum, a major branch of the Museum of Applied Arts & Sciences, is, like the Australian National Maritime Museum, a repository of *Dunbar* artefacts. I thank those at the Powerhouse who offered assistance: curatorial administration officer Sharon Dickson, rights and permissions officer Harry Ree and curator Margaret Simpson.

I am indebted to Claire Miller and Jane Fraser of Fremantle Arts Centre Press for permission to publish the diary entries of voyagers John Fitch Clark, Anne Gratton, Dr Thomas Coke Brownell and John Ramsden Wollaston who voyaged to Australia in the first half of the nineteenth century. The entries are among those collected in FACP's fine 1991 book, *The Voyage Out*, compiled by Bryce Moore, Helen Garwood and Nancy Lutton after Ms Lutton accessed diaries held by the J.S. Battye Library of West Australian History.

As always, the staff at the State Library of New South Wales were a boon to an author delving into the past of Sydney. I especially thank Tom Norquay, of the Collection Access & Description Branch, who allowed me to publish portions of the diary of Arthur Wilcox Manning relating to his hair-raising voyage from Plymouth to Sydney on the *Earl Grey* in 1839–40.

I asked Warren Fahey, folklorist, author, cultural historian and musician, who wrote and performed the ballad 'Dreadful Wreck 1857' for the 150th anniversary commemorations of the *Dunbar*, if I could reprint his lyrics in my book. Thank you, Warren.

Covid-19 thwarted my plan to visit the great shipbuilding yards and the maritime museums and archives of the United Kingdom, to pore through the documents pertaining to the clipper era, study the building of the *Dunbar* at Sunderland and uncover the life story of its legendary owner Duncan Dunbar II. So my thanks go to the curators and historians of these establishments, and especially Sue Potts, Ian Sherlock and Christopher Bell, library and engagement assistants at Sunderland Local History Library, who emailed valuable research links, and Douglas W. Smith, president of the Sunderland Antiquarian Society, who took the time and trouble to mail to me a wealth of hardcopy documents. All of this information has enriched my book.

Karen McLeod sent me information on the clipper era and a magnificent reference book, *Teak and Tide* by Nigel Costley, chronicling the preservation on the dry dock where Karen presides at Picton, New Zealand, of the 47.9 metre clipper the *Edwin Fox*. The *Edwin Fox* is the last surviving ship to transport convicts to Australia, the last Crimean War troop carrier, and one of the oldest merchant vessels extant. Karen also introduced me to two Canadian maritime scholars, professors Adrian Shubert and Boyd D. Cothran of the Department of History at York University, Toronto, who are researching the *Edwin Fox*. Adrian and Boyd helped me access the Duncan Dunbar shipping line's account books, and alerted me to the information about the *Dunbar* contained in *Lloyd's List*. In turn, I was able to provide them with details of the *Edwin Fox*'s experiences in the Crimean War, which I came upon while researching the *Dunbar*'s role in that conflict.

I was blessed to have Allen & Unwin's brilliant publishing director Tom Gilliatt and senior editor Tom Bailey-Smith shepherding this book from acceptance of manuscript to publication. Through the loss of a beloved family member, and the Covid-19 pandemic, Tom Gilliatt's enthusiasm for the *Dunbar* project never flagged and he, like Tom Bailey-Smith, was always available to assuage doubts and give encouragement and advice. *The Shipwreck* was copyedited by Susan Keogh, whose intelligent suggestions and sensitive (to the text and to my easily bruised sensibilities) editing made this book better than it otherwise would have been.

All my love, finally, to Carol, my amazing wife, and our sons, Tom and Casey. Carol accompanied me to South Head on the morning of 21 March 2021, in the middle of the worst storm Sydney had experienced for decades. We stood on the edge of The Gap and atop Jacobs Ladder and the wreck site as rain speared down from black clouds, salty sea spray stung our faces and the wild wind all but blasted us off our feet. Being drenched and buffeted by these elements, at South Head, was a kind of homage, albeit from behind a safety fence, to those whose journey to Sydney was cut so cruelly short. It seemed the least I could do.

Further reading

Bach, John, *A Maritime History of Australia*, Sydney: Pan Books, 1982.

Ball, Duncan, *Amazing Australian Shipwrecks*, Sydney: Angus & Robertson, 1987.

Bell, James, *Private Journal of a Voyage to Australia: James Bell*, Sydney: Allen & Unwin (ed. Richard Walsh), 2011.

Bradshaw, H., *A Narrative of the Melancholy Wreck of the* Dunbar; *Bradshaw's Railway Guide*, Sydney, 1857.

Bridges, Peter, *Foundations of Identity—Building Early Sydney 1788–1822*, Sydney: Hale & Iremonger, 1995.

Colwell, Max, *Ships and Seafarers in Australian Waters*, Melbourne: Lansdowne Press, 1973.

Costley, Nigel, *Teak and Tide: The Ebbs and Eddies of the* Edwin Fox, Nelson, New Zealand: Nikau Press, 2014.

Duncan, Brad, and Gibbs, Martin, *Please God Send Me a Wreck: Responses to shipwreck in a 19th century Australian community*, New York: Springer, 2015.

Duncan, Sinclair Thomas, *Journal of a Voyage to Australia*, Edinburgh: James Gemmell, George IV Bridge, 1884.

Edwards, Hugh, *Australian and New Zealand Shipwrecks and Sea Tragedies*, Sydney: Phillip Mathews, 1978.

Fryer, James, *A Narrative of the Melancholy Wreck of the* Dunbar, *Merchant Ship, on the South Head of Port Jackson, August 20th, 1857, with Illustrations of the Principal Localities*, Sydney: For the proprietors by James Fryer.

Halls, Chris, *Australia's Worst Shipwrecks*, Adelaide: Rigby, 1978.

Heads, Ian, *The Beach Club: 100 years at Balmoral 1914–2014*, Sydney: Playright Publishing Pty Ltd, 2014.

Heads, Ian, and Lester, Gary, *200 Years of Australian Sport: A glorious obsession*, Sydney: Lester Townsend Publishing Pty Ltd and Angus & Robertson Publishers, 1988.

Henderson, Graeme, *Swallowed by the Sea*, Canberra: National Library of Australia Publishing, 2016.

Hosty, Kieran, Dunbar *1857: Disaster on our doorstep*, Sydney: Australian National Maritime Museum, 2007.

FURTHER READING

Hughes, Robert, *The Fatal Shore*, London: Vintage, 2003.

Karskens, Grace, *The Colony: A history of early Sydney*, Allen & Unwin, 2010.

Loney, Jack, *Australian Shipwrecks Vol. 2 1851–1871*, Sydney: Reed, 1980.

Lubbock, Basil, *The Blackwall Frigates*, Glasgow: James Brown and Son, 1922.

Lubbock, Basil, *The Colonial Clippers*, Glasgow: Brown, Son & Ferguson Ltd, 1968.

McHugh, Evan, *Shipwrecks: Australia's greatest maritime disasters*, Melbourne: Penguin/Viking, 2003.

Mead, Tom, *The Fatal Lights*, Sydney: Dolphin Books, 1993.

Moore, Bryce, Garwood, Helen and Lutton, Nancy, *The Voyage Out: 100 years of sea travel to Australia*, Fremantle: Fremantle Arts Centre Press in association with The Library Board of Western Australia, 1991.

Mundle, Rob, *The First Fleet*, Sydney: HarperCollins, 2014.

Mundle, Rob, *Under Full Sail*, Sydney: ABC Books, 2000.

Noble, John, *Hazards of the Sea: Three centuries of challenge in southern waters*, Sydney: Angus and Robertson, 1970.

Parker, Derek, *Arthur Phillip: Australia's first governor*, Sydney: Woodslane Press, 2009.

Pembroke, Michael, *Arthur Phillip: Sailor, mercenary, governor, spy*, Melbourne: Hardie Grant, 2014.

Ritchie, John, *Lachlan Macquarie—A Biography*, Melbourne: Melbourne University Press, 1988.

Stephensen, P.R., and Kennedy, Brian, *The History and Description of Sydney Harbour*, 2nd edn, Sydney: Reed, 1980.

Stringer, Michael, *Sydney Harbour: A pictorial history from the first settlers to the present day*, Sydney: JMA Stringer & Co., 1984.

Veitch, Michael, *Hell Ship: The true story of the plague ship* Ticonderoga, *one of the most calamitous voyages in Australian history*, Sydney: Allen & Unwin, 2020.

Sources

The books listed above are valuable reading for anyone interested in the *Dunbar* and its era. Below are individual chapter sources and references.

Prologue

Bradshaw, H. 'A Narrative of the Melancholy Wreck of the Dunbar,' *Bradshaw's Railway Guide*, Sydney, 1857.

1: This Hard Land

Books, journals, reports, newspapers, periodicals and websites

Bowes-Smyth, Arthur, *A Journal of a Voyage from Portsmouth to New South Wales in the* Lady Penrhyn, *Merchantman 1787–1789*, digital version. State Library of New South Wales.

Bradley, William, *A Journey to New South Wales, December 1786–May 1792*, facsimile edition. State Library of New South Wales.

Collins, David, *An Account of the English Colony of New South Wales, With Remarks on the Dispositions, Customs, Manners Etc of the Native Inhabitants of That Country*, Project Gutenberg Australia, gutenberg.net.au/ebooks/e00010.html>, n.d., accessed 15 January 2022.

Convict Records, 'Samuel Peyton', <convictrecords.com.au/convicts/peyton/samuel/66014>, n.d., accessed 15 January 2022.

Crockett, Gary, *The Convicts Colony*, Sydney Living Museums, <sydneyliving museums.com.au/convict-sydney/convicts-colony>, 2017, accessed 15 January 2022.

Derricourt, Robin, 'South Head Signal Station', *The Dictionary of Sydney*, <dictionaryofsydney.org/entry/south_head_signal_station>, 2008, accessed 14 January 2022.

Derricourt, Robin, *South Head Sydney and the Origins of Watsons Bay*, Sydney: publication of Watsons Bay Association, 2011.

Encyclopaedia Britannica editors, 'Arthur Phillip (1738–1814)', *Encyclopaedia Britannica*, <www.britannica.com/biography/Arthur-Phillip>, n.d, accessed 14 January 2022.

Encyclopaedia Britannica editors, 'Sydney: Early Settlement', *Encyclopaedia Britannica*, <www. britannica.com/place/Sydney-New-South-Wales/History> n.d., accessed January 2022.

Hunter, John, J*ournal Kept on Board the* Sirius *During a Voyage to New South Wales, May 1787–March 1791*, MS, Collection 05, State Library of New South Wales.

Loney, Jack, *Australian Shipwrecks, Vol. 2, 1851–1871*, Sydney: A.H. & A.W. Reed, 1980.

Nagle, Jacob, *The Nagle Journal: A Diary of the Life of Jacob Nagle, Sailor, from the Year 1775 to 1841*, ed. John C. Dann, New York: Grove Press, 1988.

Phillip, Arthur, *Journals of the First Fleet by Arthur Phillip and Watkin Tench*, Sydney: Shepherd Moon, 2019.

Port Authority of New South Wales, *Marine Pilots: Keeping ships in Sydney safe for 255 years*, <www.portauthoritynsw.com.au/news-and-publications/2018-news/marine-pilots-keeping-ships-safe-in-sydney-for-225-years/>, 2018, accessed 15 January 2022.

Ships File, Mitchell Library, State Library of New South Wales.

Southwell, David, *Journal and Letters of Daniel Southwell*, Project Gutenberg Australia, <gutenberg.net.au/ebooks12/1204411h.html>, 2012, accessed 15 January 2022.

Staff writer, 'Harbour pilots', *The Dictionary of Sydney*, <dictionaryofsydney.org/entry/harbour_pilots>, 2008, accessed 15 January 2022.

Stephensen, P.R., and Kennedy, Brian, *The History and Description of Sydney Harbour*, 2nd edn, Sydney: Reed, 1980.

Twain, Mark, *Following the Equator: A journey around the world*, Mineola, New York: Dover Publications; 2000.

Watsons Bay Association, 'The Gap', <watsonsbayassociation.org/history-places/50/The-Gap/>, n.d., accessed 15 January 2022.

Woollahra Municipal Council, 'Timeline of significant events in the South Head region', <www.woollahra.nsw.gov.au/library/local_history/local_areas/timeline_of_significant_events_in_the_south_head_region>, n.d., accessed 15 January 2022.

2: A Brave New World
Books, journals, reports, newspapers, periodicals and websites

Askew, John, *A Voyage to Australia and New Zealand, Including a Visit to Adelaide, Melbourne, Sydney. Hunters River, Newcastle, Maitland, and Auckland*, Palala Press Open Library, 2018.

Bowes-Smyth, Arthur, *A Journal of a Voyage from Portsmouth to New South Wales in the* Lady Penrhyn, *Merchantman 1787–1789*, digital version. State Library of New South Wales.

Bradley, William, *A Journey to New South Wales, December 1786–May 1792*, digital edition, State Library of New South Wales.

Bridges, Peter, *Foundations of Identity: Building early Sydney 1788–1822*, Sydney: Hale & Iremonger, 1995.

Collins, David, *An Account of the English Colony of New South Wales, With Remarks on the Dispositions, Customs, Manners Etc of the Native Inhabitants of That Country*, Project Gutenberg Australia, <gutenberg.net.au/ebooks/e00010.html>, n.d., accessed 15 January 2022.

Crockett, Gary, 'The convicts' colony', *Sydney Living Museums*, <sydneyliving museums.com.au/convict-sydney/convicts-colony>, 2017, accessed 15 January 2022.

Encyclopaedia Britannica editors, 'Arthur Phillip (1738–1814)', *Encyclopaedia Britannica*, <www.britannica.com/biography/Arthur-Phillip>, n.d., accessed 14 January 2022.

Encyclopaedia Britannica editors, 'Lachlan Macquarie', *Encyclopaedia Britannica*, <www.britannica.com/biography/Lachlan-Macquarie>, n.d., accessed 17 January 2022.

Heads, Ian, and Lester, Gary, *200 Years of Australian Sport: A glorious obsession*, Sydney: Lester Townsend Publishing and Angus & Robertson Publishing, 1988.

Hunter, John, *Journal Kept on Board the* Sirius *During a Voyage to New South Wales, May 1787–March 1791*, MS, Collection 05, State Library of New South Wales.

Jevons, William Stanley, *Remarks Upon the Social Map of Sydney, 1858*, State Library of New South Wales, <acms/sl.nsw.gov.au/_transcript/2015/D00007/a1760.html>, accessed 13 April 2022.

Jordan, Robert, *The Convict Theatres of Early Australia 1788–1840*, Sydney: Currency Press, 2002.

Lemercier, Annette, 'Egan, Marian', *Dictionary of Sydney*, <dictionaryofsydney.org/entry/egan_marian>, 2012, accessed 17 January 2022.

McLachlan, N.D., 'Macquarie, Lachlan (1762–1824)', *Australian Dictionary of Biography*, vol. 2, Melbourne: Melbourne University Press, 1967.

Phillip, Arthur, *Journals of the First Fleet by Arthur Phillip and Watkin Tench*, Sydney: Shepherd Moon, 2019.

Ships File, Mitchell Library, State Library of New South Wales.

Southwell, David, *Journal and Letters of Daniel Southwell*, Project Gutenberg Australia, <gutenberg.net.au/ebooks12/1204411h.html>, 2012, accessed 15 January 2022.

Stringer, Michael, *Sydney Harbour: A pictorial history from the first settlers to the present day*, Sydney: JMA Stringer & Co., 1984.

Waterhouse, Richard, 'Bare-knuckle prize fighting, masculinity and nineteenth century Australian culture', *Journal of Australian Studies*, vol. 26, no. 73, 2002.

Waterhouse, Richard, 'Culture and Customs', *Dictionary of Sydney*, <dictionaryofsydney.org/entry/culture_and_customs>, 2008, accessed 13 April 2022.

Woollahra Municipal Council, 'Timeline of significant events in the South Head region', <www.woollahra.nsw.gov.au/library/local_history/local_areas/timeline_of_significant_events_in_the_south_head_region>, n.d., accessed 15 January 2022.

3: Bound for Sydney Cove
Author interviews
Kosta Akon, Roger Bayliss, James Hanson, Kieran Hosty, Michael Rigg, Terry Wolfe

Books, journals, reports, newspapers, periodicals and websites
Derricourt, Robin, *South Head Sydney and the Origins of Watsons Bay*, Sydney: publication of Watsons Bay Association, 2011.
Early Days at Watsons Bay, a pamphlet for St Peter's Church, n.d.
Encyclopaedia Britannica editors, 'Sydney: Early Settlement', *Encyclopaedia Britannica*, <www.britannica.com/place/Sydney-New-South-Wales/History> n.d., accessed January 2022.
Encyclopaedia Britannica editors, 'Lachlan Macquarie', *Encyclopaedia Britannica*, <www.britannica.com/biography/Lachlan-Macquarie>, n.d., accessed 17 January 2022.
Harbour Trust, 'The history of Macquarie Lightstation', <www.harbourtrust.gov.au/en/our-story/harbour-history/history-of-macquarie-lightstation>, n.d., accessed 17 January 2022.
Jateff, Emily, '"Not all beer and skittles": Sydney Harbour pilotage', Australian National Maritime Museum, <www.sea.museum/2020/08/07/not-all-beer-and-skittles-sydney-harbour-pilotage>, 7 August 2020, accessed 15 January 2022.
Lighthouses of Australia, 'Macquarie Lighthouse', <lighthouses.org.au/nsw/macquarie-lighthouse/>, n.d., accessed 17 January 2022.
Marinato, Thomas, 'Walking down Memory Lane, My Memoirs: Story and illustrations', MLMSS 5288 ADD-ON 1891, Box 1X, Mitchell Library, State Library of New South Wales.
McLachlan, N.D., 'Macquarie, Lachlan (1762–1824)', *Australian Dictionary of Biography*, vol. 2, Melbourne: Melbourne University Press, 1967.
Poland Peter, 'Two hundred years since whaling tragedy strikes Sydney Harbour', *Wentworth Courier*, 28 July 1990.
Ships File, Mitchell Library, State Library of New South Wales.
Sisley, C.J., 'Ship watchers since the early colonial times', *Wentworth Courier*, 18 June 1986.
Watsons Bay, Derricourt, Robin, 'Watsons Bay', *Dictionary of Sydney*, <dictionaryofsydney.org/entry/watsons_bay>, 2008, accessed 17 January 2022.
Watsons Bay Association, 'Aboriginal Watsons Bay', <watsonsbayassociation.org/history-places/42/Aboriginal-Watsons-Bay/>, n.d., accessed 17 January 2022.
Watsons Bay Association, 'Early Watsons Bay', <watsonsbayassociation.org/history-places/46/Early-Watsons-Bay>, n.d., accessed 17 January 2022.

Watsons Bay Association, 'Macquarie Lighthouse', <watsonsbayassociation.org/history-places/45/Macquarie-Lighthouse/>, n.d., accessed 17 January 2022.

Watsons Bay Association, 'Signal Station', <watsonsbayassociation.org/history-places/44/Signal-Station/>, n.d., accessed 17 January 2022.

Watsons Bay Association, 'The Gap', <watsonsbayassociation.org/history-places/50/The-Gap/>, n.d., accessed 17 January 2022.

Watsons Bay Association, 'Watsons Bay History', <watsonsbayassociation.org/history>, n.d., accessed 17 January 2022.

Woollahra Municipal Council, 'Timeline of significant events in the South Head region', <www.woollahra.nsw.gov.au/library/local_history/local_areas/timeline_of_significant_events_in_the_south_head_region>, n.d., accessed 15 January 2022.

4: For Posterity
Books, journals, reports, newspapers, periodicals and websites

Australian National Maritime Museum, 'Passenger ships to Australia', <www.sea.museum/collections/library/research-guides/passenger-ships-to-australia>, n.d., accessed 31 January 2022.

Bell, James, *Private Journal of a Voyage to Australia: James Bell*, ed. Richard Walsh, Sydney: Allen & Unwin, 2011.

Bridges, Peter, *Foundations of Identity—Building early Sydney 1788–1822*, Sydney: Hale & Iremonger, 1995.

Broeze, F.J.A., 'The cost of distance: shipping and the early Australian economy', *Economic History Review*, November 1975, vol. 28, no. 4, pp. 582–597.

Colwell, Max, *Ships and Seafarers in Australian Waters*, Melbourne: Lansdowne Press, 1973.

Diary: Ally Heathcote, England to Melbourne, Victoria, Onboard SS *Northumberland, 1874*; Museums Victoria

Encyclopaedia Britannica editors, 'Sydney: Early Settlement', *Encyclopaedia Britannica*, <www.britannica.com/place/Sydney-New-South-Wales/History>, n.d., accessed January 2022.

History Trust of South Australia, 'Shipwreck', *Bound for South Australia*, <boundforsouthaustralia.history.sa.gov.au/journey-content/shipwreck.html>, n.d., accessed 31 January 2022.

Immigration Museum, 'Journeys to Australia: 1850s–70s: a long and dangerous journey', <museumsvictoria.com.au/immigrationmuseum/resources/journeys-to-australia/>, n.d., accessed 31 January 2022.

Kiprop, Joseph, 'What was the clipper route?', *World Atlas*, <www.worldatlas.com/articles/what-was-the-clipper-route.html>, 30 May 2018, accessed 31 January 2022.

Maritime Museum of Tasmania, 'The journey—by sailing ship', www.maritimetas.org/collection-displays/displays/over-seas-stories-tasmanian-migrants/journey-sailing-ship>, n.d., accessed 13 April 2022.

Moore, Bryce, Garwood, Helen and Lutton, Nancy (eds), *The Voyage Out: 100 years of sea travel to Australia*, Fremantle, WA: Fremantle Arts Centre Press in Association with The Library Board of Western Australia, 1991.

Ships File, Mitchell Library, State Library of New South Wales.

State Library of New South Wales, 'Shipboard: The 19th century emigrant experience', <www.sl.nsw.gov.au/stories/shipboard-19th-century-emigrant-experience>, n.d., accessed 31 January 2022.

Willox, John, *Practical Hints to Intending Emigrants for Our Australian Colonies*, Liverpool, England: Henry Greenwood, 1858.

5: A City Comes of Age
Books, journals, reports, newspapers, periodicals and websites

Australian Government Department of Agriculture, Water and the Environment, 'Whaling: history of whaling in Australia', Department of Agriculture, Water and the Environment, <www.awe.gov.au/environment/marine/marine-species/cetaceans/whaling>, n.d., accessed 31 January 2022.

Bell, James, *Private Journal of a Voyage to Australia 1838–39*, ed. Richard Walsh, Sydney: Allen & Unwin, 2011.

Capper, John, *The Emigrant's Guide to Australia: Containing the fullest particulars relating to the recently discovered gold fields, the government regulations for gold seeking, &c.*, 2nd edn, London: George Phillip & Son, 1853.

Caryl-Sue, 'Feb 12, 1851 CE: Australian gold rush begins', *National Geographic*, <www.nationalgeographic.org/thisday/feb12/australian-gold-rush-begins/>, 6 April 2020, accessed 31 January 2022.

City of Sydney, 'History: History of City of Sydney council', *City of Sydney*, <www.cityofsydney.nsw.gov.au/history/history-city-sydney-council>, 18 September 2020, accessed 31 January 2022.

'Coroner's inquests', *Sydney Gazette and New South Wales Advertiser*, 9 September 1834.

Currey, C.J., 'Denison, Sir William Thomas (1804-71)', *Australian Dictionary of Biography*, <adb.anu.edu.au/biography/denison-sir-william-thomas-3394?>, 1972, accessed 13 April 2022.

Diary: Ally Heathcote, England to Melbourne, Victoria, Onboard SS Northumberland, 1874; Museums Victoria <collections.museumsvictoria.com.au/items/272753>, n.d., accessed 13 April 2022.

Duncan, Sinclair Thomas, *Journal of a Voyage to Australia*, Edinburgh: James Gemmell, George IV Bridge, <collections.museumsvictoria.com.au/items/272753>, n.d., accessed 13 April 2022, 1884.

Dunn, Cathy, 'Victorian fashions', *Australian History Research*, <www.australianhistoryresearch.info/victorian-fashions/>, n.d., accessed 31 January 2022.

Hill, David, *The Gold Rush: the fever that forever changed Australia*, Sydney: William Heinemann, 2011.

Immigration Museum, 'Journeys to Australia', <museumsvictoria.com.au/immigrationmuseum/resources/journeys-to-australia/>, n.d., accessed 31 January 2022.

Jevons, William Stanley, Letter 108 from William Stanley Jevons to Lucy Jevons, *Papers and Correspondence of William Stanley Jevons*, ed. R.D. Collison Black, vol. 2, London: Macmillan for the Royal Economic Society, 1973.

Lemercier, Annette, 'Egan Marian', *Dictionary of Sydney*, <dictionaryofsydney.org/entry/egan_marian>, 2012, accessed 31 January 2022.

McKillop, Bob, 'The railways of Sydney: shaping the city and its commerce', *Dictionary of Sydney*, <dictionaryofsydney.org/entry/the_railways_of_sydney_shaping_the_city_and_its_commerce>, 2016, accessed 31 January 2022.

Manning, Arthur Wilcox, *Journal of a Voyage from Plymouth to Sydney on the Earl Grey, 1839–40*, MLMSS 7390, Mitchell Library, State Library of New South Wales.

Moore, Bryce, Garwood, Helen and Lutton, Nancy (eds), *The Voyage Out: 100 Years of sea travel to Australia*, Fremantle, WA: Fremantle Arts Centre Press in Association with The Library Board of Western Australia, 1991.

State Library of New South Wales, 'Eureka! the rush for gold: gold boom', <www.sl.nsw.gov.au/stories/eureka-rush-gold/gold-boom>, n.d., accessed 31 January 2022.

State Library of New South Wales, 'Shipboard: The 19th century emigrant experience', <www.sl.nsw.gov.au/stories/shipboard-19th-century-emigrant-experience>, n.d., accessed 31 January 2022.

Swain, Edward P., *Journal of a voyage to Sydney in the ship* Duncan Dunbar *from London, 1864*, MS 92793, Australian Maritime Museum.

'Sydney incorporated as a City', 20 July 1842, New South Wales Government State Archives and Records.

Tranter, Hugh, 'The wreck of the *Edward Lombe*', *Dictionary of Sydney*, <dictionaryofsydney.org/entry/the_wreck_of_the_edward_lombe>, 2019, accessed 31 January 2022.

Trollope, Anthony, *Australia and New Zealand*, Cambridge, UK: Cambridge University Press, 2013.

Turnbull, Lucy Hughes, 'Sydney in 1858', *Dictionary of Sydney*, <dictionaryofsydney.org/entry/sydney_in_1858>, 2008, accessed 31 January 2022.

'The loss of the *Edward Lombe* in Sydney Harbour', *The Sydney Times*, 29 August 1834.

Waterhouse, Richard, 'Culture and customs', *Dictionary of Sydney*, <dictionaryofsydney.org/entry/culture_and_customs>, 2008, accessed 31 January 2022.

Wotherspoon, Garry, 'Ferries', *Dictionary of Sydney*, <dictionaryofsydney.org/entry/ferries>, 2008, accessed 31 January 2022.

'Wreck of the *Edward Lombe*', *Sydney Herald*, 28 August 1834.

6: Greyhounds of the Sea
Author interview
Mori Flapan

Books, journals, reports, newspapers, journals and websites

Australian National Maritime Museum, 'Passenger ships to Australia', <www.sea.museum/collections/library/research-guides/passenger-ships-to-australia>, n.d., accessed 31 January 2022.

Blue Peter, 'Shipbuilders of the 19th century', *Sunderland Echo*, 2014.

Blue Peter, 'The river workshops of 1852', *Sunderland Echo*, 2014.

Colwell, Max, *Ships and Seafarers in Australian Waters*, Melbourne: Lansdowne Press, 1973.

'Dunbar Death' ('The Late Mr Duncan Dunbar', 1862*), Royal Sappers and Miners in Western Australia*, <sappers-minerswa.com/ships/lincelles-1862/dunbar-death/#main>, 25 May 2015, accessed 31 January 2022.

Dunbar, Patrick, 'Person page – 37', *Dunbar Family Worldwide*, <dunbar.one-name.net/p37.htm>, n.d., accessed 31 January 2022.

Immigration Museum, 'Journeys to Australia', <museumsvictoria.com.au/immigration museum/resources/journeys-to-australia/>, n.d., accessed 31 January 2022.

Kiprop, Joseph, 'What was the clipper route?', *World Atlas*, <www.worldatlas.com/articles/what-was-the-clipper-route.html>, 30 May 2018, accessed 31 January 2022.

Lance, Kate, *Allan Villiers: voyager of the winds*, London: National Maritime Museum UK, 2009.

Lubbock, Basil, *The Blackwall Frigates*, Glasgow: James Brown & Son, 1922.

Lubbock, Basil, *The Colonial Clippers*, Glasgow: Brown, Son & Ferguson Ltd, 1968.

MacGregor, David R., *Merchant Sailing Ships 1815–1850: Supremacy of sail*, London: Naval Institute Press, 1984.

MacGregor, David R., *Merchant Sailing Ships 1850–1875: Heyday of sail*, London: Naval Institute Press, 1985.

Moore, Bryce, Garwood, Helen and Lutton, Nancy (eds), *The Voyage Out: 100 Years of sea travel to Australia*, Fremantle, WA: Fremantle Arts Centre Press in Association with The Library Board of Western Australia, 1991.

Pickworth, Dr A., 'Shipbuilding on the Wear Part 1; Local Studies Centre Fact Sheet No.10', City of Sunderland Library and Arts Centre.

Pickworth, Dr A., 'Shipbuilding on the Wear Part 2; Local Studies Centre Fact Sheet No.10', City of Sunderland Library and Arts Centre.

Willox, John, *Practical Hints to Intending Emigrants for Our Australian Colonies*, Liverpool, England: Henry Greenwood, 1858.

7: 'A Splendid Vessel'

Books, journals, reports, newspapers, periodicals and websites

Annual Surveys Report for Dunbar, 7 April 1857; 02. Annual Surveys.pdf, London, Archive and Library, Heritage and Education Centre, <hec.lrfoundation.org.uk/archive-library/documents/lrf-pun-lon638-0223a-r>, n.d., accessed 13 April 2022.

'Arrival of the wounded in the Bosporus', *The Times* (London), 9 October 1854.

Australian Broadcasting Corporation, 'Shipwrecks: Dunbar Head', ABC, <www.abc.net.au/backyard/shipwrecks/nsw/dunbar.htm>, 2003, accessed 31 January 2022.

Dunbar Family History researched by Patrick Dunbar, UK, available at Dunbar Family Worldwide, a collection of Dunbar Family Lines, <dunbar.one-name.net>, n.d., accessed 13 April 2022.

Dunbar Management Plan NSW Heritage <www.heritage.nsw.gov.au/search-for-heritage/maritime-heritage-database/>, accessed 13 April 2022.

'Dunbar Wharf and the remarkable story of Duncan Dunbar', *Isle of Dogs Life*, <isleofdogslife.wordpress.com/2015/10/21/dunbar-wharf-and-the-remarkable-story-of-duncan-dunbar/>, n.d., accessed 31 January 2022.

'*Dunbar*'s maiden voyage', *The Shipping Gazette*, 29 September 1856.

Dunbar-Nasmith, David, 'On Duncan Dunbar (I) and (II): Duncan Dunbar and his ships', text of a 2005 talk published in 2006 in Merchant Networks, an Armidale, NSW, website project in economic and maritime history by Ken Cozens and Dan Byrnes.

Figes, Orlando, *Crimea: the last crusade*, London: Penguin, 2011.

'James Green', Ancestry UK; <www.ancestry.co.uk/family-tree/person/tree/1125 57266/person/380098272978/facts>, n.d., accessed 13 April 2022.

James Green: Certificate of Competency as Master 1851, London, issued by the Lords of the Committee for Privy Council of Trade.

'List of passengers [and crew] on the Dunbar', NRS 4332, New South Wales Government State Records and Archives, <www.records.nsw.gov.au/archives/collections-and-research/guides-and-indexes/series-list/4332>, n.d., accessed 1 February 2022.

Lloyd's Registers Foundation, London, <www.lrfoundation.org.uk>, accessed 13 April 2022.

Lubbock, Basil, *The Blackwall Frigates*, Glasgow: James Brown & Son, 1922.

Lubbock, Basil, *The Colonial Clippers*, Glasgow: Brown, Son & Ferguson Ltd, 1968.

MacGregor, David R., *Merchant Sailing Ships 1815–1850: Supremacy of sail*, London: Naval Institute Press, 1984.

MacGregor, David R., *Merchant Sailing Ships 1850–1875: Heyday of sail*, London: Naval Institute Press, 1985.

Mackenzie, Captain T.A., Lieutenant and Ewart, Adjutant J.S. and Findlay, Lieutenant C. (comp. and eds), *Historical Records of the 79th Cameroon Highlanders*, London: Hamilton Adams & Co, 1887.

McNamara, Robert, 'Clipper ship: extraordinarily fast sailing ships had a brief but glorious heyday', Thought.Co, <www.thoughtco.com/clipper-ship-definition-1773367>, 30 December 2017, accessed 31 January 2022.

Marriage Certificate of James Green and Alice Wright, General Register Office, Stepney, London.

'Naval and military intelligence', *The Times* (London), 1 April 1855.

'Naval and military intelligence', *The Times* (London), 6 April 1855.

'Naval and military intelligence', *The Times* (London), 7 May 1855.

'Naval and military intelligence', *The Times* (London), 11 May 1855.

Shepherd, John A., 'The surgeons in the Crimea 1854–1856', *Journal of the Royal College of Surgeons of Edinburgh*, vol. 17, 1972.

Shipping Wonders of the World, 'Troopships and trooping', <www.shipping wondersoftheworld.com/troopships.html>, n.d., accessed 31 January 2022.

'Sir James Laing and Sons', *Grace's Guide to British Industrial History*, <www.graces guide.co.uk/Sir_James_Laing_and_Sons>, August 2021, accessed 31 January 2022.

'State of the army before Sebastopol', *The Times* (London), 21 March 1855.

Sunderland Antiquarian Society, <www.sunderland-antiquarians.org>, accessed 13 April 2022.

'The British Expedition', *The Times* (London), 2 October 1854.

The Great Circle: Precarious Voyage of Her Majesty's Convict Ship Nile *to the Swan River Colony Late 1857… and the Unexpected Aftermath*, The Australian Association for Maritime History, <jstor.org/stable/26783779>, 2018, accessed 13 April 2022.

'The Mediterranean', *The Times* (London), 7 January 1856.

The ship *Dunbar* (1854–1857), Heritage NSW, 'Maritime Heritage Database', information for *Dunbar*, <www.heritage.nsw.gov.au/search-for-heritage/maritime-heritage-database/>, n.d., accessed 31 January 2022.

'The Sick & Wounded Fund', *The Times* (London), 3 February 1855.

'The War', *London Illustrated News*, 8 April 1854.

8: Most Able Seamen
Author interview
James Hanson

Books, journals, reports, newspapers, periodicals and websites

Jevons, William Stanley, Letter 108 from William Stanley Jevons to Lucy Jevons, *Papers and Correspondence of William Stanley Jevons*, ed. R.D. Collison Black, vol. 2, London: Macmillan for the Royal Economic Society, 1973.

'List of passengers on the *Dunbar*', NRS 4332, New South Wales Government State Records and Archives, <www.records.nsw.gov.au/archives/collections-and-research/guides-and-indexes/series-list/4332>, n.d., accessed 1 February 2022.

Lubbock, Basil, *The Blackwall Frigates*, Glasgow: James Brown and Son, 1922.

Lubbock, Basil, *The Colonial Clippers*, Glasgow: Brown, Son & Ferguson Ltd, 1968.

Register of Wages and Effects of Deceased Seamen: Dunbar, BT 153, National Archives (UK).

Shaw, Lindsey, 'Two unusual artefacts from the wreck of the Dunbar', Australian National Maritime Museum, <www.sea.museum/2012/01/31/

two-unusual-artefacts-from-the-wreck-of-the-dunbar>, 31 January 2012, accessed 1 February 2012.

Ships File, Mitchell Library, State Library of New South Wales.

Simpson, Margaret, 'Sydney's most famous shipwreck—the "*Dunbar*"', *Powerhouse*, <maas.museum/inside-the-collection/2017/08/21/sydneys-most-famous-shipwreck-the-dunbar/>. 21 August 2017, accessed 1 February 2022.

Dunbar crew
Green, James
1821 Census of South Ronaldsay, courtesy of Jennie Fairs, private collection.

1845 British Merchant Seamen, courtesy of Jennie Fairs, private collection.

1848 British Merchant Seamen, courtesy of Jennie Fairs, private collection.

Baptism Certificate of Alice James Green, 13 December 1857, courtesy of Jennie Fairs, private collection.

Baptism Certificate of James Green, 6 January 1822, courtesy of Jennie Fairs, private collection.

Death Certificate of Daughter Alice James Green, 27 July 1859, courtesy of Jennie Fairs, private collection.

Death Certificate of James Green, courtesy of Jennie Fairs, private collection.

Death Certificate of Malcolm Green, courtesy of Jennie Fairs, private collection.

'Green, James', Ancestry UK, DJF full tree <www.ancestry.co.uk/family-tree/person/tree/112557266/person/380098272978/facts>, n.d., accessed 13 April 2022.

James Green: Certificate of Competency as Master 1851, London, issued by the Lords of the Committee for Privy Council of Trade, 4 June 1851.

Letter from Captain James Green to Passengers of the *Dunbar*, *Sydney Morning Herald*, 25 September 1856.

Letter from Passengers of the *Dunbar* to Captain James Green, *Empire*, 29 September 1856.

Mariners and Ships in Australian Waters, <marinersandships.com.au/>, accessed 13 April 2022.

Marriage Certificate (James Green to Alice Wright), courtesy of Jennie Fairs, private collection.

Heisch, Allan Dunbar
1840 Birth Certificate, courtesy of Jennie Fairs, private collection.

1840 UK Baptism Certificate, courtesy of Jennie Fairs, private collection.

1841 UK Census, courtesy of Jennie Fairs, private collection.

'Obituary', *Globe* (UK), 17 November 1857.

Jerram, John Ridley
1839 UK Baptism Certificate, courtesy of Jennie Fairs, private collection.

'John Ridley Jerram', *Descent – magazine of Society of Australian Genealogists*, June 2017.

'Deaths', *Empire*, 24 August 1857.

'Obituary', *Gloucester Chronicle*, 21 November 1857.

Johnson, James

1915 Deceased Estate File including Will of Johnson, courtesy of Jennie Fairs, private collection.

Blair, Richard, '*Dunbar* survivor James Johnson of the Boulevarde, Dulwich Hill [sic]', *Marrickville Heritage Society Newsletter*, May 2005.

Coronial Inquest into the Foundering of *Dunbar* and the Deaths of Those Onboard, *Sydney Morning Herald*, 25 August, 1857.

'Drogheda, Co. Louth, Ireland: A Brief History', IC Business Services, Drogheda, Ireland, <www.ireland-calling.net/drogheda.htm>, accessed 13 April 2022.

George Henry Bassett, *Louth County Guide and Directory*, Dublin 1886 (Reprinted 1998).

George Thornton, 'Johnson's Narrative to the right worshipful the mayor', *The Shipping Gazette and Sydney General Trade List*, 24 August 1857.

'James Johnson: The sole survivor', *Descent – magazine of Society of Australian Genealogists*, June 2017.

'Johnson, James', Ancestry UK, rell222, <www.ancestry.co.uk/family-tree/person/tree/9278000/person/220011897299/facts>, accessed 13 April 2022.

Kay, Thomas

1841 UK Census, courtesy of Jennie Fairs, private collection.

'Kay, Thomas', Ancestry UK, jmcarter16, <www.ancestry.co.uk/family-tree/person/tree/166574034/person/202161420816/gallery>, accessed 13 April 2022.

'Obituary', *Hampshire Telegraph*, n.d.

Pascoe, John

1851 UK Census, courtesy of Jennie Fairs, private collection.

'Obituary', *Kentish Gazette*, 1 December 1857.

'Pascoe, John', Ancestry UK, clutterbuck21, <www.ancestry.co.uk/family-tree/person/tree/45092212/person/6305003220/facts?_phsrc=ClW962&_phstart=successSource>, accessed 13 April 2022.

Simpson, Margaret, 'Sydney's most famous shipwreck—the "*Dunbar*"', Powerhouse Museum, <maas.museum/inside-the-collection/2017/08/21/sydneys-most-famous-shipwreck-the-dunbar/>. 21 August 2017, accessed 1 February 2022.

Sappie, Charles

Britain, Merchant Seamen 1851, courtesy of Jennie Fairs, private collection.

George Thornton, 'Johnson's Narrative to the right worshipful the mayor', *The Shipping Gazette and Sydney General Trade List*, 24 August 1857.

James Johnson's testimony to Coronial Inquest into the Foundering of *Dunbar* and the Deaths of Those Onboard, Register of Coroner's Inquests 1857, State Archives and Records New South Wales.

Struthers, James

'Struthers, James', Ancestry UK, quilietti1, <www.ancestry.co.uk/family-tree/person/tree/18269627/person/432080265664/facts?_phsrc=ClW984&_phstart=successSource>, accessed 13 April 2022.

'Wreck of the *Dunbar*' *Dundee, Perth and Cupar Advertiser*, 20 November 1857.

Williams, William Butler

'Deaths', *Sydney Morning Herald*, 25 August 1857.

'William Butler Williams', *Descent – magazine of Society of Australian Genealogists*, June 2017.

9: So Much to Live For
Author interviews

Laurie Alexander, Brad Duncan, Christian Garland, James Hanson, Kieran Hosty, John Lanser, Annette Lemercier, David Nutley, Steve Waller

Books, journals, reports, newspapers, periodicals and websites

Australian Broadcasting Corporation, 'Shipwrecks: Dunbar Head', ABC, <www.abc.net.au/backyard/shipwrecks/nsw/dunbar.htm>, 2003, accessed 31 January 2022.

Burke, Sir Bernard, *A Genealogical and Heraldic History of the Colonial Gentry*, London: Harrison & Sons, 1891, Google Books, <www.google.com.aubooks/A Genealogical and Heraldic History of the Colonial Gentry>, accessed 13 April 2022.

Gledhill, Percy Walter, *A Stroll through the historic Camperdown Cemetery*, Sydney: R Dey, 1946.

'List of passengers on the *Dunbar*', NRS 4332, New South Wales Government State Records and Archives, <www.records.nsw.gov.au/archives/collections-and-research/guides-and-indexes/series-list/4332>, n.d., accessed 1 February 2022.

'Maritime heritage database', information on the *Dunbar*, NSW Government: Heritage NSW, <www.heritage.nsw.gov.au/search-for-heritage/maritime-heritage-database/>, 2022, accessed 1 February 2022.

Objects through time . . . Dunbar *Shipwreck Collection c1857*, Migration Heritage Centre <www.migrationheritage.nsw.gov.au/exhibitions/objectsthroughtime/dunbar/index.html>, accessed 13 April 2022.

Ships File, Mitchell Library, State Library of New South Wales.

Passengers
Brown, Martha and Henry

1851 UK Census

Baptism Certificate of Martha Brown, 11 April 1824.

'Deaths', *Sydney Morning Herald*, 27 August 1857.

'Further particulars of the shipwreck at the Heads', *Sydney Morning Herald*, 22 August 1857.

'Obituary for David Jones', *Australian Town and Country Journal*, 5 April 1873.

SOURCES

Bynon, William

Bishop, Catherine, 'Women of Pitt Street 1858', *Dictionary of Sydney*, <dictionary ofsydney.org/entry/women_of_pitt_street_1858>, 2011, accessed 1 February 2022.

'Bynon, William', *Dictionary of Sydney*, <dictionaryofsydney.org/person/bynon_ william>, n.d., accessed 1 February 2022.

New South Wales Government Gazette, 8 September 1857.

Davidson, Cuthbert John

'Cantray House', *Luxury Portfolio International*, <www.luxuryportfolio.com/ Property/inverness-properties-cantray-house/QYEP>, n.d., accessed 13 April 2022.

'Davidson of Cantray', *Red Book of Scotland*, <redbookofscotland.co.uk/ davidson-of-cantray>, n.d., accessed 1 February 2022.

'Deaths', *Inverness Courier*, 3 December 1857.

'Lost on board the *Dunbar*', *Edinburgh Evening Courant*, 1 December 1857.

'Obituary', *Edinburgh Evening Courant*, 1 December 1857.

'Obituary', *Inverness Courier*, 1 December 1857.

Downey, Patrick J.

Assisted Bounty immigration records for P.J. Downey and his family per *Gilbert Henderson,* courtesy of Jennie Fairs, private collection.

'By Councillor McEnroe', *Empire*, 22 January 1853.

Downey, P.J., Letter forwarding a medical certificate re acting as an assessor for Cook Ward.

'Downey family', *Rootsweb*, <lists.rootsweb.com/hyperkitty/list/aus-nsw.rootsweb. com/thread/1465620/>, n.d., accessed 13 April 2022.

'Downey, Patrick', Ancestry UK, Jan Lawson17, <www.ancestry.co.uk/family-tree/ person/tree/972302/person/6061226858/facts>, n.d., accessed 13 April 2022.

'Election of city councillors', *New South Wales Government Gazette*, 30 November 1852.

'Election of a City Councillor', *NSW Government Gazette*, 14 December, 1852.

Extract on the lives of Patrick and Belinda Downey, *Australiana*, November 2015.

'From a visitor to the Heads', *Sydney Morning Herald*, 22 August 1857.

Marriage certificate (Patrick Downey to Belinda Clune), courtesy of Jennie Fairs, private collection.

'Municipal Election' *Freeman's Journal*, 25 November 1852.

'New Insolvents', *Morning Chronicle*, 18 October 1843.

'Nomination for a City Councillor', *Empire*, 11 December 1852.

'Patrick Joseph Downey', *Descent – magazine of Society of Australian Genealogists*, June 2017.

Will of P.J. Downey, courtesy of Jennie Fairs, private collection.

Egan, Marian, and Cahuac, Gertrude and Henry

Chapman, Anne Hale, 'Reminiscences of Anne Hale Chapman (nee Wilson) from 1835 to 1903', manuscript, MSS 2837, Mitchell Library, State Library of New South Wales.

'Deaths', *Sydney Morning Herald*, 27 August 1857.

Demson, Michael, 'Remembering John Cahuac: Post-Peterloo repression and the fate of radical-romantic satire', *Romantic Circles*, <romantic-circles.org/praxis/shelley_politics/praxis.2015.shelley_politics.demson.html>, September 2015, accessed 1 February 2022.

Garland, Christian, 'Three *Dunbar* Stories: The Egans', *Pioneer* magazine, September 2007.

Hosty, Kieran, Dunbar *1857: Disaster on our doorstep*, Sydney: Australian National Maritime Museum, 2007.

Lemercier, Annette, 'Egan, Marian', *Dictionary of Sydney*, <dictionaryofsydney.org/entry/egan_marian>, 2012, accessed 17 January 2022.

McCormack, Terri, 'Egan, Daniel', *Dictionary of Sydney*, 2010, <dictionaryofsydney.org/entry/egan_daniel#ref-uuid=dad095b0-ea6a-87b0-b3ef-e287517c0a28>, 2010, accessed 1 February 2022.

Mellefont, Jeffrey, 'Faces from the *Dunbar* disaster', *Signals* magazine, March–May 2008.

Neil, Marie H., *Valley of the Macleay: The history of the Kempsey and Macleay River district*, Sydney: Wentworth Books, Sydney, 1972.

Portrait: Marianne Egan and her children Gertrude Evans Cahuac and Henry William Cahuac, <www.costumecocktail.com/2016/10/04/marianne-egan-with-her-children-gertrude-evans-cahuac-henry-william-cahuac-1857/>, n.d., accessed 13 April 2022.

'The *Dunbar*', *Bell's Life in Sydney*, 31 October 1857.

'The *Dunbar*', *Hobart Town Mercury*, 30 September 1857.

'The Late Mrs Egan', *Freeman's Journal*, 7 November 1857.

Walsh, G.P., 'Egan, Daniel (1803?–1870)', *Australian Dictionary of Biography*, vol. 4, Melbourne: Melbourne University Press, 1972.

Healing, Daniel, Elizabeth, Louisa, Frederick and George

Baptism certificates of Daniel Healing and Mercy, Elizabeth, William and George Healing, at Cheltenham Parish Church, 12 October 1834.

'Daniel Healing', *Descent – magazine of Society of Australian Genealogists*, June 2017.

'Deaths', *Empire*, 27 August 1857.

'Deaths', *Gloucestershire Chronicle*, 21 November 1857.

'Dreadful Loss', *Gloucestershire Chronicle*, 21 November 1857.

'Healing, Daniel', Ancestry UK, wrag44, <www.ancestry.co.uk/family-tree/person/tree/43459145/person/12661633555/facts>, n.d., accessed 13 April 2022.

Marriage certificate of Elizabeth and Daniel Healing, courtesy of Jennie Fairs, private collection.

'Stealing an umbrella', *Cheltenham Journal & Gloucestershire Fashionable Weekly Gazette*, 7 May 1853.

Holl, John

1851 UK Census

'Holl, John', Ancestry UK, Christine Parsons 952, <www.ancestry.co.uk/family-tree/person/tree/54358461/person/190091656746/facts>, n.d., accessed 13 April 2022.

'Obituary of Robert Holl', *Dubbo Liberal & Macquarie Advocate*, 1 September 1925.

Hunt, Sarah and Emily

Birth certificate of Sarah Hunt, courtesy of Jennie Fairs, private collection.

'Hunt, Robert Fellowes', Ancestry UK, belindacaldwell1, <www.ancestry.co.uk/family-tree/person/tree/13818987/person/-1435052/facts>>, n.d. accessed 13 April 2022.

Jevons, William Stanley, *Papers and Correspondence of William Stanley Jevons*, ed. R.D. Collison Black, vol. 2, London: Macmillan for the Royal Economic Society, 1973.

Lanser, John, 'Three *Dunbar* Stories: Robert Hunt', *Pioneer* magazine, September 2007.

Martin, Megan, 'Robert Hunt, chemist, photographer and deputy Mint master', Sydney Living Museums, <sydneylivingmuseums.com.au/stories/robert-hunt-chemist-photographer-and-deputy-mint-master>, n.d., accessed 1 February 2022.

Sydney Monthly Overland Mail, 10 September 1857.

James, Adrian de Jongh

'Deaths', *Sydney Morning Herald*, 24 August 1857.

'James, Adrian de Yonge', Ancestry UK, pvcow, <www.ancestry.co.uk/family-tree/person/tree/51026481/person/390054234247/facts>, n.d., accessed 13 April 2022.

'The Late Mr Adrian De Yongh James', *Sydney Morning Herald*, 5 September 1857.

Logan, Ida, Arthur and Charles

'Further particulars of the shipwreck at the Heads', *Sydney Morning Herald*, 22 August 1857.

'Mrs Logan', *Hobart Town Courier*, 19 June 1835.

Skinner, Graeme, 'Maria Logan and Family', *Australharmony* (an online resource towards the history of music and musicians in colonial and early Federation Australia), <www.sydney.edu.au/paradisec/australharmony/logan-maria.php> 10 October 2017, accessed 1 February 2022.

'Sydney Heads, death by drowning of three Logan children', *Sydney Morning Herald*, 20 August 1857.

'The Chapel Royal', *Austral-Asiatic Review*, 11 November 1838.

'The Logans', *Sydney Monthly Overland Mail*, 10 September 1857.

Macquoid, Thomas Hyacinth

Lea-Scarlett, Errol, *Queanbeyan: District and people*, Queanbeyan, NSW: Queanbeyan Municipal Council, 1968.

'Obituary', *Empire*, 25 August 1857

Meyer, Abraham, Julia, Lazarus, Julia, Morris, Lewis, Rachel, Hannah

Harrison, Donald H., 'The Jewish victims in an Australian tragedy', *San Diego Jewish World*, <www.sdjewishworld.com/2018/03/29/the-jewish-victims-in-an-australian-tragedy>, 29 March 2018, accessed 1 February 2022.

'Hart, Julia', Ancestry UK, Brenda Willis15, <www.ancestry.co.uk/family-tree/person/tree/62951891/person/48588155144/facts>, n.d. accessed 13 April 2022.

Lea-Scarlett, Errol, *Queanbeyan: District and people*, Queanbeyan, NSW: Queanbeyan Municipal Council, 1968.

Levi, John S., *These Are the Names: Jewish lives in Australia 1788–1850*, Melbourne: Melbourne University Press, 2013.

'Meyer, Abraham', Ancestry UK, Brenda Willis15, <www.ancestry.co.uk/family-tree/person/tree/62951891/person/172029331830/facts>, n.d. accessed 13 April 2022.

'Meyers', *Goulburn Herald*, 29 August 1857.

'Mr Solomon Meyer (1823–1902)', Parliament of New South Wales, <www.parliament.nsw.gov.au/members/Pages/member-details.aspx?pk=530>, n.d., accessed 1 February 2022.

'Myers [sic] funeral', *Sydney Morning Herald*, 26 August 1857.

'The Loss of the *Dunbar*', *Goulburn and County of Argyle Advertiser*, 29 August 1857.

'The starving Jews in Palestine', *Empire*, 4 September 1854.

Tuck, Dan, *From the Tablelands to the Sea: A contextual history*, report for the former Pristine Waters Council Area (Ulmarra and Nymboida Shires), Clarence Valley Council LGA, <www.clarenceconversations.com.au/ulmarra-nymboida-heritage-study>, April 2018, accessed 1 February 2022.

'Wreck of the *Dunbar*', *Dundee, Perth and Cupar Advertiser*, 20 November 1857.

'Wreck of the *Dunbar*', *Sydney Morning Herald*, 26 August 1857.

SOURCES

Mylne, Annie, Letitia, John and Thomas

Bawden, Thomas, 'Eatonswill station, celebrated for its hospitality', *The Bawden Lectures: the first fifty years of settlement*, 5th edn, Grafton, NSW: Clarence River Historical Society, 1997.

Clarence River Historical Society, 'Timeline links: Grafton and the early days on the Clarence—the story of the Mylne brothers', Clarence River Historical Society, <www.clarencehistory.org.au/html/mylne_bro.html>, n.d., accessed 1 February 2022.

Clarence Valley Historical Society, 'Clarence Valley Timeline', *New England's History*, Jim Belshaw, <newenglandhistory.blogspot.com/2008/03/clarence-valley-timeline.html>, 7 March 2008, accessed 1 February 2022.

'Further particulars of the shipwreck at the Heads', *Sydney Morning Herald*, 22 August 1857.

Hon. East India Company Records. search.findmypast.co.uk/search-world-Records/british-india-office-births-and-baptisms.

Mylne, Tom, *Mylnefield Mylnes in Scotland, in Australia*, <mylnefieldmylne.wixsite.com/family>, 2016, accessed 1 February 2022.

Will of John Mylne, *New South Wales Will Books 1800–1952*, <www.findmypast.co.uk/>, n.d., accessed 13 April 2022.

Will of Thomas Mylne, *New South Wales Will Books 1800-1952*, <www.findmypast.co.uk/>, n.d., accessed 13 April 2022.

'Wreck of the *Dunbar* and loss of 122 lives', *Dundee, Perth and Cupar Advertiser*, 20 November 1857.

Peek, Samuel and Caroline

City of Sydney, 'Samuel Peek', *Discover Sydney's Aldermen*, <www.sydneyaldermen.com.au/alderman/samuel-peek/>, 2022, accessed 1 February 2022.

'Dreadful loss of the Australian packetship *Dunbar* with upwards of 150 lives', *Gloucestershire Chronicle*, 21 November 1857.

'Further particulars of the shipwreck at the Heads', *Sydney Morning Herald*, 22 August 1857.

May, T., and Regan, A. *Chronology of S. Peek and Co, Sydney Tea and Coffee Merchant, Issuer of the Tea Stores Token. Tea Stores*, Sydney NSW. Museums Victoria Collection, 2005, <collections.museumsvictoria.com.au/articles/2488>, n.d., accessed 18 February 2022.

'Peek, Samuel', Ancestry UK, Kingston100, <www.ancestry.co.uk/family-tree/person/tree/68676003/person/36221557691/facts?_phsrc=ClW997&_phstart=successSource>, n.d., accessed 13 April 2022.

'Samuel Peek, Alderman', <www.sydneyaldermen.com.au/alderman/samuel-peek/www.gosford.nsw.gov.au>, n.d., accessed 13 April 2022.

Watson, J. Frederick, *The History of Sydney Hospital from 1811 to 1911, Internet Archive*, <archive.org/details/historyofsydneyh00wats/page/210/mode/2up?q=peek>, 1911, accessed 1 February 2022.

308

Severne, Edward
Biographical notes courtesy of Jennie Fairs, private collection.
Lea-Scarlett, Errol, *Queanbeyan: District and people*, Queanbeyan, NSW: Queanbeyan Municipal Council, 1968.
New South Wales Government Gazette, 1852.

Simmons, Isaac
City of Sydney, 'James Simmons', *Discover Sydney's Aldermen*, www.sydney aldermen.com.au/alderman/james-simmons/>, 2022, accessed 1 February 2022.
'Further particulars of the shipwreck at the Heads', *Sydney Morning Herald*, 22 August 1857.
'Isaac Simmons Jr', *Descent – magazine of Society of Australian Genealogists*, June 2017.

Steane, John
1818 Applications for Marriage Licences in Hampshire.
1858 UK Probate Calendar, courtesy Jennie Fairs, private collection.
Brigstocke, Captain, RN, Inspecting Commander of the Coastguard of the Isle of Wight, 'Trial between Mr. John Dennett's Rockets and Captain Manby's Mortar 1827', Report on a comparative trial made at Freshwater, between the rockets and Captain Manby's mortar, *Coastguards of Yesteryear*, <www.coastguardsofyesteryear.org/articles.php?article_id=116>, 18 June 2007, accessed 1 February 2022.
'Captain Steane', *Evening Standard* (London), 17 November 1857.
'From a visitor to the Heads', *Sydney Morning Herald*, 22 August 1857.
Gledhill, Percy Walter, *A Stroll through the historic Camperdown Cemetery*, Sydney: R Dey, 1946.
'Steane, John', Ancestry UK, Jill Beatrice Taylor, <www.ancestry.co.uk/family-tree/person/tree/105933744/person/222133430582/facts>, n.d. accessed, 13 April 2022.

Tindal, Francis
'Frederick Colquhoun Tindal', *Design and Art Australia Online*, <www.daao.org.au/bio/frederick-colquhoun-tindal/>, n.d., accessed 13 April 2022.
'Melancholy end', *Bucks Herald* (UK), 21 November 1857.
'Tindal, Frederick Colquhoun (1831–)', *Trove*, <nla.gov.au/nla.party-1475196>, 2011, accessed 1 February 2022.

Troughton, Charles
'Deaths', *Morning Post* (UK), 20 November 1857.
'Deaths', *Newcastle Journal* (UK), 28 November 1857.
'Deaths', *Sydney Morning Herald*, 26 August 1857.

SOURCES

'The late Mr CJ Troughton', *Newcastle Journal* (UK), 12 December 1857.
'The late wreck', *Empire*, 28 August 1857.

Waller, Kilner, Hannah Maria, Arthur, Edward, John, Kate, Maria, Mary
Author interview:
Steve Waller

Books, journals, reports, newspapers, periodicals and websites
'Deaths', *Sydney Morning Herald*, 25 August 1857.
'From a visitor to the Heads', *Sydney Morning Herald*, 22 August 1857.
'Funeral', *Sydney Morning Herald*, 24 August 1857.
'Obituary', *Cardiff and Merthyr Guardian, Glamorgan, Monmouth and Brecon Gazette*, 28 November 1857.
'Obituary', *Launceston Examiner*, 17 September 1857.
Rowbotham, Jill, 'Link to historic wreck is family's fortune', *The Australian*, 16 August 2007.
'The *Dunbar* wreck', *Launceston Examiner*, 23 May 1907.
'Verses to the Waller family', *Launceston Examiner*, 17 September 1857.
Waller, Kilner, Ancestry UK, philmoritz, <www.ancestry.co.uk/family-tree/person/tree/4623984/person/-411621032/facts>, n.d. accessed 13 April 2022.
Waller, Kilner, Letter, *Essex Standard*, 7 April 1854.
Waller, Kilner, Letter, *Moreton Bay Courier*, 13 February 1857.
Waller, Kilner, Letters, *Sydney Morning Herald*, 24 February 1857, 11 May 1857.
'Wreck of the *Dunbar*', *Empire*, 8 September 1857.

10: Life on the *Dunbar*
Author interviews
Kieran Hosty, Steve Waller

Books, journals, reports, newspapers, periodicals and websites
'Mr Solomon Meyer (1823–1902)', Parliament of New South Wales, <www.parliament.nsw.gov.au/members/Pages/member-details.aspx?pk=530>, n.d., accessed 1 February 2022.

11: 'Breakers Ahead!'
Author interviews
James Hanson, Kieran Hosty, Meg Keneally, John Lanser, Sandy Peacock, Damien Parkes, Mike Plant, Peter Poland, Stirling Smith, John Stanley, Steve Waller, Terry Wolfe

Books, journals, reports, newspapers, periodicals and websites
Bradshaw, H., *A Narrative of the Melancholy Wreck of the* Dunbar; *Bradshaw's Railway Guide*, Sydney, 1857.
Colonial Architect Papers Re *Dunbar*, copy of 2/642 A, Archives Office of New South Wales.

310

SOURCES

Dictionary of Sydney staff writer, 'Dunbar shipwreck', *Dictionary of Sydney*, <dictionaryofsydney.org/entry/dunbar_shipwreck>, 2008, accessed 2 February 2022.

'From a visitor to the Heads', *Sydney Morning Herald*, 22 August 1857.

Fryer, James, *A Narrative of the Melancholy Wreck of the* Dunbar, *Merchant Ship, on the South Head of Port Jackson, August 20th, 1857, with Illustrations of the Principal Localities*, Sydney: For the proprietors by James Fryer.

'Further particulars of the shipwreck at the Heads', *Sydney Morning Herald*, 2nd edn, 1.15 p.m., 22 August 1857.

'Further particulars of the shipwreck at the Heads', *Sydney Morning Herald*, 24 August 1857.

'Historical feature: The wreck of the *Dunbar*', *The Sun*, 31 December 1990.

'Loss of Sunderland Built Ship', *Newcastle Guardian*, 21 November 1857.

'Loss of the *Dunbar*', *Dublin Evening Mail*, 16 November 1857.

Martin, T.C., *The Wrecking of the* Dunbar, Sydney: Woollahra History and Heritage Society, 1992.

'Melancholy shipwreck: loss of the *Dunbar* with all onboard', *Empire*, 22 August 1857.

'Notice of Manifest of Goods Per *Dunbar*', *Sydney Morning Herald*, 22 August 1857.

'Publicans; Licensing Meeting', *Bathurst Free Press and Mining Journal*, 5 September 1857.

Ships File, Mitchell Library, State Library of New South Wales.

"Shipwreck at the Heads', *Sydney Morning Herald*, 3rd edn, 22 August 1857.

'Shipwrecks—great loss of life', *Leeds Times*, 14 November 1857.

'The dreadful loss of the Australian clipper *Dunbar*, with 70 passengers and 54 crew', *Morning Chronicle* (London), 16 November 1857.

The Emeu, 'Narrative of the Wreck of the *Dunbar*', *Sydney Morning Herald*, 10 September 1857.

'The late wreck', *Empire*, 26 August 1857.

'The locality of the wreck', *Empire*, 24 August 1857.

'The loss of the *Dunbar* August 1857', Information sheet 4, Woollahra Library Local History Centre, n.d.

'The loss of the *Dunbar*', *Sydney Morning Herald*, 24 August 1857.

'The Wreck of the *Dunbar*', Archives in Brief 67, State Records New South Wales.

'The wreck of the *Dunbar*, Australian clipper', *The Times* (London), 17 November 1857.

'The wreck of the *Dunbar*, Australian clipper and loss of 140 lives', *Daily News*, (London), 16 November 1857.

'Time warp: remembering the day of the *Dunbar*', *Village Voice Eastern Harbourside*, July 2007.

'Tragic voyage rocks a proud infant colony', *The Daily Telegraph*, 20 August 2007.

Warden, Ian, *Australian History Live! Eyewitness accounts from the past*, Canberra: National Library Australia, 2013.

'Woman dreams as ship in death throes on rocks', *Adelaide Advertiser*, 8 August 1984.

Woodward, Jack, 'Wreck of *Dunbar* a "great tragedy"', *Wentworth Courier*, 15 August 1984.

'Wreck of the *Dunbar*', *Adelaide Advertiser*, 12 September 1857.

'Wreck of the *Dunbar*', *Empire*, 25 August 1857.

'Wreck of the *Dunbar*', *Empire*, 10 September 1857.

'Wreck of the *Dunbar* and great loss of life', *Leeds Mercury*, 17 November 1857.

'Wreck of the *Dunbar* (from a correspondent)', *Empire*, 27 August 1857.

'Wreck of the *Dunbar*: further intelligence', *Empire*, 2nd edn, 12 noon, 22 August 1857.

12: Bad Tidings
Books, journals, reports, newspapers, periodicals and websites

Bradshaw, H., *A Narrative of the Melancholy Wreck of the* Dunbar; *Bradshaw's Railway Guide*, Sydney, 1857.

Captain Robert Pockley's testimony to *Dunbar* coronial inquest from Register of Coroner's Inquests 1857, State Archives and Records New South Wales.

Excerpts from *Ancestor Treasure Hunt—The Pockley Family & Descendants in Australia 1842–1976* by R.V. Pockley, 1977. (Can be accessed at Mitchell Library, the State Library of New South Wales.)

'From a visitor to the Heads', *Sydney Morning Herald*, 22 August 1857.

'Further particulars', *Sydney Morning Herald*, 24 August 1857.

'Further particulars of the shipwreck at the Heads', *Sydney Morning Herald*, 22 August 1857.

'Further particulars of the shipwreck at the Heads', *Sydney Morning Herald*, 2nd edn, 1.15 p.m., 22 August 1857.

Fryer, James, *A Narrative of the Melancholy Wreck of the* Dunbar, *Merchant Ship, on the South Head of Port Jackson, August 20th, 1857, with Illustrations of the Principal Localities*, Sydney: For the proprietors by James Fryer.

Graham, James, 'South Head Signal Master's Log Book entries on the wreck of the *Dunbar*', copy, gift of E. Hanley, Australian National Maritime Museum.

Heads, Ian, *The Beach Club: One hundred years at Balmoral—The Balmoral Beach Club 1914–2014*, Sydney: Playright Publishing Pty Ltd, 2013.

Jevons, W.S., letter from William Stanley Jevons to his sister, *Papers and Correspondence of William Stanley Jevons*, ed. R.D. Collison Black, vol. 2, London: Macmillan for the Royal Economic Society, 1973, p. 301.

King, Hazel, 'McLerie, John (1809–1874)', *Australian Dictionary of Biography*, <adb.anu.edu.au/biography/mclerie-john-4127>, 1974, accessed 2 February 2022.

Meacham, Steve, 'Shipwreck that shook Australia to the core', *Sydney Morning Herald*, 18 August 2007.

Mead, Tom, 'My dear sir, I beg to inform you that a ship has been wrecked', *Wentworth Courier*, 18 February 1987.

'Melancholy shipwreck: loss of the *Dunbar* with all onboard', *Empire*, 22 August 1857.

'Notice of Manifest of Goods Per *Dunbar*', *Sydney Morning Herald*, 22 August 1857.

Pockley, Captain Robert, official report to Hon Stuart Donaldson, Parliamentary Paper 2, September 1857.

'Pockley, Robert Francis (1823–1892)', Obituaries Australia, <oa.anu.edu.au/obituary/pockley-robert-francis-16344/text28304>, 3 October 1892, accessed 2 February 2022.

Pockley, R.V., *Ancestor Treasure Hunt: The Pockley family and descendants in Australia 1842–1976*, Sydney: Wentworth Books, 1977 (incorporates Harbour Master Robert Pockley's diary, original in family's possession).

Pockley, Simon, 'The Pockley family: Robert Francis Pockley (born 10-03-1823)', *The Pockley Family—History, Descendants, Family Trees and Related Material*, <pockley.org/family/pockley0008.html>, n.d., accessed 2 February 2022.

Ships File, Mitchell Library, State Library of New South Wales.

'Shipwreck at the Heads', *Sydney Morning Herald*, 3rd edn, 22 August 1857.

The Emeu, 'Narrative of the Wreck of the *Dunbar*', *Sydney Morning Herald*, 22 August 1857.

'The late wreck', *Empire*, 26 August 1857.

'The locality of the wreck', *Empire*, 24 August 1857.

'The loss of the *Dunbar*', *Sydney Morning Herald*, 24 August 1857.

Woodward, Jack, 'Wreck of *Dunbar* a "great tragedy"', *Wentworth Courier*, 15 August 1984.

'Wreck of the *Dunbar*', *Empire*, 25 August 1857.

'Wreck of the *Dunbar*', *Empire*, 10 September 1857.

'Wreck of the *Dunbar* (from a correspondent)', *Empire*, 27 August 1857.

'Wreck of the *Dunbar*: further intelligence', *Empire*, 2nd edn, 12 noon, 22 August 1857.

13: 'A Feeling of Intense Melancholy'

Books, journals, reports, newspapers, periodicals and websites

Bradshaw, H., *A Narrative of the Melancholy Wreck of the* Dunbar; *Bradshaw's Railway Guide*, Sydney, 1857.

City of Sydney, 'George Thornton', *Discover Sydney's Aldermen*, <www.sydney aldermen.com.au/alderman/george-thornton/>, n.d., accessed 2 February 2022.

'From a visitor to the Heads', *Sydney Morning Herald*, 22 August 1857.

Fryer, James, *A Narrative of the Melancholy Wreck of the* Dunbar, *Merchant Ship, on the South Head of Port Jackson, August 20th, 1857, with Illustrations of the Principal Localities*, Sydney: For the proprietors by James Fryer.

'Further particulars', *Sydney Morning Herald*, 24 August 1857.

'Further particulars of the shipwreck at the Heads', *Sydney Morning Herald*, 22 August 1857.

'Further particulars of the shipwreck at the Heads', *Sydney Morning Herald*, 2nd edn, 1.15 p.m., 22 August 1857.

King, Hazel, 'McLerie, John (1809–1874)', *Australian Dictionary of Biography*, <adb.anu.edu.au/biography/mclerie-john-4127>, 1974, accessed 2 February 2022.

McCormack, Terri, 'Thornton, George', *Dictionary of Sydney*, <dictionaryofsydney. org/entry/thornton_george>, 2011, accessed 2 February 2022.

McLerie, John, 'Law and Order in the Pioneering Days of NSW', The Thin Blue Line, Australian Police, <www.australianpolice.com.au/nsw-police-history-index/ police-commissioners-of-nsw/john-mclerie/>, n.d. accessed 13 April 2022.

Meacham, Steve, 'Shipwreck that shook Australia to the core', *Sydney Morning Herald*, 18 August 2007.

'Melancholy shipwreck: loss of the *Dunbar* with all onboard', *Empire*, 22 August 1857.

'Mr George Thornton (1819–1901)', Parliament of New South Wales, n.d., <www. parliament.nsw.gov.au/members/formermembers/Pages/former-member-details.aspx?pk=491>, n.d., accessed 2 February 2022.

Rutledge, Martha, 'Thornton, George (1819–1901)', *Australian Dictionary of Biography*, <adb.anu.edu.au/biography/thornton-george-4720/text7827>, 1976, accessed 2 February 2022.

'Shipwreck at the Heads', *Sydney Morning Herald*, 3rd edn, 22 August 1857.

The Emeu, 'Narrative of the Wreck of the *Dunbar*', *Sydney Morning Herald*, 22 August 1857.

'The late wreck', *Empire*, 26 August 1857.

'The locality of the wreck', *Empire*, 24 August 1857.

'The loss of the *Dunbar*', *Sydney Morning Herald*, 24 August 1857.

Thornton, George, 'Johnson's narrative to the right worshipful the mayor', *The Shipping Gazette and Sydney General Trade List*, August 24 1857.

'Wreck of the *Dunbar*', *Empire*, 25 August 1857.

'Wreck of the *Dunbar*', *Empire*, 10 September 1857.

'Wreck of the *Dunbar* (from a correspondent)', *Empire*, 27 August 1857.

'Wreck of the *Dunbar*: further intelligence', *Empire*, 2nd edn, 12 noon, 22 August 1857.

Woodward, Jack, 'Wreck of *Dunbar* a "great tragedy"', *Wentworth Courier*, 15 August 1984.

14: A Miraculous Rescue

Author interview

James Hanson

Books, journals, reports, newspapers, periodicals and websites

Birth certificate of Helga Olafsson (Woolier), courtesy Jennie Fairs, private collection.

Bradshaw, H., *A Narrative of the Melancholy Wreck of the* Dunbar; *Bradshaw's Railway Guide*, Sydney, 1857.

'Bravery', *Sydney Morning Herald*, 24 August 1857.

City of Sydney, 'George Thornton', *Discover Sydney's Aldermen*, <www.sydney aldermen.com.au/alderman/george-thornton/>, n.d., accessed 2 February 2022.

'*Dunbar*', Woollahra Municipal Council, <www.woollahra.nsw.gov.au/library/local_history/local_history_fast_facts/d>, n.d., accessed 2 February 2022.

'From a visitor to the Heads', *Sydney Morning Herald*, 22 August 1857.

Fryer, James, *A Narrative of the Melancholy Wreck of the* Dunbar, *Merchant Ship, on the South Head of Port Jackson, August 20th, 1857, with Illustrations of the Principal Localities*, Sydney: For the proprietors by James Fryer.

'Further particulars', *Sydney Morning Herald*, 24 August 1857.

'Further particulars of the shipwreck at the Heads', *Sydney Morning Herald*, 22 August 1857.

'Further particulars of the shipwreck at the Heads', *Sydney Morning Herald*, 2nd edn, 1.15 p.m., 22 August 1857.

Gibbney, H.J., and Smith, Ann G., (comp. and eds), 'Pockley, Robert F.', *A Biographical Register 1788–1939*: notes from the name index of the *Australian Dictionary of Biography, vol. 2*, Canberra: *Australian Dictionary of Biography*, 1987.

Icelandic Australian Association of NSW, 'Arni Olafsson Thorlacius', IAA of NSW, <iaa.asn.au/arni-olafsson-thorlacius-2/>, n.d., accessed 2 February 2022.

McCormack, Terri, 'Thornton, George', *Dictionary of Sydney*, <dictionaryofsydney.org/entry/thornton_george>, 2011, accessed 2 February 2022.

'Melancholy shipwreck: loss of the *Dunbar* with all onboard', *Empire*, 22 August 1857.

'Mr George Thornton (1819–1901)', Parliament of New South Wales, n.d., <www.parliament.nsw.gov.au/members/formermembers/Pages/former-member-details.aspx?pk=491>, accessed 2 February 2022.

Power, Julie, '121 Dead: how one man survived "saddest episode" in Sydney history', *Sydney Morning Herald*, 20 August 2018.

Rutledge, Martha, 'Thornton, George (1819–1901)', *Australian Dictionary of Biography*, <adb.anu.edu.au/biography/thornton-george-4720/text7827>, 1976, accessed 2 February 2022.

'Shipwreck at the Heads', *Sydney Morning Herald*, 3rd edn, 22 August 1857.

The Emeu, 'Narrative of the Wreck of the *Dunbar*', *Sydney Morning Herald*, 22 August 1857.

'The late wreck', *Empire*, 26 August 1857.

'The locality of the wreck', *Empire*, 24 August 1857.

'The loss of the *Dunbar*', *Sydney Morning Herald*, 24 August 1857.

Thornton, George, article contributed to *Sydney Morning Herald*, 22 August 1857.

'Wreck of the *Dunbar*', *Empire*, 25 August 1857.

'Wreck of the *Dunbar*', *Empire*, 10 September 1857.

'Wreck of the *Dunbar* (from a correspondent)', *Empire*, 27 August 1857.

'Wreck of the *Dunbar*: further intelligence', *Empire*, 2nd edn, 12 noon, 22 August 1857.

15: Beyond Belief
Books, journals, reports, newspapers, periodicals and websites

Bradshaw, H., *A Narrative of the Melancholy Wreck of the* Dunbar; *Bradshaw's Railway Guide*, Sydney, 1857.

'Bravery', *Sydney Morning Herald*, 24 August 1857.

'From a visitor to the Heads', *Sydney Morning Herald*, 22 August 1857.

Fryer, James, *A Narrative of the Melancholy Wreck of the* Dunbar, *Merchant Ship, on the South Head of Port Jackson, August 20th, 1857, with Illustrations of the Principal Localities*, Sydney: For the proprietors by James Fryer.

'Further particulars', *Sydney Morning Herald*, 24 August 1857.

'Further particulars of the shipwreck at the Heads', *Sydney Morning Herald*, 22 August 1857.

'Further particulars of the shipwreck at the Heads', *Sydney Morning Herald*, 2nd edn, 1.15 p.m., 22 August 1857.

'Melancholy shipwreck: Loss of the *Dunbar* with all onboard', *Empire*, 22 August 1857.

Old Chum, 'Sidelights on the wreck of the *Dunbar*', *Truth*, 21 June 1925.

'Shipwreck at the Heads', *Sydney Morning Herald*, 3rd edn, 22 August 1857.

The Emeu, 'Narrative of the Wreck of the *Dunbar*', *Sydney Morning Herald*, 22 August 1857.

'The late wreck', *Empire*, 26 August 1857.

'The locality of the wreck', *Empire*, 24 August 1857.

'The loss of the *Dunbar*', *Sydney Morning Herald*, 24 August 1857.

'The wreck of the *Dunbar* 20th August, 1857', *The Illustrated Sydney News*, 15 September 1887.

'Wreck of the *Dunbar*', *Empire*, 25 August 1857.

'Wreck of the *Dunbar*', *Empire*, 10 September 1857.

'Wreck of the *Dunbar* (from a correspondent)', *Empire*, 27 August 1857.

'Wreck of the *Dunbar*: further intelligence', *Empire*, 2nd edn, 12 noon, 22 August 1857.

16: The Dead House

Books, journals, reports, newspapers, periodicals and websites

'Bodies recovered and identified by their friends', *Empire*, 25 August 1857.

Bradshaw, H., *A Narrative of the Melancholy Wreck of the* Dunbar; *Bradshaw's Railway Guide*, Sydney, 1857.

'Deaths: William Butler Williams', *Sydney Morning Herald*, 25 August 1857.

'Dramatis Personae—Examiners', entry for Haynes Gibbes Alleyne (1814–1882), The University of Sydney School of Medicine Online Museum, <sydney.edu.au/medicine/museum/mwmuseum/index.php/Dramatis_Personae_-_Examiners#Haynes_Gibbes_Alleyne.281814.E2.80.931882.29>, n.d., accessed 2 February 2022.

Fryer, James, *A Narrative of the Melancholy Wreck of the* Dunbar, *Merchant Ship, on the South Head of Port Jackson, August 20th, 1857, with Illustrations of the Principal Localities*, Sydney: For the proprietors by James Fryer.

'Gorman, John Valentine', *Dictionary of Sydney*, <dictionaryofsydney.org/person/gorman_john_valentine>, n.d., accessed 2 February 2022.

Lyons, Mark, 'Raphael, George Joseph (1818–1879)', *Australian Dictionary of Biography*, <adb.anu.edu.au/biography/raphael-joseph-george-4451>, 2006, accessed 2 February 2022.

Register of Coroner's Inquests 1857, State Archives and Records New South Wales.

'The Dead-House, Circular Quay', letter, *Sydney Morning Herald*, 5 March 1881.

The Emeu, 'Narrative of the Wreck of the *Dunbar*', *Sydney Morning Herald*, 22 August 1857.

'Viewing the dead', *Empire*, 24 August 1857.

'William Butler Williams', *Descent – magazine of Society of Australian Genealogists*, June 2017.

'Wreck of the *Dunbar*', *Bathurst Free Press and Mining Journal*, 5 September 1857.

'Wreck of the *Dunbar*', *Empire*, 10 September 1857.

17: How and Why

Books, journals, reports, newspapers, periodicals and websites

'Inquest', *Empire*, 24 August 1857.

'Inquest on the bodies', *Sydney Morning Herald*, 25 August 1857.

Register of Coroner's Inquests 1857, State Archives and Records New South Wales.

'The *Dunbar*', *Maitland Mercury & Hunter River General Advertiser*, 3 September 1857.

The Emeu, 'Narrative of the Wreck of the *Dunbar*', *Sydney Morning Herald*, 22 August 1857.

'The verdict of the Coroner's jury', *Sydney Morning Herald*, 26 August 1857.

'Wreck of the *Dunbar*', *Empire*, 10 September 1857.

'Wreck of the Dunbar', *Sydney Morning Herald*, 26 August 1857.

18: The City Weeps
Books, journals, reports, newspapers, periodicals and websites

Bradshaw, H., *A Narrative of the Melancholy Wreck of the* Dunbar; *Bradshaw's Railway Guide*, Sydney, 1857.

Camperdown Cemetery: Society of Australian Genealogists, <ag.org.au/Camperdown-Cemetery>, n.d., accessed 13 April 2022.

'Deaths', *Sydney Morning Herald*, 24 August 1857.

'Deaths', *Sydney Morning Herald*, 25 August 1857.

'Deaths', *Sydney Morning Herald*, 26 August 1857.

'Deaths', *Sydney Morning Herald*, 27 August 1857.

'Deaths', *Sydney Morning Herald*, 10 September 1857.

Fryer, James, *A Narrative of the Melancholy Wreck of the* Dunbar, *Merchant Ship, on the South Head of Port Jackson, August 20th, 1857, with Illustrations of the Principal Localities*, Sydney: For the proprietors by James Fryer.

Gledhill, Percy Walter, *A Stroll through the historic Camperdown Cemetery*, Sydney: R Dey, 1946.

'James Green', Monument Australia, <monumentaustralia.org.au/themes/people/tragedy/display/23208-james-green>, n.d., accessed 2 February 2022.

'Myers [sic] funeral', *Sydney Morning Herald*, 26 August 1857.

Register of Coroner's Inquests 1857, State Archives and Records New South Wales.

'The *Dunbar*: black swan', *Empire*, 31 August 1857.

The Emeu, 'Narrative of the Wreck of the *Dunbar*', *Sydney Morning Herald*, 22 August 1857.

'The funeral', *Empire*, 10 September 1857.

'The funeral', *Sydney Morning Herald*, 25 August 1857.

'Two bodies recovered', *Sydney Morning Herald*, 31 August 1857.

'Wreck of the *Dunbar*', *Empire*, 10 September 1857.

19: Recriminations
Books, journals, reports, newspapers, periodicals and websites

A Fisherman, 'The *Dunbar*', letter to the editor, *Empire*, 31 August 1857.

'Gossip of the week', *Bell's Life in Sydney & Sporting Reviewer*, 29 August 1857.

'No generous man will refuse a tear to the memory of Captain Green', *Sydney Morning Herald*, 25 August 1857.

'The *Dunbar* and her commander', *Empire*, 10 September 1857.

The Emeu, 'Narrative of the Wreck of the *Dunbar*', *Sydney Morning Herald*, 22 August 1857.

'The rule', *Empire*, 27 August 1857.

'Wreck of the *Dunbar*', *Empire*, 10 September 1857.

'Wreck of the *Dunbar* (from a correspondent)', *Empire*, 27 August 1857.

20: Disorder in the House
Books, journals, reports, newspapers, periodicals and websites

Graham, James, 'South Head Signal Master's Log Book entries on the wreck of the *Dunbar*', copy, gift of E. Hanley, Australian National Maritime Museum.

'Harbour safety', *Empire*, 27 August 1857.

'Legislative Assembly: Additional Lighthouse', *Sydney Morning Herald*, 27 August 1857.

Light, Pilot and Navigation Board Report, New South Wales State Archives. Minute Book [Light, Pilot and Navigation Board] AONSW NRS-9608 (6/5080).

New South Wales Legislative Assembly, Robert F Pockley's Report, *Parliamentary Papers, 'Wreck of the Ship* Dunbar', ordered to be printed 2 September 1857.

New South Wales Legislative Assembly, *Parliamentary Papers, 'Wreck of the Ship* Dunbar'.

New South Wales Parliamentary Papers, Votes & Proceedings of the Legislative Assembly, 21—1st Parliament 1857, 21 August 1857, 2 September 1857, 20 October 1857, 28 October 1857, 30 October 1857, 4 November 1857, 10 November 1857, 13 November 1857.

21: Keepsakes and Chronicles
Author interviews

Kieran Hosty, John Lanser, Stirling Smith

Books, journals, reports, newspapers, periodicals and websites

'Australia: Shipwrecks and loss of life', *Leeds Times*, 14 November 1857.

Bennett, Samuel, 'The Wreck of the *Dunbar*', collection of the Australian National Maritime Museum. The poem can be viewed on Trove at nla.gov.au/nla.obj-76415276/view?partId=nla.obj-76415326.

Bradshaw, H., *A Narrative of the Melancholy Wreck of the* Dunbar; *Bradshaw's Railway Guide*, 1857.'*Dunbar*', *Bell's Life in Sydney and Sporting Reviewer*, 5 September 1857.

Fryer, James, *A Narrative of the Melancholy Wreck of the* Dunbar, *Merchant Ship, on the South Head of Port Jackson, August 20th, 1857, with Illustrations of the Principal Localities*, Sydney: For the proprietors by James Fryer.

Kendall, Henry, '*Dunbar*, 1857', New South Wales Government: Office of Environment and Heritage, <www.environment.nsw.gov.au/maritimeheritage app/research.aspx?id=97>, n.d., accessed 2 February 2022.

'Loss of the *Dunbar*', *Dublin Evening Mail*, 16 November 1857.

'Narrative of the wreck', *Empire*, 28 August 1857.

Shaw, Lindsey, 'Two unusual artefacts from the wreck of the Dunbar', Australian National Maritime Museum, <www.sea.museum/2012/01/31/two-unusual-artefacts-from-the-wreck-of-the-dunbar>, 31 January 2012, accessed 1 February 2012.

'The dreadful loss of the Australian clipper ship *Dunbar*, with 70 passengers and 54 crew', *Morning Chronicle* (London), 16 November 1857.

The Emeu, 'Narrative of the Wreck of the *Dunbar*', *Sydney Morning Herald*, 22 August 1857.

'The late wreck' *Empire*, 28 August 1857.

'The wreck of the *Dunbar*, Australian clipper, and loss of 140 lives', *London Daily News*, 16 November 1857.

'Wreck of the *Dunbar*', *Dundee, Perth, and Cupar Advertiser*, 20 November 1857.

'Wreck of the *Dunbar*', *Empire*, 27 August 1857.

'Wreck of the *Dunbar* and great loss of life', *Leeds Mercury*, 17 November 1857.

'Wreck of the *Dunbar*: new publications', *Empire*, 5 September 1857.

22: Lightning Strikes Twice
Books, journals, reports, newspapers, periodicals and websites

'*Catherine Adamson*', *Shipping Gazette and Sydney General Trade List*, 4 February 1856.

Gregory, Mackenzie J., 'Two shipwrecks off Sydney Heads and the building of Hornby Light', *Naval Historical Review*, vol. 26, no. 2, June 2005.

Watson, Captain J.H., 'Ships that have passed', *Sea, Land and Air*, December 1918.

23: Reforms
Author interviews
Brad Duncan, Kieran Hosty, Stirling Smith

Books, journals, reports, newspapers, periodicals and websites

'Additional Lighthouse for Port Jackson', Paper to the Treasury by Robert F. Pockley, *New South Wales Parliamentary Papers*, 29 October 1857.

Colonial Architect Papers Re *Dunbar* (AO NSW COD393, Archives Office of NSW, State Archives and Records New South Wales.

Derricourt, Robin, *South Head Sydney and the Origins of Watsons Bay*, Sydney: Watsons Bay Association, 2011.

Dictionary of Sydney staff writer, 'Harbour pilots', *Dictionary of Sydney*, <dictionary ofsydney.org/entry/harbour_pilots>, 2008, accessed 15 January 2022.

'Harbour safety', *Empire*, 27 August 1857.

'History of pilotage, NSW 1842–1954', *Sydney Morning Herald*, 25 April 1934.

'Hornby Light', Woollahra Library Local History Centre Information Sheet 3.

'Hornby Light and Cottages Group, Watsons Bay', National Trust Listing Sheet, 1976.

Jateff, Emily, '"Not all beer and skittles": Sydney Harbour pilotage', Australian National Maritime Museum, <www.sea.museum/2020/08/07/not-all-beer-and-skittles-sydney-harbour-pilotage>, 7 August 2020, accessed 15 January 2022.

Johnstone, James, 'New South Wales Colonial: 1858–1900 The First Telegraph Line', *Telegrams in Australia: 1854–1988*, <telegramsaustralia.com/Forms/Colonial/NSW/Lines%20%20&%20admin/NSW%20first%20line.html>, n.d., accessed 2 February 2022.

'Legislative Assembly—wreck at the Heads', *Sydney Morning Herald*, 26 August 1857.

'Legislative Assembly: Additional Lighthouse', *Sydney Morning Herald*, 27 August 1857.

Letters and despatches of Captain Henry Mangles Denham, Denison Family Papers, National Library of Australia.

Light, Pilot and Navigation Board Report, New South Wales State Archives. Minute Book, AONSW NRS-9608 (6/5080)

Lighthouses of Australia Inc., 'Hornby Lighthouse', Lighthouses of Australia Inc., <lighthouses.org.au/nsw/hornby-lighthouse/>

NSW Legislative Assembly; Robert F. Pockley's Report, Parliamentary Papers, 'Wreck of the Ship *Dunbar*', ordered to be printed 2 September 1857.

New South Wales Parliamentary Papers, Votes & Proceedings of the Legislative Assembly, 21—1st Parliament 1857, 21 August 1857, 2 September 1857, 20 October 1857, 28 October 1857, 30 October 1857, 4 November 1857, 10 November 1857, 13 November 1857.

Port Authority of New South Wales, 'Marine pilots: keeping ships safe in Sydney for 225 years', 27 March 2018, accessed 2 February 2022.

Report of the Light, Pilot and Navigation Board, with Minutes of Evidence, 1857, State Archives and Records New South Wales.

'The awful wreck', *Sydney Morning Herald*, 17 November 1857.

'The *Dunbar*', *Sydney Morning Herald*, 28 August 1857.

'The *Dunbar*', *The Shipping Gazette and Sydney General Trade List*, 24 August 1857.

24: Three Lives
Author interview
James Hanson

Books, journals, reports, newspapers, periodicals and websites
Johnson, James

1915 Deceased Estate File including Will of James Johnson, courtesy of Jennie Fairs, author's collection.

Blair, Richard, '*Dunbar* survivor James Johnson of the Boulevarde, Dulwich Hill [sic]', *Marrickville Heritage Society Newsletter*, May 2005.

'Death of *Dunbar*'s only survivor', *Nepean Times*, 24 April 1915.

Find A Grave. Source: Carolyn [ID 46783077], <www.findagrave.com/memorial/154591517/james-j-johnson>, n.d., accessed 13 April 2022.

'James Johnson', *Descent – magazine of Society of Australian Genealogists*, June 2017.

'List of subscriptions for James Johnson', *Sydney Morning Herald*, 12 October 1857.

'Johnson, James', Ancestry UK, rell222, <www.ancestry.co.uk/family-tree/person/tree/9278000/person/220011897299/facts>, n.d. accessed 13 April 2022.

James Johnson, Cemetery Transcription Library, Sandgate Cemetery, New South Wales.

'Memories of the *Dunbar*', *Sunday Telegraph*, 27 August 1981.

'Obituary: Mr James J. Johnson', *Freeman's Journal*, 29 April 1915.

Register of Coroner's Inquests 1857, State Archives and Records New South Wales.

Thornton, George, 'Johnson's narrative to the right worshipful the mayor', *The Shipping Gazette and Sydney General Trade List*, August 24 1857.

'Whitbread vs Hatch', *Sydney Morning Herald*, 25 November 1857.

Thornton, George

City of Sydney, 'George Thornton', *Discover Sydney's Aldermen*, <www.sydneyaldermen.com.au/alderman/george-thornton/>, n.d., accessed 2 February 2022.

McCormack, Terri, 'Thornton, George', *Dictionary of Sydney*, <dictionaryofsydney.org/entry/thornton_george>, 2011, accessed 2 February 2022.

'Mr George Thornton (1819–1901)', Parliament of New South Wales, <www.parliament.nsw.gov.au/members/formermembers/Pages/former-member-details.aspx?pk=491>, n.d., accessed 2 February 2022.

Rutledge, Martha, 'Thornton, George (1819–1901)', *Australian Dictionary of Biography*, <adb.anu.edu.au/biography/thornton-george-4720/text7827>, 1976, accessed 2 February 2022.

'Thornton, George (1819-1901)', *Australian Town and Country Journal*, 30 November 1901.

Thornton, George, 'Johnson's narrative to the right worshipful the mayor', *The Shipping Gazette & Sydney General Trade List*, 24 August 1857.

Woolier, Antonio

'Antonio Woollier [sic]', *Empire*, 25 August 1857.

'Antonio Woollier [sic], *Sydney Morning Herald*, 22 September 1857.

'Betting at the Epsom races', *Bendigo Advertiser*, 14 January 1873.

Birth certificate of Helga Florence Woolier, November 14 1868, Victoria Births, Deaths and Marriages.

'Bravery', *Sydney Morning Herald*, 24 August 1857.

'Central Criminal Court', *Maitland Mercury and Hunter River General Advertiser*, 9 July 1863.

'Central Police Court', *Empire*, 17 March 1863.

Death certificate of Antonio Woolier, 5 November 1889, Victoria Births, Deaths and Marriages.

'Frederick Perry', *Empire*, 10 March 1863.

Icelandic Australian Association of NSW, 'Arni Olafsson Thorlacius', IAA of NSW, <iaa.asn.au/arni-olafsson-thorlacius-2/>, n.d., accessed 2 February 2022.

'Insolvent estate of Antonio Woolier', *NSW Government Gazette,* 18 August 1862.

'Notes of the week' *Sydney Morning Herald*, 11 July 1863.

'The *Dunbar*', *Sunday Times*, 6 May 1906.

'The first case under the new Gambling Act: Antonio Woolier', *Argus*, 6 November 1872.

'The Gulf diggings', *Goulburn Herald*, 1 May 1861.

'The pen and paint brush', *Bell's Life in Sydney and Sporting Reviewer*, 19 September 1857.

'The Recent Wreck', *Empire*, September 3 1857.

Thornton, George, 'Johnson's narrative to the right worshipful the mayor', *The Shipping Gazette & Sydney General Trade List*, 24 August 1857.

Woolier, A., *The Backer's Guide For the Year 1874 by A Woolier, Containing Pedigrees and Performances of Horses Engaged in the Metropolitan Stakes and the Melbourne Cup*, Melbourne: BM Lucas, 1874.

25: Unreliable Memories
Books, journals, reports, newspapers, periodicals and websites

'After 48 years, sole survivor's story', *The Sun*, 20 August 1905.

James, George, 'Wreck of the *Dunbar*', letter to the editor, *Sydney Morning Herald*, 30 August 1887.

'The *Dunbar* Wreck', *Sydney Morning Herald*, 16 July 1910.

'The *Dunbar*'s anchors', letter from R.L. Siddins to *Sydney Morning Herald*, 22 July 1910.

'The wreck of the *Dunbar*', *Sydney Morning Herald*, 24 August 1887.

Thornton, George, 'Wreck of the *Dunbar*: the rescuer', letter to the editor, *Sydney Morning Herald*, 25 August 1887.

26: All That Remains
Author interviews

Myffanwy Bryant, Brad Duncan, Mori Flapan, Kieran Hosty, David Nutley, Harry Rees, Stirling Smith

Books, journals, reports, newspapers, periodicals and websites

'An historic wreck: the *Dunbar*'s anchors discovered after 50 years', *Sydney Morning Herald*, 15 July 1907.

Australian Broadcasting Corporation, 'Shipwrecks: Dunbar Head', ABC, <www.abc.net.au/backyard/shipwrecks/nsw/dunbar.htm>, 2003, accessed 31 January 2022.

'Ballina recalls colonial tragedy', *Ballina Shire Advocate*, 16 August 2007.

Cock, Anna, 'Sydney history goes under the hammer', *Daily Telegraph*, 25 August 2001.

Colman, Mike, *Ben Cropp: Blood in the water*, Sydney: Park Street Press, 2006.

Cropp, Ben, *Whale of a Shark*, Adelaide: Rigby Limited, 1969.

Crosson, Bruce, *After the* Dunbar, Sydney: booklet published by Woollahra History and Heritage Society, 1997.

Dobbyn, Alan, 'Divers go down today to try to save the *Dunbar* wreckage', *Sydney Morning Herald*, 7 June 1980.

'*Dunbar* anchors: all four located', *Sydney Morning Herald*, 7 July 1910.

'*Dunbar* anchors: where the wreck occurred', *Sydney Morning Herald*, 23 July 1910.

Dunbar; Australasian Underwater Cultural Heritage Database, Australian Government Department of Agriculture, Water and the Environment, <environment. gov.au,shipwreck/public/wreck/wreck.do?key=517>, n.d. accessed 13 April 2022.

Heritage Branch website, 'The ship *Dunbar* (1854–1857)', <www.heritage.nsw. gov.au/maritime/wrk_dunbar.htm>, n.d., accessed 13 April 2022.

Morcombe, John, 'Relics of the *Dunbar*', *Manly Daily*, 30 August 2007.

Nutley, David, Dunbar *Wreck Inspection Report, New South Wales Department of Planning 1991*, Sydney: Heritage Branch, Department of Planning.

Nutley, David, 'The tragedy of the *Dunbar*', *Heritage Conservation News*, June 1991.

Nutley, David and Smith, Tim, Dunbar *1854–1857 Conservation Management Plan*, Sydney: Marine Archaeology Program, NSW Heritage Office, 1992.

Objects Through Time . . . Dunbar *Shipwreck Collection 1857*, Migration Heritage Centre, <www.migrationheritage.nsw.gov.au/exhibitions/objectsthroughtime/ dunbar/index.html>, n.d., accessed 13 April 2022.

O'Connor, Kim, 'Maritime Museum to buy *Dunbar* relics', *Wentworth Courier*, 7 December 1994.

O'Connor, Kim, 'Plaque to mark *Dunbar* sinking', *Wentworth Courier*, 9 September 1992.

O'Connor, Kim, 'Signal station's bicentenary mark', *Wentworth Courier*, 24 January 1990.

Robson, Frank, 'Treasure hunters of the deep', *Sydney Morning Herald Good Weekend* magazine, 15 January 1994.

Royal Australian Historical Society, 'The Dunbar Anchor', *Journal and Proceedings*, <nla.gov.au/nla.obj-596682683/view?partId=nla.obj-596733307#page/n93/ mode/1up>, 1918, accessed 2 February 2022.

Sautelle, Edwin S., letter to *Empire*, 20 August 1907.

'Save the *Dunbar* treasure', *Wentworth Courier*, 30 November 1994.

'Secret treasure up for sale', *The Sun*, 27 November 1994.

'The recovered anchors', *Sydney Morning Herald*, 22 July 1910.

'The sovereign wreck'. *Fathom: Skindiving in Australia*, vol. 1, no. 4.

'The wreck of the *Dunbar*: Nat Williams tells the stories behind the library's treasures', *Unbound: The National Library of Australia Magazine*, December 2017.

Williams, Mary-Louise, '*Dunbar* shipwreck collection', *Signals* magazine, March–May 1995.

Wolfe, A., *The* Dunbar *Group Statement of Significance;* Sydney, Heritage Office, 1990.

Woodward, James, 'Diver gets some treasure off his chest', *Sydney Morning Herald*, 16 October 1993.

'Wreck of fifty years ago: remains of the *Dunbar* found', *The Examiner*, May 1907.

'Wreck of the *Dunbar*', *Inverell Times*, 23 August 1907.

'Wreck of the *Dunbar*: the scene located: Sydney pilot's narrative', *Sydney Morning Herald*, 28 July 1910.

27: Last Respects

Author interviews

Laurie Alexander, Roger Bayliss, Christian Garland, James Hanson, John Lanser, Annette Lemercier, Peter Poland, John Stanley, Steve Waller

Books, journals, reports, newspapers, periodicals and websites

Bertrand, I., 'Lovely, Louise Nellie (1895–1980)', *Australian Dictionary of Biography*, vol. 10, Melbourne: Melbourne University Press, 1986.

'Death of the Hon. Daniel Egan', *Australian Town and Country Journal*, 22 October 1870.

Doolan, Shirley (comp.), *A Brief History of the Memorial to Those Who Were Drowned on the* Dunbar *and* Catherine Adamson *Sailing Ships in 1857*, Sydney: Shirley Doolan, 2007.

'*Dunbar* commemorations and *Dunbar* folk opera', *Marrickville Heritage Society* newsletter, vol. 24, no. 1, July 2007.

'*Dunbar* shipwreck, 150th anniversary', *Eastern Suburbs Spectator*, 27 July 2007.

Egan, Paul, *St John's Darlinghurst: Serving the Cross, a Short History*, Sydney: Paul Egan, 2008.

Garland, Christian, 'Three *Dunbar* Stories: The Egans', *Pioneer* magazine, September 2007.

Knott, Peta, 'Tokens of a tragedy', *Signals* magazine, March–May 2001.

Lanser, John, 'Three *Dunbar* Stories: Robert Hunt', *Pioneer* magazine, September 2007.

Lanser, John, 'Three *Dunbar* Stories: The Greens', *Pioneer* magazine, September 2007.

'Marking ship's dead', *Canberra Times*, 20 August 2007.

Martin, Megan, 'Robert Hunt, chemist, photographer and deputy Mint master', Sydney Living Museums, <sydneylivingmuseums.com.au/stories/robert-hunt-chemist-photographer-and-deputy-mint-master>, n.d., accessed 1 February 2022.

Maynard, Roger, 'Australia mourns "Angel of the Gap" Don Ritchie, the man who talked 160 out of suicide', *The Independent* (UK), 16 May 2012.

Mellefont, Jeffrey, 'Faces from the *Dunbar* disaster', *Signals* magazine, March–May 2008.

O'Connor, Kim, '*Dunbar* remembered', *Wentworth Courier*, 1 August 2007.

Power, Julie, '121 Dead: how one man survived "saddest episode" in Sydney history', *Sydney Morning Herald*, 20 August 2018.

Robert Hunt: Australian Pioneer Photographer (1830–1892), University of Sydney Museums.

Terry, Martin, *Maritime Paintings of Early Australia*, Melbourne: Miegunyah Press, 1998.

'The stained glass detective and the wreck of the *Dunbar*', *Simply Australia*, 2 January 2007.

'The Wreck of the *Dunbar* 1857 Commemorative Service', booklet published by St Stephen's Newtown.

Wade, John, 'Loss of the *Dunbar*', *Antiques in New South Wales*, December 1987–April 1998.

Wood, David, 'Police re-enact the heroic rescue of James Johnson from the *Dunbar* wreck at Watsons Bay', *Wentworth Courier*, 22 August 2018.

Writer, Larry, 'The caretakers', *The (Sydney) Magazine*, March 2017.

Epilogue: The Bay
Author interviews
Kosta Akon, Tony Baine, Roger Bayliss, John Blondin, Jim Boyce, James Hanson, Peter Poland, Michael Rigg, Mike Rose, Terry Wolfe

Books, journals, reports, newspapers, periodicals and websites
Crosson, Bruce, 'The tree of knowledge', *Bay Lief*. n.d.

Dignam, Anne, 'Watsons Bay cliff walk', *Weekend Notes*, <www.weekendnotes.com/watsons-bay-cliff-walk/>, 8 April 2013, viewed 2 February 2022.

Maynard, Roger, 'Australia mourns "Angel of the Gap" Don Ritchie, the man who talked 160 out of suicide', *The Independent* (UK), 16 May 2012.

Nutley, David and Smith, Tim, Dunbar *1854–1857 Conservation Management Plan*, Sydney: Marine Archaeology Program, NSW Heritage Office, 1992.

Watsons Bay Association, *The Gap*, information sheet.

Wolfe, A., *The* Dunbar *Group Statement of Significance*; Sydney, Heritage Office, 1990.

Woodward, Jack, 'Man-eaters hung at the bay', *Eastern Herald*, 11 February 1988.

Index